WHAT IT MEANS TO BE HUMAN

WHAT IT MEANS TO BE
human

THE CASE FOR THE BODY
IN PUBLIC BIOETHICS

O. Carter Snead

Harvard University Press

Cambridge, Massachusetts • London, England

2020

Library of Congress Cataloging-in-Publication Data

Names: Snead, O. Carter, author.
Title: What it means to be human : the case for the body in
public bioethics / O. Carter Snead.
Identifiers: LCCN 202001IIII | ISBN 9780674987722 (cloth)
Subjects: LCSH: Human body—Law and legislation—United States. |
Bioethics—United States. | Abortion—Law and legislation—United States. |
Human reproductive technology—Law and legislation—United States. |
Terminal care—Law and legislation—United States. | Human experimentation
in medicine—Law and legislation—United States. |Medical laws and
legislation—United States.
Classification: LCC KF390.5.H85 S64 2020 | DDC 174.20973—dc23
LC record available at https://lccn.loc.gov/202001IIII

for Leigh

CONTENTS

WHAT IT MEANS TO BE HUMAN

Introduction

In America, law and policy are made through often messy processes of discourse, deliberation, and democratic forms of decision-making. This entails grappling with contested matters of deep importance, including competing and divergent visions of how we should live and what we owe to one another. This is certainly the case for public bioethics—the governance of science, medicine, and biotechnology in the name of ethical goods.

In our public bioethics discourse, contending sides frequently invoke abstract principles or rely on premises that do not reflect the full complexity of lived reality. This, in turn, leads to the adoption of laws and policies that fail to address the full range of human needs, often to the severe detriment of the weakest and most vulnerable. But what if we could create an alternative governing vision that stems from a shared foundational understanding of human experience and identity? What if the law and policy of American public bioethics accurately reflected our lived experience, shared values, hopes, fears, and needs? What if there was a new way of governing ourselves on matters touching the most intimate and defining issues facing humankind? This book aims to offer such a new path forward for public bioethics, rooted in what it means to be and flourish as a human being, in light of what and who we really are.

Public bioethics is fundamentally concerned with human vulnerability, dependence, frailty, and finitude. It is about procreation, pregnancy, babies, wasting illness, devastating injury, desperate enrollees in clinical trials, fearful patients, the disabled, the elderly, the dying, and the dead. Public bioethics is uniquely complex and complicated, dealing with novel and powerful scientific techniques, clinical practices, and biotechnologies applied in service of "health" and "wholeness"—concepts that are both elusive and disputed. Public bioethics is a realm of strong and often bitter disagreement, touching as it does on intimate and essential matters such as the meaning of parenthood, obligations to children and our elders, the claims of the sick and disabled, our freedom, our flourishing, our very conception of self, as well as the boundaries of the moral and legal community. It involves literal life and death issues such as the core "vital conflicts" over the law governing abortion, assisted reproductive technology, and end of life care. And there are set dichotomies of conservative versus liberal and secular versus religious that bring us even further from agreement or a shared understanding. How, then, should we seek to govern ourselves in this complex, contested, and vital domain?

To govern ourselves wisely and humanely, we must start at the beginning, namely, the normative foundation for law and policy in this area. We must begin with what it means to be human.

This book will argue that the current law concerning the core "vital conflicts" of American public bioethics is grounded in a gravely incomplete and thus false vision of human identity and flourishing. It is a vision that defines the human being fundamentally as an atomized and solitary *will*. It equates human flourishing solely with the capacity to formulate and pursue future plans of one's own invention. By contrast, the law in this domain views the natural world and even the human body itself as merely inchoate matter to be harnessed and remade in service of such projects of the will.

But human beings do not live as mere atomized wills and there is more to life than self-invention and the unencumbered pursuit of a destiny of our own devising. The truth is that persons are *embodied* beings, with all the natural limits and great gifts this entails. We experience our world, ourselves, and one another *as* living (and dying) bodies. Because we are bodies, vulnerability, mutual dependence, and natural limits are inextricable features of our lived human reality. And, for reasons that will be explored below, our embodiment situates us in a particular relationship to one another, from which emerge obligations to come to the aid of vulnerable others, including especially the disabled, the elderly, and children. But because the law governing several of the core vital conflicts of American public bioethics rests on a vision of human identity and flourishing that does not consider embodiment as essential to its account of the person, it fails to recognize these obligations, and leaves the weakest and most vulnerable members of the human community invisible and unprotected.

As is true for all areas of law and policy, if public bioethics is to effectively protect and promote the flourishing of human beings, it must be rooted in a conception of human identity that corresponds to embodied, lived reality. Public bioethics must therefore be grounded in the whole truth of who we are and how we stand in relation to one another as vulnerable, mutually dependent, finite, and embodied beings.

Accordingly, this book will reframe and resituate three principal contemporary issues of public bioethics within what will be termed an "anthropological" paradigm. Law and public policy are irreducibly normative, aiming at goods to be pursued and promoted, as well as harms to be avoided or remediated. Despite efforts to avoid appeals to "comprehensive" visions of the good in policy debates and lawmaking, all legislative, regulatory, and judicial authorities, along with the public and academic discourse that ground and sustain them, unavoidably rely on contested but mostly undeclared visions of what it means to be and thrive as a human being. This is, *a fortiori*, true of public bioethics. For this reason, the first task at hand is to subject the core disputes of American public bioethics to a searching, inductive *anthropological* analysis that will uncover, illuminate, and critique the conception of human identity and flourishing that underwrites current law and policy.

To understand why a new framework is needed and how it might be integrated into law and policy, we must first explore the history and practicalities of American *public* bioethics. Accordingly, Chapter 1 traces the historical trajectory of public bioethics in the United States with special attention to three signal events at its inception that illustrate the legal, ethical, and political paradigm that persists to the present day. Chapter 2 reflects on the problem (and solution) of anthropology—offering an account of the book's primary mode of inquiry, and an exploration and critique of "expressive individualism," the vision of human identity and flourishing that animates key conflicts of American public bioethics. Following that is a more in-depth exploration of these perennial vital conflicts of American public bioethics at the beginning and end of human life, including the disputes over: the law of abortion (Chapter 3); the regulation of assisted reproduction (Chapter 4); and issues concerning the law of end-of-life decision-making, with a special focus on the refusal or termination of life-sustaining measures, and physician-assisted suicide (Chapter 5).

These critiques will show that American law and policy in these domains rest on an image of the human being that does not reflect the lived experience of embodied human reality in all its complexity. Instead, it relies on a partial and incomplete vision of human identity that closely tracks what both sociologist Robert Bellah and philosopher Charles Taylor have identified as "expressive individualism," in which persons are conceived merely as atomized individual wills whose highest flourishing consists in interrogating the interior depths of the self in order to express and freely follow the original truths discovered therein toward one's self-invented destiny.[1] Expressive individualism, understood in this sense, equates being fully human with finding the unique truth within ourselves and freely constructing our individual lives to reflect it.

As it emerges in American public bioethics, this anthropological frame decisively privileges cognition and will in defining personal identity, supplies the content for normative (and legal) concepts such as "health" and "human dignity," and dictates the very boundaries of the moral and legal community. It dualistically distinguishes will and cognition from the body and treats the body itself as primarily a tool for pursuing one's own freely chosen goals. It understands human relationships as transactional, formed by agreements, promises, and consent for the mutual benefit of the parties involved.

People thus encounter one another as collaborative or contending wills, pursuing their own individual goals. Claims of unchosen obligations and unearned privileges are unintelligible within this framework. In this paradigm, the goods of autonomy and self-determination enjoy pride of place among ethical and legal principles. Law and government exist chiefly to create the conditions of freedom to pursue one's invented future, unmolested by others and perhaps even unimpeded by natural limits.

It is a vision that rejects the teleological conception that "natural givens" are a useful guide to interpreting the world of physical reality and embraces a more modern and instrumental vision of humankind's relationship to the natural world, and indeed, to the human body itself.

Because this regnant anthropology of American public bioethics is, to borrow the words of Alasdair MacIntyre, "forgetful of the body," it is inadequate as a foundation for laws and policies responsive to the lived realities of vulnerability, mutual dependence, and finitude that comprise the human context of this domain.[2] It is true, of course, that human beings exist as individuated, free, and particular selves. And there can be great value in the exploration of the vast interior of the self to discover and express the authentic and original meaning found there that serves as a guide to one's future plans, and even as a transgressive witness against wrongheaded and repressive customs.

But this is only a partial and incomplete picture of the fullness of lived human reality. The anthropology of expressive individualism alone cannot make sense of our fragility, neediness, and natural limits. Worse still, it cannot offer a coherent, internally consistent account of our obligations to vulnerable others, including children, the disabled, and the elderly.

What is needed, and what this book offers, is an anthropological corrective, an augmentation to the foundations of American public bioethics. To govern ourselves wisely, justly, and humanely, we must begin by *remembering the body* and its meaning for the creation and implementation of law and policy.

To that end, this book articulates and defends a more capacious account of human identity that embraces not only the truth and reality of human freedom and particularity, but also the vulnerability, mutual dependence, and finitude that result from our individual and shared lives as embodied beings. Building upon this richer anthropological account, the book argues— following Alasdair MacIntyre—that for both their basic survival and their flourishing, embodied (vulnerable) human beings depend on networks of "uncalculated giving and graceful receiving" constituted by other people who are willing to make the good of others' their own, regardless of what this might offer by way of recompense.[3] By first depending on these networks, and then participating in them, individuals become the sort of people who can care for others in this same way. This transformation of persons from needy consumers of unconditional care and support to mature uncalculating caregivers for others, of course, guarantees the sustainability of these essential networks. But, more importantly, it also helps people to develop into what an embodied being *should* become, namely, the kind of people who make the good of others their own. Put most simply and directly, by virtue of their embodiment, human beings are *made for love and friendship*.

The cultivation of memory and the moral imagination are a crucial means of understanding ourselves more fully and seeing "the other" to whom we owe obligations of care and protection. If we remember that we are embodied, we will better understand ourselves as whole, living *organisms* rather than mere wills inhabiting instrumental bodies ("re-membering" as re-integration of body and mind). If we remember that our embodiment renders us vulnerable and dependent upon the beneficence of others for our very lives and self-understanding, we will more clearly grasp our obligations of just generosity and reciprocal indebtedness to those others who are likewise vulnerable ("re-membering" as re-binding ourselves to one another in the body of the community). If we remember that as living human bodies, we all pass through stages of life when our will, judgment, strength, and beauty are inchoate, obscured, compromised, or annihilated, we will be able to more readily recognize others as fellow members of the human community with claims on us, despite the sometimes distressing disguises of age, illness, and disability ("remembering" as an essential tool of recognition).

The pathway to a richer, more human public bioethics requires not only acknowledging the limits and necessities of embodiment but embracing the great gifts and opportunities that only embodied human life affords. Thus, this book proposes a new array of goods, practices, and principles suitable for governing a polity of relational, needful, finite, and embodied persons. Drawing upon MacIntyre's "virtues of acknowledged dependence," these include the practices of just generosity, hospitality, misericordia (accompaniment of others in their suffering), gratitude, humility, Michael Sandel's (and William May's) "openness to the unbidden," tolerance of imperfection, solidarity, dignity, and honesty.[4] In other words, the practices of authentic friendship.

After applying this analysis and argument to the current law of abortion, assisted reproduction, and end-of-life decision-making, the book concludes by arguing that the proposed anthropological vision rooted in human embodiment is truer, better, and more beautiful than the alternative that currently grounds these vital conflicts of American public bioethics. Unlike the regnant paradigm that undergirds the law, this conception of human identity and flourishing makes sense of our embodiment, vulnerability, and complex relationships to vulnerable others, including especially children, the disabled, and the elderly. It also enables a more coherent account of both equality and human freedom.

This discussion serves as a first point of entry into the thorny questions and complexities of *how* a pluralistic nation can and should integrate normative concepts regarding the nature of human identity and flourishing into law and policy. And it will offer general principles and policy goals that follow from the proposed augmentation of the anthropological foundations of public bioethics.

Some of these ideas may prove surprising and challenging both for those who identify themselves as liberal or progressive, as well as for those who describe themselves as conservative and libertarian. Taking seriously the meaning of embodiment for public bioethics leads to conclusions that do not fit easily—or perhaps at all—into current American political categories. But the hard work of translating the general principles and prescriptions of a more human public bioethics into concrete, operational laws and policies must wait for the next phase of inquiry.

Lastly, before proceeding, it is worthwhile to recall that even though it draws upon works of philosophy, political theory, science, and even literature, this is, finally, a book about the law. The discussion concerns the anthropological premises and assumptions on which the law relies as revealed through an inductive analysis of its doctrine and application. There are no claims made about the motivations, commitments, or premises of individual people in their decision-making. Of course, the law shapes and reflects the goods people hold dear and the harms they seek to avoid, and so the analysis that follows is relevant to personal decision-making. But the anthropological premises of the law and that of the individual person are not necessarily the same. The inquiry and argument of this book is focused on the former.

Finally, this book is a *proposal* of an alternative governing vision that resonates more truly with our lived experience, shared values, hopes, fears, and needs. Accordingly, the criteria for evaluating the proposal should be tailored to the standards of the public square, where the aim is political persuasion rather than apodictic philosophical proof. There are no demonstrable first

principles offered here—only axioms, postulates, and proposi-
tions, to be judged by reason and experience. But this is the way
of law, politics, and public policy. In the end, this book is a proposal offered in the spirit of friendship, anchored in the firm
belief that we can only govern ourselves wisely, humanly, and
justly if we become the kind of people who can make each
other's goods our own.

I

A Genealogy of
American Public Bioethics

The core argument of this book is that the normative grounding of American public bioethics is a vision of human identity and flourishing that does not fully reflect the lived reality in which the relevant legal and political issues arise. American law and policy concerning bioethical matters are currently animated by a vision of the person as atomized, solitary, and defined essentially by his capacity to formulate and pursue future plans of his own invention. The "natural" world and even the human body are, by contrast, understood as merely inchoate matter to be harnessed and remade in service of such projects of the will. This incomplete and thus false picture of life as humanly lived makes a very poor foundation for the law and policy of bioethics. The truth is that persons live (and die) as *embodied* beings, with all the natural limits and great gifts this entails. Thus, the real human context in which the issues of public bioethics emerge is characterized by vulnerability, mutual dependence, and finitude. The asymmetry between the law's current anthropological premises and the lived reality that it seeks to govern renders American public bioethics incapable of responding wisely, justly, and humanely to many of the pitched vital conflicts that define this domain. Indeed, because of its inadequate vision of human identity and flourishing, the relevant law and policy cannot offer a coherent account of our own vulnerability, dependence, and relationships to vulnerable others, including especially children, the disabled, and the elderly. What is needed, therefore, is an "anthropological" corrective to resolve this asymmetry, and to integrate into public bioethics fitting goods, practices, and virtues suitable to governing a polity of embodied human beings.

To understand why such a corrective is needed and how it might be integrated into law and policy, it is necessary first to explore in some depth the unique field under consideration, namely, American *public* bioethics. Accordingly, this chapter will set forth a brief thematic historical narrative meant to illuminate the procedural, substantive, and human paradigm of American public bioethics, established at its inception and continuing to the present day. This genealogy will lay a general framework for the more granular inductive anthropological analysis and critique of American public bioethics in the chapters that follow.

WHAT IS PUBLIC BIOETHICS?
HISTORY AND HUMAN CONTEXT

The story of American public bioethics is a succession of political and legal reactions to the reported use, abuse, and exploitation of the weakest and most vulnerable members of the human pop ulation. It is a history of mutual dependence, neediness, and finitude. It is a story that begins with the practice of human subjects research.

Why did the practice of human subjects research precipitate the crises from which American public bioethics emerged in response? The answer lies in its very definition and purpose, which reveal that despite its importance for the pursuit of health and wholeness, it is a species of activity fraught with potentially profound ethical and personal risks to all involved.

Human subjects "research" is a term defined in federal law as "systematic investigation . . . designed to develop or contribute to generalizable knowledge."[1] It is essential for understanding human biological functioning and the mechanisms of action of drugs, devices, and medical interventions that may (or may not) offer safe and efficacious means of preventing or treating diseases and injuries. When directed toward common lethal diseases, such research can save lives. In the face of existential public health threats, human subjects research may save communities or even entire nations. Unsurprisingly, biomedical research thus enjoys widespread public support, and its most prominent practitioners are sometimes rightly hailed as genuine heroes for the common good.

However, the primary goal of this research is not for researchers to care for and cure those who serve as subjects. Instead, researchers use human subjects as tools to evaluate untested interventions or to understand the natural progress of disease without treatment. Often the human subjects involved are profoundly vulnerable—gravely ill and suffering. While both researcher and subject surely hope that the latter will receive a benefit through his participation, this is not the fundamental aim of the endeavor. The goal is to obtain information about the safety and efficacy of possible medical treatments. The human subjects involved are, by design, *means* and *instruments* to the development of this knowledge.

Accordingly, the aims and metrics for success are not the same for clinicians and researchers. Clinicians are single-mindedly focused on restoring their patients to health and wholeness. The interests and goals of doctor and patient are thus perfectly aligned, even in the application of experimental therapy. The success of clinical care is measured by healing or, failing that, diminished suffering. By contrast, the researcher seeks generalizable knowledge through the rigorous and systematic application of the scientific method. For the researcher, an experiment definitively showing that an untested medical intervention is ineffective or even dangerous is *successful* in that it produces useful generalizable knowledge.

The challenge for human subjects researchers is to find a way to conduct this research while remaining faithful to foundational principles of ethics, justice, and human rights that bind us all. They traditionally do so by securing informed consent. Providing such consent allows subjects to freely participate in the research enterprise, knowing and appreciating the risks to life, limb, and the expectations involved. Thus, by the exercise of their own autonomy and self-determination, the human subjects themselves transform the nature of the transaction from objectification to collaboration.

But does this protect human subjects from exploitation and abuse? What about those who are incapable of informed consent because of cognitive impairments resulting from immaturity, disability, low intelligence, or lack of sophistication? What about those subjects whose capacity to consent is impaired by circumstances such as incarceration, serving as soldiers bound to strict rules of obedience and chain of command, or belonging to a community beset by systemic racial injustice? What about those who are so desperate for a cure that their perceptions and understanding are compromised? These are serious questions that emerge in dramatic fashion in the historical narrative of American public bioethics.

Therefore, in its essence, research involving human subjects presents an ethically fraught and volatile human context, rife with potential peril for all involved. Even under the best possible circumstances, research involving human subjects involves management and distribution of serious risks, and the engagement with potentially profound conflicts involving justice, human dignity, freedom, and the common good. At its worst, research involving human subjects can be the occasion for the darkest forms of exploitation, abuse, and deep violence. It is from this crucible that American public bioethics emerged.

Scholars and commentators mark the beginning of American public bioethics in different ways, but there are three signal moments that particularly illustrate how crucial human embodiment is for wise and just governance in this domain. Moreover, these events set in motion a cascade of political and legal responses that laid the foundation for a framework that endures today. The first was the publication by the *New*

England Journal of Medicine of Henry K. Beecher's "Ethics and Clinical Research," a 1966 article detailing twenty-two examples of unethical experiments involving human subjects.[2] The second was the publication on July 25, 1972, of the details of the infamous federal "Tuskegee Study of Untreated Syphilis in the Negro Male" in the *Washington Evening Star.*[3] Third, on April 10, 1973, an article by Victor Cohn published on the front page of the *Washington Post* reported for the first time on debates at the National Institutes of Health on whether to fund research involving "newly delivered human fetuses—products of abortions—for medical research before they die."[4]

Each of these three episodes began with a public scandal involving the abuse of vulnerable individuals treated as objects by researchers or clinicians, followed by a governmental response. This response included information gathering and debate with discussion of the moral and legal boundaries of the community, as well as the tensions between scientific progress and respect for the dignity, autonomy, and bodily integrity of marginalized and exploited individuals. The governmental response finally culminated in official action such as passage of a statute, administrative regulations, judicial decision, or issuance of an advisory report. Solutions looked primarily to the ethical goods of autonomy and self-determination as the key safeguards against future abuses.

BEECHER SOUNDS THE ALARM

Henry Knowles Beecher was an eminent practitioner and professor of anesthesiology at Harvard University, and also an active clinical research scientist. He had a profound interest in the shocking research abuses perpetrated by the Nazi "doctors" against more than seven thousand documented concentration camp captives, including Jews, Gypsies, Soviet prisoners, Poles, Catholic priests, political prisoners, and homosexuals. He carefully studied classified U.S. military documents detailing these atrocities, along with the proceedings of the Nuremberg "Doctor's Trial" itself (1946–47), which culminated in the conviction of sixteen defendants, including seven who were put to death.

During the Nuremberg Doctor's Trial, the defendants raised the argument that the United States was not itself a paragon of research ethics and had its own sordid past. Indeed, on cross-examination a key witness for the prosecution admitted that until the trial there were no human subjects protections codified in the United States. In fact, the first such code, "Principles of Ethics Concerning Human Beings," was adopted by the American Medical Association in 1946 precisely in response to the Doctor's Trial.

From his study of these documents Beecher was moved to explore the lack of protections for human subjects of research in the United States as well as the past exploitation of vulnerable populations in America. On March 22, 1965, he delivered a lecture at the Brook Lodge Symposium for Science Writers in Kalamazoo, Michigan (sponsored by the Upjohn Company), detailing more than a dozen experiments conducted that presented no therapeutic benefits to the human subjects involved and for which no consent had been provided. His speech provoked a spirited response both from the medical research community and the lay public.[5]

For the next year he continued to write and speak about the issue, as he worked to compile a carefully documented and illustrative study meant to demonstrate the scope and gravity of the problem.

On June 16, 1966, the *New England Journal of Medicine* published the fruits of Beecher's painstaking labors in an article with the unremarkable title "Ethics and Clinical Research." In the article, Beecher argued that "unethical or questionably ethical procedures are not uncommon," and documented twenty-two published research papers in which human subjects received no therapeutic benefits.[6] In all but two examples, there was no mention whatsoever of consent. Many of the human subjects were incapable of meaningful consent due to cognitive incapacity or extenuating circumstances. Indeed, many of the individuals affected had no idea that they were enrolled in a biomedical research project at all. The human subjects involved were profoundly vulnerable. These included soldiers, indigent patients of a charity hospital, institutionalized children with severe intellectual disabilities, the elderly, the terminally ill, and chronic alcoholics suffering from liver disease.

The cases Beecher cited included protocols in which researchers withheld known effective treatments, resulting in direct and grave harm to the participants.[7] For example, in one study of rheumatic fever, investigators intentionally withheld penicillin from one hundred and nine military servicemen with streptococcal infections. They were never informed that they were part of an experiment. Two of these servicemen developed acute rheumatic fever and one developed acute nephritis.[8] In another study of relapse rates of Typhoid Fever, efficacious treatment was withheld from a group of charity hospital patients, twenty-three of whom died "who would not have been expected to succumb if they had received specific therapy."[9]

Other cases involved the intentional exposure of subjects to infectious diseases or other dangerous agents. The two most notorious examples involved the "artificial induction of hepatitis . . . carried out in an institution for mentally defective children" (later revealed to be Willowbrook State School in Staten Island), and the deliberate injection of live cancer cells into elderly patients of New York's Jewish Chronic Disease Hospital.[10] In the first case, the parents of the cognitively disabled children acceded to the administration of the virus, but "nothing is said of what was told them concerning the appreciable hazards involved."[11] In the second case, the hospitalized patients were "merely told they would be receiving 'some cells'" but "the word cancer was entirely omitted."[12]

Beecher did not provide any identifying information for the researchers or institutions involved, but the twenty-two examples cited were drawn "from leading medical schools, university hospitals, private hospitals, governmental military departments (the Army, the Navy, and the Air Force), governmental institutes (the National Institutes of Health), Veterans Administration hospitals and industry."[13] The institutions hosting the research included such luminaries as Harvard University and the NIH Clinical Center. These ethically suspect research projects had passed peer review and were published in elite journals including both the *New England Journal of Medicine* and the *Journal of the American Medical Association*. Beecher detailed the powerful institutional and personal pressures that induce researchers to aggressively pursue their work with human subjects, including new sources of financial support, requirements for academic tenure and promotion, hunger for prestige, as well as a genuine passion to pursue knowledge for the sake of itself or to relieve human suffering.

Even though Beecher's assessment included the assurance that "American medicine is sound, and most progress in it soundly attained," and his proposed solutions were modest (he thought that calling public attention to these ethical lapses would be a sufficient corrective), the article shocked the medical research community and the public.[14] The front pages of major national newspapers covered the scandals and Congress directed the National Institutes of Health to investigate. And, as will be discussed below, Beecher's article (and his testimony) played an essential role in the Congressional hearings that culminated in the federal statute that led to American public bioethics.

INJUSTICE IN TUSKEGEE

On July 25, 1972, an article appeared on the front page of the *Washington Evening Star* entitled "Human Guinea Pigs: Syphilis Patients Died Untreated," by Associated Press reporter Jean Heller.[15] The next day, this shameful story of exploitation, deception, and neglect of hundreds of poor black men and their families by U.S. Public Health Service researchers dominated the headlines throughout the country. The details were shocking. In 1932, researchers from the federal government commenced the "Public Health Service Study of Untreated Syphilis in the Male Negro in Macon County, Alabama." It was to be a "natural history" study of the progression of the devastating and deadly disease without any significant medical intervention. The disease was rampant in Macon County, a community of poor, mostly uneducated black sharecroppers. Indeed, Macon had the highest syphilis rate in the nation. The researchers lured their subjects—600 men in all—with vague and deceptive advertisements promising testing and treatment for "bad blood" for "colored people." Of the 600 men enrolled, 301 had evidence of latent syphilis and 299 served as a control group. Original records and protocols of the study are scant, but it is clear that the initial plan was to study the men for six months. Later, however, the decision was taken to follow the men until they died and perform investigative autopsies. Ultimately, the study lasted *forty years*.[16]

Investigators never made any mention of syphilis to the participants, nor did they disclose the then-known consequences of failing to treat the disease. They also failed to inform participants of the known risks of transmission of infection to sexual partners or children. There was, in fact, no evidence whatsoever of any attempts to secure meaningful consent of any sort. The participants were merely told that they were being tested for "bad blood." They were subject to invasive testing, including spinal taps. As an inducement to participate in the study, men were offered rides to the doctor, free lunches, and stipends to offset the costs of burial following the investigative autopsy.[17]

Not only did the investigators deceive the participants and withhold crucial information about the study and its risks, they actively took steps to *prevent the patients from obtaining needed care.* The men were deprived of effective management of their symptoms, and it has been reported that the investigators even successfully persuaded local medical care providers (along with their partners at the Tuskegee Institute) not to diagnose or treat them so that the natural history of the disease could be observed without disruption. Most shocking of all, even though penicillin was developed as a highly effective intervention for syphilis in the 1940s and became widely available shortly thereafter, the investigators deliberately withheld such treatment.[18]

The human toll on these poor men and their families was staggering. Many had their lives cut short by the disease. Those who survived suffered its ravages, including severe pain, skin lesions, neurological dysfunction, bone and joint defects, cardiovascular disease, paralysis, and dementia. Still others unwittingly passed the disease to their spouses and children.

In 1966, a low-level U.S. Public Health Service venereal disease researcher, Peter Buxton, learned of the study and reported his alarm to colleagues, who almost entirely ignored him. When his superiors took no action, he brought the story to a journalist friend who referred him to AP reporter Jean Heller who published her findings, described in detail above, in July 1972. A civil rights class action lawsuit was filed on behalf of survivors against the government and was later settled for ten million dollars.[19]

Alongside the ethical breaches reported by Beecher, the scandalous injustices of Tuskegee comprise the second major precipitating event from which American public bioethics emerged. But before turning to the governmental responses engendered by these events, it is necessary to consider one final scandal that further catalyzed the development of this distinctive field of law and policy.

RESEARCH ON JUST-ABORTED, EX UTERO, BUT STILL-LIVING INFANTS

Between April 10 and April 15, 1973, the *Washington Post* ran three separate front-page articles detailing a previously unreported debate at the National Institutes of Health regarding a proposal to fund research involving the use of "newly-delivered human fetuses—products of abortion—before they die."[20] The first article (April 10) related that thirteen months earlier NIH had received an internal recommendation to proceed with such research, though it had more recently chosen to "consider the ethics of the matter afresh" in light of the scandal of the Tuskegee syphilis study. Two years prior, another NIH advisory committee proposed the use of such newly-delivered aborted children provided they were of a certain age (no more than twenty weeks), weight (no more than 1.1 pounds), and length (no more than 9.8 inches, crown to heel). There were reports from Great Britain and elsewhere that researchers had been "obtaining months-old fetuses for research and keeping them alive for up to three or four days" *ex utero*. One American researcher asserted that U.S. scientists were conducting similar experiments abroad with NIH funding. This was disputed by other NIH officials. One federal official, the scientific director for the Child Health Institute, noted that federal support for such research is controversial because of "an articulate Catholic minority who disagrees" and "a substantial and articulate black minority" who oppose abortion.[21]

This comment proved prescient, as detailed in the second *Washington Post* article published three days later (April 13), when more than 200 Catholic high school students gathered in the NIH auditorium to protest and put pointed questions to federal officials. The protest was organized by a group from Stone Ridge Country Day School of the Sacred Heart, led by three students, including 17-year-old Maria Shriver, the daughter of Eunice and Sargent Shriver, and the niece of Senator Edward Kennedy, and his deceased brothers, the late Senator Robert and President John F. Kennedy. (She would, of course, go on to have a distinguished career as a journalist and serve as First Lady of California.) In response to the students, Dr. Robert Berliner, NIH Deputy Director for Science, asserted in a written statement that the agency "does not now support" such research and that there are "no circumstances at present or in the foreseeable future that would justify NIH support."[22]

Two days later (on April 15), the *Washington Post* published yet another article, this time describing the work of two American scientists who had on separate occasions traveled to Finland to conduct experiments on newly aborted, *ex utero* but still-living infants. One scientist, Dr. Jerald Gaull, stated that he would remove the brain, lungs, liver, and kidneys while the child's heart was still beating. The other doctor (chief of Pediatrics at Cleveland Metropolitan General Hospital) would take a blood sample while the child was still connected to her mother by the umbilical cord. After the cord was severed, but before cessation of the heartbeat, he would surgically remove various organs. These scientists justified their practices first by appealing to the useful knowledge such experiments might yield in service of maternal-fetal health, and second, because the just-aborted infants were too biologically immature (given their under-developed lungs) to survive outside of the womb for an extended period of time.[23]

Such scientists would travel abroad to countries where abortions were performed later in pregnancy by caesarean section, affording ready access to newly-removed and still-living neonates. Dr. Gaull indicated that he had traveled to Finland for a period of a month, during which time he could perform five or six procedures per day. He stated that he and colleagues had "even studied the whole intact fetus, injecting radioisotopes and following certain chemical reactions. We have in Europe studied the transfer of amino acids from mother to fetus while the umbilical cord was still intact." Another scientist, Dr. Abraham Rudolph, injected "radioactively labeled microspheres" into an intact living post-abortion infant still attached to her mother by the umbilical cord in order to study blood circulation in the fetus. Another scientist interviewed suggested that dozens of researchers conducted similar experiments. A 1971 NIH nonfederal study section recommended that researchers be allowed to artificially maintain the life of post-abortion neonates for at least three or four hours. This proposal does not appear to have been accepted as formal NIH policy, though NIH-funded researchers seem to have engaged in research on still-living aborted neonates abroad.[24]

Published articles in scholarly journals likewise confirmed the use and destruction of living newly aborted babies in research, including experiments that intentionally extended their lives *ex utero* solely for the sake of the investigation. One such experiment was reported in the *American Journal of Obstetrics and Gynecology,* and involved efforts to develop an artificial placenta.[25] Another paper published in the *Transactions of the American Pediatric Society* described the decapitation of living newly aborted *ex utero* infants (at 12–20 weeks gestation) followed by perfusion of their brains with chemical markers in order to study fetal brain metabolism.[26]

Much of the lay public was shocked by the reports of these experiments, and NIH leaders quickly sought to reassure them that these were not sponsored projects that enjoyed the support of federal taxpayer dollars. But as will be detailed below, this was not the end of the story, but rather only the beginning.

These three public scandals—the ethical abuses reported by Beecher, the Tuskegee scandal, and controversial experiments on aborted but still-living *ex utero* nonviable infants—formed a troika of events that spurred a governmental response that would lay both the procedural and substantive groundwork for American public bioethics for years to come.

THE KENNEDY HEARINGS

It began in February of 1973. The U.S. Senate Subcommittee on Health of the Committee on Labor and Public Welfare, led by Senator Edward Kennedy, convened a series of hearings in response to practices and developments in biomedical science and medicine that he believed raised profound ethical, legal, political, and social challenges. The hearings lasted eleven days in all, including ten meetings of the subcommittee from February through July of 1973, and one in July 1974 (one week after the passage of a significant federal statute—the direct fruit of the previous year's hearings).

But these were not the first Congressional hearings on bioethical issues. Years before, in 1968, Senator Walter Mondale initiated seven days of hearings aimed at passing a joint resolution creating a federal "Commission on Health Science and Society" to provide oversight and guidance on bioethical questions of public import. Mondale was reacting to reports of the first human heart transplant by Dr. Christiaan Barnard of South Africa as well as various questions concerning genetic manipulation that prefigured the current debates over human cloning and gene editing. But it is also clear that he had in mind the 1966 article of Henry Knowles Beecher, who provided testimony at the hearing recapitulating his arguments about the professional and financial pressures motivating increasingly aggressive forms of human subjects research. But Mondale's initiatives foundered until Senator Kennedy commenced his own efforts in 1973.

The Kennedy hearings were formally framed around three legislative proposals under consideration: Senate Bills 878 and 974, and Joint Resolution 71. S.B. 878 and S.B. 974, aimed, respectively, to provide oversight of federally sponsored research involving human subjects and to provide training in the ethical, legal, social, and policy dimensions of biomedical research. The third proposal, Senate Joint Resolution 71, was for the creation of a national bioethics advisory commission in the same spirit as the 1968 Mondale proposal.

Individual hearings were divided by topic. The first hearings focused on ethical risks and abuses involving pharmaceutical research using vulnerable populations, including the controversial "off-label" use of DepoProvera and DES as experimental contraceptives. A second set of hearings explored the ethical challenges of research involving the neurosurgical or pharmacological manipulation of brain and behavior, as well as research involving genetic screening and engineering. A third set of hearings focused on research done on vulnerable subjects, including prisoners, and a discussion of what was termed "outrageous research abuses." This included the experimental use of a dangerous midterm abortion procedure in May of 1972 by Dr. Kermit Gosnell, which led to serious complications for sixty percent of a group of poor minority women bused from Chicago to Philadelphia to receive the procedure.[27] The fourth round of hearings focused entirely on the Tuskegee syphilis study scandal. A fifth hearing, held a year later, was dedicated to examining the controversial use of living just-aborted *ex utero* newborns in research.

Despite the wide-ranging subject matter of the first four rounds of Kennedy hearings in 1973, three recurring elements ran throughout the discussion: namely, the work of Henry Knowles Beecher, the abuses of Tuskegee, and to a lesser extent, research involving unborn children during and after abortion. This last issue resurfaced prominently in the final Kennedy bioethics hearing dedicated entirely to exploring this controversial matter.

Beecher was everywhere. His research (especially his 1966 article) was invoked in nearly every hearing. He testified directly in the third set of hearings on research abuses of vulnerable human subjects. Symbolically and substantively, he served as a living prophetic witness warning against the powerful temptation to use and exploit the vulnerable in biomedical research to gain prestige, professional advancement, the promise of funding, as well as the noble pursuit of useful knowledge.

The Tuskegee scandal was a ubiquitous element of the hearings, anchoring its inception and sustaining its investigative work. In written testimony submitted for the first hearing, Senator Hubert Humphrey directly invoked the abuses of Tuskegee and quoted Beecher's observation that "[l]ay subjects, sick or well, are not likely to understand the full implications of complicated procedures, even after careful explanation."[28] In the third round of hearings relating to vulnerable human subjects and "outrageous" research abuses, numerous witnesses cited Tuskegee as a constant refrain. Members of the Tuskegee Syphilis Study Ad Hoc Advisory Committee (created by the Assistant Secretary of Health, Education, and Welfare) testified about their investigation of the incident. Fred Gray, a prominent civil rights attorney who had represented Rosa Parks, testified about his work on behalf of victims of the Tuskegee experiments, followed by the testimony of two Tuskegee survivors, Lester Scott and Charles Pollard. A fourth round of hearings lasting four days was dedicated entirely to investigating the Tuskegee scandal and hearing from those involved. Throughout all the hearings, the Tuskegee incident served as a stark and constant reminder that all American institutions—even the federal government itself—are capable of unspeakable abuse and profound injustice in the name of biomedical progress.[29]

Research involving aborted though still-living newborns was also a feature of the 1973 hearings. In the second round of hearings (held on February 23 and March 6), nearly sixty pages of written testimony and supporting materials were submitted describing examples of and raising grave concerns about such research. Though less prominent during the Kennedy hearings of 1973, the issue and the public controversy that it occasioned proved central to the legislative action following those hearings and prompted a hearing entirely dedicated to live fetal research, held in 1974.

THE BIRTH OF AMERICAN PUBLIC BIOETHICS

While the 1973 Kennedy hearings themselves marked an essential moment in the inception of public bioethics as a field of law, policy, and politics in America, the legislative action in which the hearings culminated was even more momentous. In effect, it constituted the first legal mandate for the government to identify and implement bioethical principles and regulations in the name of the state.

The National Research Act was signed into law by Richard Nixon on July 12, 1974. In part it aimed to facilitate and promote excellence in biomedical research through federal training and funding programs. But more significantly, it was the concrete statutory response to the scandals and concerns that surfaced and were examined during the Kennedy hearings. Title II of the Act created the National Commission for the Protection of Human Subjects of Biomedical and Behavioral Research. It was to be an eleven-member advisory council composed of experts drawn from a variety of disciplines including medicine, law, ethics, theology, philosophy, health management, government affairs, and the sciences. It provided that five members (though no more than five of the eleven) should be actively involved in research with human subjects.[30]

The National Commission was empowered by the new law "to identify the basic ethical principles which should underlie the conduct of biomedical and behavioral research involving human subjects." The Commission was tasked with focusing on the question of the contours and meaning of "informed consent" in the context of research. In a clear response to the abuses flagged by Beecher, the Commission was charged to articulate standards for the ethical conduct of research involving "children, prisoners, and the institutionalized mentally infirm."[31]

As a first order of business, the Commission was tasked with exploring the question of research involving "living fetuses," and was directed to provide a report on this topic no later than four months after its members assumed office.[32] It was also instructed to explore the ethics of psychosurgery, another topic of the Kennedy hearings. Even more broadly, the Commission was directed to undertake a special "comprehensive study of the ethical, legal, and social implications of advance in biomedical and behavioral research and technology."[33] The Commission was empowered to hold hearings, take testimony, access information from federal agencies, and provide recommendations to the President, Congress, and the Secretary of Health, Education, and Welfare. The National Research Act ordered the Secretary to publish such recommendations, invite public comment, and either act on them expeditiously or publish his or her reasons for declining to do so in the Federal Register, the official daily journal of the U.S. government. In short, the National Research Act created a commission with the power to make presumptively actionable recommendations to the U.S. government on the bioethical issues that scandalized the American public for nearly a decade.

But the act did still more. It added a provision that the Secretary of HEW must establish regulations requiring that institutions receiving funding or support under the new law demonstrate that they have established an Institutional Review Board to review protocols involving human subjects and provide for their protection. Furthermore, the Secretary was charged with promulgating regulations that would govern the conduct of such research. Finally, the National Research Act imposed a moratorium on federally funded research "on a living human fetus, before or after the induced abortion of such fetus, unless such research is done for the purpose of assuring the survival of such fetus."[34] The ban was to remain in place until Congress received and considered the report of the National Commission.

Exactly one week after President Nixon signed the National Research Act, Senator Kennedy convened the fifth and final hearing, focused solely on the question of fetal research, including aborted but still-living (though imminently dying) newborns.[35] It was meant to provide a forum for wide ranging public discussion in advance of the National Commission's work on the issue. Kennedy aimed to obtain information about the means, ends, benefits, and harms of such research, and to explore how it related to the controversial matter of abortion. *Roe v. Wade,* decided just eighteen months prior, roiled the public square and disrupted the legal and policy landscape by announcing a constitutional right to abortion and a new jurisprudential framework for its regulation that altered the laws of all fifty states.

Testimony and documentary evidence offered at the hearing described many of the same experiments reported by the *Washington Post* a year earlier. There was also discussion of experiments in which unborn children slated for abortion were deliberately exposed to rubella in order to study its mechanism of transmission and effects (for purposes of vaccine development) after the abortion was completed.

Kennedy called witnesses on both sides of the debate. Nobel Laureate Dr. Frederick Robbins, Dean of Medicine at Case Western Reserve University, and Dr. Richard Berman, Chairman of Pediatrics at Columbia University, offered support for the research, citing its benefits for biomedical science and clinical practice, and noting that the unborn or aborted but still-living newborns involved were inexorably dying in any event. On the other side, Dr. Andre Hellegers, Professor of Obstetrics and Gynecology and Director of the Kennedy Institute of Ethics at Georgetown (founded by and named for Senator Kennedy's family), and Patricia Policastro, a grassroots pro-life activist and advocate for the cognitively disabled, argued that it was gravely unjust, abusive, and exploitative to manipulate and inflict additional injuries on living human subjects slated for abortion (or just aborted) in research that would provide them with no benefit. In response to the argument that the research was justified because such children were going to die in any event, Dr. Hellegers replied, "[I]f you are not going to make it [meaning, survive] anyway, it is not a warranty to be experimented upon."[36]

For her part, Policastro provided testimony and documentary evidence recounting controversial examples of live fetal experimentation. For example, she recalled student protests at Stanford University in response to a university researcher experimenting on living fetuses. She provided a statement by one of the student protest organizers that "[Dr. Goodlin's] experiments have involved cruel acts, such as slicing open the rib cages of still living aborted fetuses in order to observe their hearts."[37] Her written testimony also recapitulated some of the documentary evidence submitted a year before during the second round of Kennedy hearings.

The hearing concluded and the National Commission commenced its analysis of research on living fetuses immediately after its members were chosen and seated. Their work and the report in which it culminated relied on the evidence presented during the Kennedy hearings. It also animated and influenced the creation of the strict federal regulations on research involving living fetuses destined for abortion that are detailed further below.

AN ENDURING BLUEPRINT
FOR AMERICAN PUBLIC BIOETHICS

The Kennedy hearings, the National Research Act, and the events to which they were a response set in place a procedural and substantive foundation that endures to the present day.

Procedurally, from its inception to today, American public bioethics has been a reactive form of governance. Scandals occur and the political branches (or occasionally the judiciary, as in the case of abortion) respond. The initial reaction nearly always includes an attempt at fact-finding, most frequently by convening a well-familiar cast of characters—eminent scientists, famous clinicians, patients' groups, philosophers, theologians, activists, government officials, and not infrequently, a representative of the U.S. Conference of Catholic Bishops. The discourse and debate in these hearings feature a recurring thrust-and-parry over scientific freedom, biomedical progress, and efforts to relieve suffering on the one hand, and, on the other, the competing and constraining goods of respect for the dignity and autonomy of persons, as well as the practice of humility and the corollary injunction against "playing God."

Hearings are often followed by formal state action (such as the National Research Act) that attempts to address public concerns, even if only temporarily, like the moratorium on research involving aborted but still-living newborns. Such legislation often provides a broad-strokes mandate, and delegates authority to the administrative state—executive branch agencies such as the Department of Health and Human Services or federal advisory bodies like the National Commission—to flesh out the details in a more fine-grained manner, usually in the form of promulgated regulations which bind with the force of law. The events of 1973 and 1974 are thus emblematic of this enduring procedural blueprint.

The events of 1973 and 1974 show that public bioethics is uniquely complex and complicated. Not only does it concern the rapidly evolving and multifarious fields of biomedical science and biotechnology, but the most difficult ethical, legal, and policy questions feature the possibility of great goods seamlessly interwoven with potentially catastrophic wrongs. The researchers described by Beecher, the U.S. Public Health officials in Tuskegee, and the American doctors traveling to Europe to experiment on newly aborted still-living infants all intended their work to serve humanitarian ends for precisely the kinds of subjects they exploited and abused. In their minds, they were trying to salvage some good from a tragic circumstance that they did not create—the children of Willowbrook were at severe risk for hepatitis in any event, the men of Tuskegee were infected with syphilis and unlikely to get effective care because of their socioeconomic plight and racial injustice, and the *ex vivo* neonates were imminently dying (as intended by the abortion) and beyond the reach of rescue. The data to be gleaned from these research projects would be valuable. But the deeper truth is that these researchers intentionally exploited these intellectually disabled children, poor African American sharecroppers, and just-aborted but still-living newborns, subjecting them to risks, manipulation, and painful nontherapeutic interventions that would be regarded as intolerably unethical if performed without consent on able-bodied adults of sound mind and sophistication. The researchers embraced the tragic circumstances as a warrant to conscript these unfortunate victims into *yet another* extractive project to serve someone else's ends, with no benefits to themselves.

More complicated still are the issues posed by enormously powerful biotechnologies that can be equally used for good or ill. The Kennedy hearings featured discussion of novel techniques of neurological or genetic modification. The technologies themselves were (as all are) neutral and merely instrumental. They could be used, respectively, both for therapies for mental illness or heritable disease, or they could be used to exert unprecedented and unjust psychological control over others, or to pursue eugenic aspirations. This admixture of good intentions and development of genuinely beneficial biomedical knowledge combined with the possibility of great harms and even wickedness is characteristic of many of the issues of public bioethics, making it a distinctively complicated field of law and policy.

The events at the birth of American public bioethics likewise illustrate that the core disputes in this domain are *vital* conflicts, literally presenting matters of life and death. Conflicts concern the boundaries of the moral and legal community, inside of which one is protected by the law and enjoys the care and concern of others, but outside of which one may be objectified and even destroyed with impunity for the benefit of others. The children of Willowbrook, the elderly of the New York Jewish Chronic Disease hospital, and the people of Tuskegee were singled out for abuse and mistreatment because their marginal social status rendered them largely defenseless in the face such injustices. They were effectively invisible until their mistreatment was exposed by the more powerful. For the just-aborted newborns, the situation was even more dramatic. Their very moral status as human beings was (and remains) contested. As will be discussed extensively in Chapter 3, the question of membership in the human community that anchors the abortion controversy (which, of course, erupted on the national scene in 1973) infuses the perennial conflicts of American public bio-ethics. Across the spectrum of public matters concerning those individuals at the margins of life's beginning and end (and the liminal moments in between), the normative questions of "Who counts?" and "Whose good counts as part of the common good?" are ubiquitous.

The scandals uncovered by Beecher, of Tuskegee, and in-volving research on living just-aborted infants (and the state action taken in response) likewise manifest the final distinctive feature of American public bioethics: it is bitterly contested and vexed. This should not be surprising, given that it is fundamen-tally concerned with the nature, meaning, and consequences of birth, life, death, procreation, parenthood, childhood, race, pov-erty, illness, scientific freedom, autonomy, dignity, equality, and justice. Public bioethics squarely and unavoidably poses the questions of "Who are we and what do we owe to one another?"—matters about which people differ and feel very strongly, to say the least.

In much of American law and policy there may be a "live and let live" *modus vivendi* available, where governmental neu-trality can simply make space for different forms of private or-dering, each according to the diverse normative commitments of various members of the polity. But American public bioethics presents vital conflicts where either through action or inaction, the state must take sides. Does the search for useful biomedical knowledge justify intentionally using and harming disabled children, the senile elderly, stigmatized minorities, and just-aborted newborns? Does the very moral and legal status of an individual depend on her circumstances (such as when she will die imminently because of terminal illness or someone else's decision to end her life), her condition of dependence, or how useful or burdensome she is judged to be by others? Put another way, American public bioethics unavoidably trades in vital conflicts among "comprehensive" theories of the good. State neutrality is frequently not a coherent option.

The events of 1973 and 1974 illustrate the singular substantive nature of American public bioethics. They make clear that public bioethics emerges in response to the lived realities and consequences of the individual and shared lives of *embodied* beings. Human embodiment entails vulnerability, the finitude of natural limits, and mutual dependence. These direct effects of embodiment motivate the pursuit of great goods, but also create the possibility of profound exploitation and abuse, as we have seen in the proceeding events. The search for biomedical knowledge and the practice of medicine aim to ameliorate the afflictions of the body—disease, injury, and senescence. But those very afflictions create the human vulnerability that exposes the weak to exploitation by researchers. The intellectually disabled children at Willowbrook, the elderly patients of the New York Jewish Chronic Disease Hospital, the men suffering from syphilis in Tuskegee, and the just-aborted but still-living newborns in Scandinavia were easily conscripted into involuntary, harmful, and nontherapeutic research projects precisely because their bodily conditions and diminished social standing impeded their agency and robbed them of their voices.

And, finally, the events at the birth of American public bioethics also usefully point toward the most commonly invoked legal or public policy solution, rooted in a particular vision of the human being as fundamentally an individual choosing self. Thus, the solution to the problems of abuse and exploitation was to seek refuge in legal mechanisms nested in the goods of *autonomy* and *self-determination*, designed primarily to secure the informed exercise of free will by rational, able-minded persons.

THE DECADES THAT FOLLOWED

In the nearly five decades that followed, three particular *vital conflicts*, namely, the legal and policy disputes regarding abortion, assisted reproduction, and end-of-life decision-making, have been persistent features of the landscape, and have largely defined American public bioethics. These vital conflicts are the foci of the inductive anthropological analysis that comprise the heart of this book. It is thus worth briefly sketching out in a general way the arc of American public bioethics to illustrate the durability of these vital conflicts across time, and to prepare the way for the discussion in later chapters of how embodiment is an essential element to consider when evaluating the current American legal framework.

1970s

For the remainder of the 1970s, in direct reaction to highly publicized events, the principal issues of American public bioethics included the law and policy of human subjects protections, fetal research, gene transfer research, assisted reproduction, abortion, and end-of-life decision-making. In 1974, the Department of Health, Education, and Welfare (HEW) promulgated regulations implementing the National Research Act, including rules relating to pregnant women, fetuses, prisoners, and the work of Institutional Review Boards in overseeing research with human subjects.

In 1975, the National Commission issued its first report "Research on the Fetus," in which it recommended that HEW could ethically support research involving fetuses slated for abortion "provided such research is carried out within the guidelines for all other nontherapeutic research directed toward the fetus *in utero*" that is intended to be brought to term.[38] They additionally recommended that HEW could support research involving a just-aborted, nonviable but living newborn, so long as certain criteria were met, including that the newborn was "less than 20 weeks gestational age, no significant changes are introduced into the abortion procedure in the interest of research alone, and no intrusion into the fetus is made which alters the duration of life."[39] Moreover, the Commission advised that the research protocol should not affect the decision, timing, and method of abortion. The Commission stated that such newborns are entitled to the respect owed to "dying subjects," whose human dignity warranted appropriate treatment.[40] The Commission also recommended the creation of a national ethical review body to evaluate cases presenting difficult questions involving these criteria. Accordingly, HEW propounded regulations by adopting these recommendations and creating an "Ethics Advisory Board" (EAB), charged with reviewing and approving proposals seeking federal funding for research in this domain.

Not surprisingly, in the wake of the Supreme Court's 1973 *Roe v. Wade* decision, the issue of abortion dominated the American public bioethical landscape throughout that decade (and every decade thereafter). In response, Congress moved quickly to protect the rights of conscientious objectors. In 1974, Congress passed the so-called "Church Amendments" (named for their sponsor, Idaho Democratic Senator Frank Church), which extended conscience protections to those individuals and entities with religious or moral objections to performing or assisting performance of abortions and sterilizations. The Church Amendments also prohibited institutions that receive certain forms of federal support from discriminating against health care providers because they performed or refused to perform abortions on conscientious grounds.[41] Also, in 1976, Congress passed an appropriations restriction colloquially known as the "Hyde Amendment," forbidding the use of Medicaid funds to pay for most abortions. The law has changed slightly over time, but in its essence has been reauthorized every year since.[42] In 1977, in *Maher v. Roe*, the U.S. Supreme Court upheld as constitutional a state regulation that restricted Medicaid funding for first-trimester abortions to those procedures deemed "medically necessary."[43]

In 1976, end-of-life decision-making emerged as a signal issue in American public bioethics with the New Jersey Supreme Court decision *In re Quinlan*. The case involved a dispute over the proper care for a profoundly cognitively disabled woman between her father, who wished to discontinue life-sustaining measures (namely, her ventilator) and her health care providers, who refused. Ultimately, the Supreme Court of New Jersey held that Quinlan's right to privacy entailed the freedom to choose to discontinue life-sustaining measures, and that this right could be exercised by her proxy decision-makers.[44] Though the ventilator was removed, Quinlan surprisingly continued to breathe unaided and died nine year later in 1985.[45]

In 1978, Louise Brown—the first baby who had been conceived by *in vitro fertilization*—was born. That same year, the HEW Ethics Advisory Board (EAB) agreed to review a research proposal involving in vitro fertilization. Federal regulations required EAB evaluation prior to authorization of federal funding by HEW of any project involving IVF. The EAB deliberated and concluded in a 1979 report that research involving human in vitro fertilization is "ethically defensible but still legitimately controverted."[46] It also recommended that human IVF research is acceptable from an ethical standpoint, subject to certain criteria. It further recommended that HEW provide support for such research, though the EAB refrained from addressing the level of funding. This EAB report (though never implemented) proved to be a crucial development for the public bioethics matters touching and concerning both assisted reproduction and research involving human embryos.

The final key development of the 1970s for public bioethics in America was the publication in 1979 of the "Belmont Report" by the National Commission. This report constituted the Commission's response to the charge in the National Research Act to articulate the "basic ethical principles that should underlie the conduct of biomedical and behavioral research involving human subjects." The Commission identified three such ethical principles, namely "respect for persons," "beneficence," and "justice." Respect for persons entails respect for autonomous decision-making and protection of those incapable of such choices. "Beneficence" is a principle that imposes the obligations first, to do no harm, and second, to seek to maximize benefits while minimizing risks. Finally, "justice" is a norm concerned with fairly allocating the burdens and benefits of scientific research involving human subjects.[47]

Much of the report is dedicated to discussing how these principles might be applied, with special emphasis on informed consent, risk assessment, and selection of subjects. The report has had enormous worldwide impact on the discourse and practice of human subjects research, despite its failure to define and explore in-depth key concepts, most importantly the meaning of "persons." Subsequent application of the Belmont Report by policymakers and commentators alike has shifted emphasis from respect for persons generally to one narrow aspect discussed in the report, namely, the good of personal autonomy. This shift both reflects and reinforces the vision of human identity and flourishing (expressive individualism) critiqued in the chapters that follow.

As the decade drew to a close, the National Commission's term expired, and Congress created by statute a successor entity in the executive branch entitled The President's Commission for the Study of Ethical Problems in Medicine and Biomedical and Behavioral Research.

1980s

The 1980s saw the continuation of law and policy disputes over abortion, fetal research, assisted reproduction, and research involving human subjects, but also witnessed the emergence of new conflicts regarding the definition of death, end-of-life decision-making on behalf of disabled newborns, and related matters of organ transplantation policy.

Reacting to developments in medical techniques enabling clinicians to artificially sustain respiration and circulation—the traditional indicators of biological life, the absence of which signaled "death"—the President's Commission issued a report in 1981 that sought to offer a new uniform definition of death, faithful to the physiological realities of the phenomenon and applicable across a wide variety of ethical, legal, and public policy contexts. Specifically, in its report, succinctly entitled "Defining Death," the President's Commission proposed the Uniform Determination of Death Act, which provided that "an individual who has sustained either (1) irreversible cessation of circulatory and respiratory functions, or (2) irreversible cessation of all functions of the entire brain, including the brain stem, is dead."[48] This proposal was approved by the National Conference of Commissioners on Uniform State Laws, the American Bar Association, and the American Medical Association. It has since been adopted as the law in nearly every state in the union, thus transforming the American landscape of criminal law, tort law, estate law, insurance law, and the law and policy of organ donation.

Around the same time, in 1982 and 1983, a series of reports emerged about parents refusing consent for life-saving medical treatments for their disabled newborns that would otherwise be provided to healthy babies. In one case from Indiana, parents of a newborn ("Baby Doe") with Down's Syndrome refused consent to correct an esophageal atresia and directed that food and water be withheld. The hospital objected and filed suit, but the baby died before the Indiana Supreme Court could hear the case. In another case from New York, a private citizen unsuccessfully tried to intervene on behalf of a child with spina bifida whose parents had declined a life-prolonging intervention. Led by President Reagan and his Surgeon General, the federal government sought to intervene first by administrative rule, ostensibly implementing a federal statute prohibiting discrimination on the basis of disability. The rule directed facilities receiving federal funding to take steps to prevent the neglect of disabled newborns. In 1986, a fractured Supreme Court held in *Bowen v. American Hospital Association* that the federal regulation was invalid because it exceeded the authority of the underlying disabilities statute it was meant to implement.[49] While this case was being litigated, Congress embedded federal protections for disabled newborns by amendment of the Child Abuse Prevention and Treatment Act, which was passed in October of 1984.[50]

Closely connected to the question of death and dying, the issue of organ donation and transplantation likewise emerged in the 1980s as a core issue in American public bioethics. In response to a shortage in donor organs, a demand for transplantations, and lack of clarity regarding the law concerning property in human remains, Congress adopted the National Organ Transplant Act (NOTA) in 1984.[51] The law was designed to create a national procurement framework that would promote donation of organs. But it also clearly forbade the buying and selling of organs for transplantation out of ethical concerns regarding commodification of the body and exploitation of the poor.

Just as in the 1970s, the issues of human subjects protections, fetal research, and abortion remained active concerns for lawmakers, judges, and the public at large. The Department of Health and Human Services in 1981 revised federal regulations regarding Institutional Review Boards to conform to recommendations by the National Commission, and the FDA followed suite, within the boundaries of their statutory authority. In 1982, the President's Science Adviser in the Office of Science and Technology Policy created a committee tasked with developing a common federal policy for protection of human subjects. This proposed policy was published in 1986 and adopted in 1991 by multiple federal agencies as the "Common Rule."[52]

The public struggle over the ethics, law, and policy regarding
ɪ fetal research continued. In 1985, Congress passed the Health Research Extension Act, which reauthorized the National Institutes of Health (the primary research funding arm of the federal government), prohibiting federal support for research on nonviable newborns or newborns of uncertain viability unless the intervention was meant to "enhance the well-being or meet health needs of the fetus or enhance the probability of its survival to viability; or will pose no added risk of suffering injury, or death to the fetus." Moreover, the law provided that in federal human subjects regulations the risk standard must "be the same for fetuses which are intended to be aborted and fetuses which are intended to be carried to term." The act also created the "Biomedical Ethics Advisory Committee," which was to study the "nature, advisability, and biomedical and ethical implications" of exercising any waiver of the human subjects protections applicable to live fetal research.[53] The BEAC met only twice and its work was stymied over abortion politics. Its ap-

propriations were halted and its term expired in 1990 without making any recommendations.

In 1988, the public question shifted its focus from research on living fetuses and newborns to research involving cadaveric fetal tissue. Assistant Secretary for Health and Human Services Robert Windom announced a moratorium on transplantation research with fetal tissue taken from abortions until an advisory committee could examine the question and report back. In December 1988, the NIH Human Fetal Tissue Transplantation panel issued a report responding to the questions posed by Windom and recommending that such research receive federal support subject to certain conditions.

For example, the decision to terminate the pregnancy and consent to the abortion must be prior to and separate from the decision to donate fetal tissue for research; the pregnant woman may not designate the transplant-recipient of the tissue; the pregnant woman should not be induced to terminate pregnancy for the sake of providing tissue; prior informed consent of the pregnant woman should be obtained before using the tissue in research; and the timing and method of abortion should not be influenced by the potential uses of fetal tissue.

No action was taken on the NIH report until November 1989, when the Secretary of HHS advised the Director of NIH that he intended to continue indefinitely the moratorium for federal funding on research involving transplantation of human fetal tissue derived from induced abortions.

Abortion likewise loomed large in the 1980s, with several important decisions of the Supreme Court. Two decisions bookending the decade bear particular mention. First, in *Harris v.*

McRae, the U.S. Supreme Court affirmed the constitutionality of the Hyde Amendment.[54] Second, in 1989, in a fractured opinion in *Webster v. Reproductive Health Services,* the Court affirmed the constitutionality of a Missouri law that, among other things, banned the use of public employees and facilities for performance or assistance of elective abortions.[55] A plurality of Justices pointedly refused to overturn *Roe v. Wade,* to the chagrin of some Justices and to the relief of others. Thus, *Webster* signaled that the jurisprudence of abortion was unstable and remained a source of contention among the justices along multiple lines of concern.

Finally, assisted reproduction emerged once again as a key locus of public bioethical controversy at the end of the 1980s, with the high-profile case of *In re Baby M.* This case featured a dispute between a surrogate, Mary Beth Whitehead, and prospective parents including William Stern (whose sperm was used to impregnate Whitehead) and his wife Elizabeth. Following the birth of the baby, Whitehead changed her mind and sought custody of the child. The Sterns, in turn, sued to enforce the surrogacy contract. The New Jersey Supreme Court held in 1988 that the contract was invalid on the grounds that such agreements violated public policy. On remand, the New Jersey Family Court concluded that the "best interests of the child" would be served by awarding custody to Mr. Stern, with rights of visitation granted to Whitehead.[56]

1990s

Into the 1990s American public bioethics was dominated by the issues of abortion, fetal tissue research, embryo research, assisted reproduction, end-of-life decision-making, and assisted suicide. The events of this decade will be unpacked in further detail in the chapters that follow.

The first (and only) federal statute governing the practice of assisted reproduction—the Fertility Clinic Success Rate and Certification Act—was passed in 1992. It provided a mostly voluntary consumer protection framework, requiring clinics to report certain information relevant to patients (for example, success rates), published annually by the Centers for Disease Control. It also offered a model laboratory certification program, which appears never to have been adopted in the United States by researchers or practitioners of IVF.[57] That same year, in the influential case of *Davis v. Davis,* the Supreme Court of Tennessee decided that while frozen IVF embryos are, legally speaking, neither "persons" nor "property," in a custody dispute between a former married couple, the husband's desire to destroy the embryos in order to avoid procreation should prevail over the wife's desire to donate them to another infertile couple.[58]

The most important Supreme Court precedent in the jurisprudence of abortion was decided in 1992, in the case of *Planned Parenthood v. Casey.* A three-judge plurality affirmed the "core-holding" of *Roe v. Wade* but adopted a new and ostensibly more permissive framework for evaluating state and federal restrictions on abortion. Under the new rule, states could regulate abortion prior to viability so long as they did not impose an "undue burden" on a woman's ultimate right to terminate her pregnancy. After viability, the state could restrict abortion, so long as such laws had a rational basis and included exceptions for cases in which a woman's life or health were endangered by the continued pregnancy.[59] The Court did not specify what constituted an "undue burden," but affirmed all but one of the challenged restrictions of the Pennsylvania Abortion Control Act, including a 24-hour waiting period, an informed consent provision, and a parental consent requirement. The framework set forth in *Casey* endures to the present day and governs all efforts to regulate abortion at both state and federal levels.

Congress and the newly elected President Clinton had an immediate and outsized impact on the long simmering debate over the government's role in fetal tissue research.

President Clinton lifted the administrative moratorium on research involving fetal tissue procured from induced abortions. More importantly, Congress passed (and Clinton signed) the NIH Revitalization Act of 1993, which included a number of important provisions. First, it set in place a framework for the federal support of fetal tissue research, imposing restrictions that meant to insulate the decision for and manner of providing an abortion from the choice to donate fetal tissue for research. The new law included informed consent provisions requiring the pregnant woman to warrant that she is not permitted to designate (or even know the identity of) any recipient of transplantations of the procured tissue. Moreover, the attending physician must sign a statement averring that the woman's consent to the abortion was obtained prior to seeking consent for tissue donation, and that "no alteration of the timing, method, or procedures used to terminate the pregnancy was made solely for the purposes of obtaining the tissue." The act also prohibited any person from buying or selling fetal tissue for valuable consideration.[60]

The NIH Revitalization Act likewise had an important impact on the federal funding of embryo research—an issue that would become the most hotly-contested question in American public bioethics for two decades. The act revoked the HHS regulation requiring Ethics Advisory Board approval for NIH research funding proposals involving IVF embryos. President Clinton directed NIH Director Harold Varmus to convene an NIH Human Embryo Research Panel to offer recommendations for federal funding criteria and procedures. The Panel submitted its recommendations in September 1994, most of which were accepted by the President. Before President Clinton's NIH could authorize funding, however, party control of Congress changed hands from Democrat to Republican, and the new majority adopted in 1996 an appropriations rider known as the "Dickey-Wicker Amendment" (named for its sponsors), forbidding federal funding for research "in which" embryos are created, destroyed, or subjected to more than the minimal risks allowed by federal human subjects regulations for fetuses *in utero*.[61] This new law seemed to foreclose the possibility of federal funding for research involving IVF embryos.

The next year, the birth of "Dolly the Sheep," who had been conceived by cloning (somatic cell nuclear transfer), electrified the scientific community and captured the imagination of the public worldwide. In reaction to this event, there was a cascade of proposed legislative activity at the state, federal, and international levels seeking to ban different applications of human cloning. While these efforts met some success at the state and intergovernmental levels, the U.S. Congress was never able to settle on legislation banning or regulating human cloning.

In 1998, the first published reports of isolating human embryonic stem cells by researcher James Thomson of the University of Wisconsin reinvigorated the desire of the scientific community and its allies in government to find some way to support this work through federal funding.[62] This at first seemed a difficult task, as the Dickey Amendment forbade funding for research involving the destruction of living human embryos—a necessary step in procuring embryonic stem cells. In response to this challenge, President Clinton charged the General Counsel of HHS, Harriet Rabb, to analyze the precise language of the Amendment in order to discern whether and how federal funding for embryonic stem cell research might nevertheless be possible under the relevant law. In 1999, Rabb submitted a memorandum arguing that because the Dickey Amendment only prohibited funding for research "in which" embryos are destroyed, the federal government could nonetheless lawfully provide funding for research on cultured embryonic stem cell *lines,* so long as it did not subsidize the prior embryo-destroying act from which such lines were derived. Satisfied by her legal analysis, President Clinton began to make arrangements to provide funding to this new domain of research. However, the 2000 election of President Bush would frustrate his designs.

The beginning of human life was not the only locus of dispute in American public bioethics in this decade; there were also momentous developments concerning the law and policy of death. In 1990, in a case called *Cruzan v. Director, Missouri Department of Health,* a bare majority of the U.S. Supreme Court appeared to recognize a right to decline life-sustaining measures, but affirmed as constitutional a state law requiring proof by the exacting standard of clear and convincing evidence of an incompetent patient's desire to discontinue life support (in this case, artificial nutrition and hydration).[63]

Four years later, the state of Oregon adopted by referendum the nation's first law legalizing physician-assisted suicide. The measure was approved by a 51.3 percent to 48.7 percent vote.[64] Implementation of the law was delayed due to a court injunction, but ultimately went into effect in 1997.

Finally, in 1997, in companion cases *Washington v. Glucksberg* and *Vacco v. Quill*, the Supreme Court unanimously decided that there is no right to physician-assisted suicide in the U.S. Constitution. Accordingly, the Court held that state laws banning physician-assisted suicide do not violate the Constitution's due process or equal protection clauses.[65]

2000S

As the calendar turned to the first decade of the new millennium, American public bioethics was primarily consumed by debates over embryonic stem cell research. The issues of abortion and end-of-life decision-making were also prominent matters of public debate and governance. These developments figure prominently in the discussion in subsequent chapters.

From his inauguration in January 2001, the question of whether and how to provide federal funding for embryonic stem cell research was perhaps the most watched and hotly debated policy matter confronting President Bush's new administration. On August 9, 2001, President Bush announced his policy in the first televised address by a U.S. President entirely devoted to public bioethics.[66] President Bush announced a policy meant to advance the science of stem cell research without facilitating or creating incentives for the future use and destruction of human embryos. Concretely, by Executive Order, he would offer funding for research on stem cells derived from nonembryonic sources (for example, "adult" stem cells), as well as for research on existing embryonic stem cell *lines* derived before the announcement of the new policy. There would be no funding for any research on embryonic stem cell lines derived after the policy, as this might create incentives to destroy embryos (a necessary step in creating such stem cell lines). President Bush would later veto two Congressional attempts to liberalize the policy.

Meanwhile, states around the country adopted their own laws concerning embryonic stem cell research and the related matter of human cloning. Some states moved to ban these practices, whereas others moved to fund them. Most notably, in 2004, the state of California voted by referendum to approve Proposition 71, allocating $3 billion for stem cell research and amending the state Constitution to make cloning for biomedical research an enumerated right.[67]

Also in 2004, Congressman Dave Weldon of Florida successfully attached an appropriations rider that forbade the issuing of any patent "on claims directed to or encompassing a human organism," including human embryos, though it was silent and thus permissive of the issuance of patents on embryonic stem cell lines.[68] This provision was consistent with a proposal under discussion by President Bush's Council on Bioethics, later published in its 2004 report, *Reproduction and Responsibility: The Regulation of New Biotechnologies*. This appropriations provision was later permanently codified in 2011 as part of the America Invents Act.

In 2005, the United States joined a majority of member states at the United Nations in voting for the Declaration on Human Cloning, a nonbinding measure calling for the banning of all forms of human cloning. That same year at UNESCO, member states adopted unanimously the Universal Declaration on Bioethics and Human Rights.

In 2007, two papers published in the journals *Science* and *Cell* described a revolutionary development for "reprogramming" somatic cells to a pluripotent state, perhaps rendering them the functional equivalent of embryonic stem cells. The new cells, dubbed "induced pluripotent stem cells" (iPSCs), could be created without the controversial step of using and destroying human embryos.[69] One of the researchers involved, Shinya Yamanaka, would receive the 2012 Nobel Prize in recognition of this work. President Bush, responding in part to a white paper of his Council on Bioethics ("Alternative Sources of Human Pluripotent Cells") issued an Executive Order in 2007 meant to provide enhanced support for this new and promising avenue of research.

In March 2009, President Obama revoked all of his predecessor's executive orders regarding embryonic stem cell funding, and announced that he would adopt a policy offering funding to "responsible, scientifically worthy stem cell research, including embryonic stem cell research, to the extent permitted by law."[70] The NIH published guidelines in July 2009 implementing this order.

The first decade of the twenty-first century also saw a great deal of activity in the domain of abortion law and policy. In

2000, the Supreme Court struck down as unconstitutional dozens of state laws banning intact dilation and extraction abortions, a controversial procedure known as "partial birth abortion."[71] In 2003, the U.S. Congress passed and President Bush signed a more refined federal version of these laws known as the Partial Birth Abortion Ban Act. During the late 1990s, Congress had passed similar bills twice, but President Clinton had vetoed them. The 2003 law was immediately enjoined as it made its way to the Supreme Court, which affirmed the law as constitutional in *Gonzales v. Carhart*, announced in 2007.[72]

In response to reports of newborns surviving abortions and being left to die without medical aid, Congress passed the Born-Alive Infants Protection Act of 2002. The act clarified that in federal law and policy the words "person," "human being," "child," and "individual" include "every infant member of the species homo sapiens who is born alive at any stage of development."[73] In this way, the law meant to extend the protections of federal law (including provisions mandating emergency medical care) even to infants born alive following an abortion. However, the law did not provide for any specific mechanisms or enforcement nor penalties for its violation.

In 2004, responding to the highly publicized case of the murder of Laci Peterson and her unborn child Conner, Congress enacted the Unborn Victims of Violence Act (also called Laci and Conner's Law). The bill made it a separate crime to cause the death of or bodily injury to an unborn child at any stage of development in the commission of certain specified violent federal crimes.[74]

In 2005, the Hyde-Weldon amendment was added to the HHS appropriations bill, which provided that no federal funding would be authorized "for any federal agency or program, or to a state or local government" if they subject any individual or entity to discrimination on the grounds that they do not "provide, pay for, provide coverage of, or refer for abortions."[75] This rider has been attached to every subsequent HHS appropriations bill to the present day.

In 2006, following a recommendation by the President's Council on Bioethics in its 2004 report *Reproduction and Responsibility: The Regulation of New Biotechnologies,* Congress passed the Fetus Farming Prohibition Act, which banned the knowing solicitation or receipt of human fetal tissue donated following a pregnancy deliberately initiated to provide research materials, or derived from a human embryo or fetus gestated in the uterus of a nonhuman animal.[76]

Once again, in addition to the issues of embryo research and abortion, end-of-life decision-making resurfaced as a matter of public contention. In 2005, literally every branch of the U.S. and Florida governments were embroiled in a controversy about the treatment of Theresa Marie Schiavo, a profoundly cognitively disabled woman. Schiavo's parents and husband had been locked in a bitter disagreement over continuing provision of artificial nutrition and hydration. After the Florida courts ordered life-sustaining measures to be terminated, the Florida legislature passed a law allowing the Governor to stay the judicial order to provide time to appoint a guardian for Schiavo and to investigate the matter. The Florida Courts ultimately declared this law unconstitutional, after which the U.S. Congress passed Terri's

Law, granting federal jurisdiction to hear civil rights claims on her behalf. Ultimately, the federal courts declined to hear any claims and Schiavo died from dehydration.

In 2008, the state of Washington became the second state to legalize physician-assisted suicide by referendum. In 2009, the Montana Supreme Court declared that physician-assisted suicide was not prohibited under current state law.

2011 TO PRESENT

From 2011 to the present, the dominant public bioethics questions in America have likewise centered on end-of-life matters, abortion, and research involving gene modification, including "gene editing" of human embryos, all of which are highly relevant to the analysis of the "vital conflicts" of public bioethics in Chapters 3, 4, and 5.

In 2012 Jennifer Doudna and coauthors published "A Programmable Dual-RNA-Guided Endonuclease in Adaptive Bacterial Immunity" in *Science,* describing a technique for "site-specific DNA cleavage" and "RNA-programmable genome editing."[77] The following year, Feng Zhang and coauthors published "Genome Engineering Using the CRISPR-Cas9 System" in *Nature* discussing the use of similar techniques "to facilitate efficient genome engineering."[78] These papers (and the related patent disputes among the competing research teams) created a sensation around the world, raising the possibility of revolutionary targeted medical treatments and perhaps even ecological interventions at the genomic level. Intense debate focused on the possibility of modification that would effect heritable changes—altering the so-called "germ line," and thus transforming the genetic constitution of future generations. Alongside the optimism and curiosity arose deep worries about potential biosafety threats arising from unintentional or perhaps even intentional applications of these powerful techniques. In 2015, the journal *Protein & Cell* published a paper describing how researchers in China had used CRISPR-Cas9 to edit the genomes of living human embryos (which were later discarded).[79] In response to these developments, the National Academies of Science convened an International Summit on Gene Editing in 2015. That same year, Congressman Robert Aderholt attached an amendment to an appropriations bill preventing the Food and Drug Administration from considering or approving any research proposal "in which a human embryo is intentionally created or modified to include a heritable genetic modification."[80]

Relatedly, the ethical, legal, and policy questions regarding the creation, modification, and destruction of human embryos were sharpened further in 2017, when George Church and co-authors published "Addressing the Ethical Issues Raised by Synthetic Human Entities with Embryo-Life Features."[81] This same year, researcher Shoukhrat Mitalipov successfully edited the genomes of human embryos (later discarded) at the Oregon Health Sciences University.[82]

In 2019, the first children subject to germline gene editing were born. Lulu and Nana, twin girls from China, had their embryonic genomes edited by American-trained scientist, He Jiankui, to modify gene CCR5, associated with HIV-resistance.[83] The announcement was met with widespread criticism and condemnation.

The second decade of the millennium also featured a flurry of activity surrounding the question of death and dying. In 2012, the citizens of Massachusetts defeated a ballot measure to legalize physician-assisted suicide. A year later, the Vermont Legislature legalized the practice in that state. This was followed by legalization of physician-assisted suicide in California and Colorado in 2016, and the District of Columbia in 2017, Hawaii in 2018, and New Jersey and Maine in 2019.

In 2013, there was a widely publicized dispute between the family of a disabled thirteen year old named Jahi McMath and the hospital caring for her about whether she was properly diagnosed as "brain dead" (and thus legally deceased under relevant law). A judge concluded that she was, but the hospital released her and the family transferred her to another location for care. She died at home in 2018.[84] Relatedly, in 2015 there was a dispute between a cancer patient, Chris Dunn, and a Texas hospital over whether further life-sustaining treatment for him should be withdrawn on the grounds of futility. The conflict centered on the application of a state law in Texas which authorizes physicians to discontinue care over the objections of the patient and his representatives. Dunn pled for continued life-sustaining measures in response to efforts by his treating physicians who sought to terminate such care. Though the hospital prevailed in court, it continued to provide care for him voluntarily until his natural death shortly thereafter.[85]

Finally, the second decade of the twenty-first century saw further developments in the law and jurisprudence of abortion. States passed a series of laws during this period to regulate and restrict abortion, nearly all of which were challenged in court immediately upon passage. HB2, passed by the Texas legislature in 2013, provides an illustrative example. Its fetal pain law sought to ban abortions after twenty weeks. In response to the prosecution of Dr. Kermit Gosnell for infanticide, manslaughter, and other shocking abuses in his unsanitary and illegal abortion practice in Philadelphia, HB2 sought to impose more stringent regulations on abortion clinics. Specifically, the law required abortion providers to have hospital admitting privileges within a certain geographic radius of their practice, and required abortion clinics to meet extensive standards applicable to ambulatory surgical centers. Both of these provisions were struck down by the U.S. Supreme Court as unconstitutional in a 5–3 decision announced in 2016 (*Whole Woman's Health v. Hellerstedt*).[86]

A VISION

Since its inception, the field of public bioethics has captured the attention of the political and judicial branches of government, and the imaginations of citizens across the nation. It is an area of law and policy uniquely oriented to the challenges of human embodiment and public matters involving the protection of persons who are vulnerable, dependent, or confronted with the finitude of natural limits. It is a domain of complex, bitterly contested public questions of great moment concerning the unborn, children, the disabled, the elderly, the infertile, stigmatized minorities, and the dying.

Despite the manifold human dimensions and complexity of these disputes, a closer investigation reveals that the legal, political, and theoretical resources deployed to resolve them are relatively limited and simplistic, focusing mostly on legal mechanisms and analytic categories restricted to the ethical framework of autonomy and self-determination. While these goods and principles are important, and well suited to resolving conflicts among free and independent individuals operating at the height of their cognitive powers, they are not adequate for the lived reality of dependence, vulnerability, and diminished freedom that characterizes the human context of public bioethics.

At its foundation, American public bioethics has a reductive and incomplete vision of human flourishing and identity, and because of this it is unable to respond fully and coherently to the challenges intrinsic to the individual and shared lives of embodied beings, namely, the experience of vulnerability, dependence, and natural limits. American public bioethics falls short as a form of law and policy because it is rooted in a mistaken *anthropology*. In other words, American public bioethics is operating from a flawed *anthropological* point of departure, which leads in turn to inadequate legal tools of analysis.

Improving American public bioethics thus requires a revision of its anthropological foundations. Through an "anthropological" analysis in the next chapter I will provide a brief discussion of the errors of this field, along with the beginnings of an augmented account of human identity and flourishing that provides a better and truer foundation for law and policy in this domain.

It is to these questions that the next chapter turns.

2

An Anthropological Solution

Everyone has an anthropology. There is no not having one. If a
man says he does not, all he is saying is that his anthropology is
implicit, a set of assumptions he has not thought to call into
question.

—WALKER PERCY, "REDISCOVERING *A CANTICLE*
FOR LEIBOWITZ" IN *Signposts in a Strange Land*

What do law, policy, and politics have to do with "anthropology," defined in its original sense as an account of what it
means to be human? At the very deepest level, law and public
policy exist *for the protection and flourishing of persons*. Thus, all
law and public policy are necessarily built upon presuppositions
about what it means to be and thrive *as persons*. Accordingly,
the pathway to the deepest understanding of the law requires a
searching anthropological inquiry. The wisdom, justice, and intelligibility of the law's means and ends are fully graspable only
once its underlying vision of human identity and flourishing is
uncovered and assessed.

This is no small task. The question of human identity has bedeviled humankind since the emergence of the capacity for self-reflection. As ethicist James Gustafson observed, this question is "probably as old as critical human self-consciousness."[1] In his 1944 "An Essay on Man," German philosopher Ernst Cassirer noted that in the history of philosophy, the matter of human self-knowledge has been "the Archimedean point, the fixed and immovable center of all thought."[2] Augustine lamented "I have become a puzzle to myself and this is my infirmity."[3] And the Psalmist famously asked the creator of the universe, "What is man that you should be mindful of him?"[4]

Even the very definition of "person" is itself perennially vexed. The word is etymologically connected to the Latin word "persona," which referred to the mask worn by ancient Etruscan and Roman stage actors, through which their voices (and thus their roles) were expressed. As philosopher Kenneth Schmitz has observed, this connection to speech led Latin teachers of grammar to adopt the term "person" for the singular and plural forms of verb conjugation.[5] It is also connected to the Greek word "prosopon," variously translated as face, mask, stage character, and eventually person. From Boethius's famous definition of "person" offered in the sixth century ("an individual substance of a rational nature"), to Locke's ("a thinking intelligent being that has reason and reflection and can consider itself as itself"), to Joseph Fletcher's more recent multiple "indicators of human-hood," and Mary Anne Warren's "five traits which are most central to the concept of personhood," the substance and even intelligibility of "person" (and who counts as a person) as a descriptive and normative matter have been vigorously contested.[6]

Indeed, German phenomenologist Max Scheler lamented that the advance of knowledge across the disciplines has resulted in more rather than less perplexity on this matter: "We have a scientific, philosophical, and theological anthropology which know nothing of each other. . . . The ever growing multiplicity of sciences studying man has much more confused and obscured than elucidated our concept of man."[7]

And yet, any legal and policy apparatus that aims at the protection of persons and the promotion of their flourishing necessarily depends upon a prior, if unstated, vision of who and what persons are. This is, *a fortiori*, true of American public bioethics, which regularly engages the "boundary" question of *who counts* as a person—as a member of the legal and moral community whose rights and interests must be respected, whose good must be considered as an element of the common good. When it enters the law, the grounding vision of human identity and flourishing can mean the difference between life and death (or even how these concepts are defined).

Relatedly, as will be discussed further below, sociologist John Evans has shown empirically that one's anthropological premises strongly correlate with one's view of the scope and substance of human rights.[8] Different anthropologies expand or contract the circle of human concern and protection.

The primary substantive claim of this book emerges from an inductive legal analysis (that is, taking the law as it currently exists) meant to uncover the "anthropology"—the premises about human identity and flourishing—of American public bioethics. That is, when interrogated from an anthropological perspective, the law and policy in this area are in certain core matters deeply flawed, especially as evidenced by its response to those who are vulnerable, dependent, or particularly constrained by natural limits.

These defects in law and policy follow directly from the adoption of a reduced and incomplete vision of persons that fails to take seriously the meaning and consequences of human embodiment. To remedy this problem, the law must expand and augment its grounding conception of human identity and flourishing and integrate goods, practices, and principles that are appropriate to the fully lived reality of embodied human beings.

Before turning to the specific case studies that bear out this proposition (and point a possible way forward), it is necessary to identify and offer a preliminary discussion and critique of the anthropological conception—the vision of human identity and flourishing—that will emerge in the inductive analysis in the chapters that follow as the key anchor and driver of the law and policy of some of the core vital conflicts in American public bioethics. Put most succinctly, the dominant anthropology of American public bioethics in these conflicts most closely resembles what social scientist Robert Bellah first termed "expressive individualism."[9]

EXPRESSIVE INDIVIDUALISM

From 1979 to 1984, sociologist Robert Bellah and colleagues conducted interviews with 200 individuals, in efforts to identify and understand how Americans understood themselves as persons and how they derived meaning for their lives. In the 1985 classic *Habits of the Heart*, Bellah detailed his team's findings and identified a vison of human identity and flourishing that he dubbed "expressive individualism." Across a variety of contexts, both public and private, people interviewed by Bellah affirmed the view that the individual person considered in isolation is the fundamental and defining normative reality. Bellah found that human flourishing consists in the expression of one's innermost identity through freely choosing and configuring life in accordance with his or her own distinctive core intuitions, feelings, and preferences.

This unique anthropology combining individualism and this sense of "expressivism" has been further explored, deepened, and critiqued in various ways by contemporary philosophers such as Charles Taylor, Alasdair MacIntyre, Michael Sandel, and others. As will be shown in the chapters that follow, this is the anthropology that underwrites some of the core vital conflicts of American public bioethics. The work of these thinkers is thus highly valuable for the task of illuminating and critiquing this domain of law and policy.

But first, it is necessary to more specifically and succinctly summarize the vision of human identity and human flourishing that will emerge from the following chapters' inductive analyses of concrete domains of law and policy.

The anthropology of American public bioethics begins with the premise that the fundamental unit of human reality is the individual person, considered as separate and distinct from the manner in which he is or is not embedded in a web of social relations. Persons are identified with and defined by the exercise of their will—their capacity for choosing in accordance with their wants and desires. Thus, this conception of personhood decisively privileges cognition as the indispensable criterion for membership in this category of beings. In this way, it appears to be dualistic, distinguishing the mind from the body. The mind and will define the person, whereas the body is treated as a contingent instrument for pursuing the projects that emerge from cognition and choice. Moreover, under this anthropological approach, capacity for cognition is not only the hallmark of individual personhood, it defines the very boundaries of the world of persons versus nonpersons. (This, of course, becomes of crucial importance when operationalized in the vital legal and policy conflicts of American public bioethics.) Thus, given its singular focus on the thinking and choosing atomized self, the anthropology of American public bioethics represents a strong form of *individualism*.

The anthropology of American public bioethics is likewise strongly *expressivist* in its conception of human flourishing. As used here, "expressivism" holds that individuals thrive insofar as they are able to freely create and pursue the unique projects and future-directed plans that reflect their deeply held values and self-understanding. These projects and purposes emerge from *within* the self; neither nature, "natural givens," nor even the species-specific endowments and limits of the human body, dictate the ends of individual flourishing. Put another way, the anthropology of American public bioethics is strongly anti-teleological. It does not recognize natural "ends" that guide understanding of the flourishing of the individual human.

Within the anthropological framework of American public bioethics, it seems that human relationships and social arrangements are likewise judged in light of how well or poorly they serve the self-defining projects of the individual will. Under this account, individuals encounter one another as atomized wills. These individuals come together in collaboration to pursue mutually beneficial ends and separate when such goals are reached or abandoned. Or perhaps they encounter one another as adversaries, who must struggle to overbear one another in order to achieve their self-defined and self-defining objectives.

Accordingly, the anthropology of expressive individualism elevates the principles of autonomy and self-determination above other competing values in the hierarchy of ethical goods, such as beneficence, justice, dignity, and equality. When operationalized in law and policy, the focus turns to eliminating obstacles, perhaps even including natural limits, that impede the pursuit of the self-defining projects of the will. As will be seen, given its history, tradition, and culture, in *American* public bioethics, the primary mechanism toward this end is the assertion of "negative" rights.

The concepts of "individualism" and "expressivism" have received a great deal of attention—both positive and negative—from philosophers, theologians, writers, and artists from antiquity to the present day. There is a rich and extensive literature exploring, critiquing, and disputing these notions. There are, to be sure, many "individualisms," variously attacked and defended by theorists across the history of ideas. Philosopher Roderick Long has offered a fascinating and lengthy taxonomy of individualisms and individualists stretching from Plato's rendering of Callicles (in *Gorgias*), Glaucon, Adeimantus, and Thrasymachus (in *Republic*), through the works of Hobbes, Adam Smith,

Locke, up to twentieth-century figures including economic theorists such as Frederich Hayek.[10] Philosopher Tibor Machan has offered his own detailed historical and analytic account, alongside a defense of his preferred form of individualism.[11] One theater of intellectual reflection and contestation regarding individualism has been the "libertarian versus communitarian" debates of the latter part of the twentieth century, featuring such eminences as Nozick, Taylor, Sandel, Bellah, and MacIntyre. Still another anthropological counterproposal set forth in opposition to individualism has been "personalism," championed in a variety of forms by such diverse thinkers as Emmanuel Mounier, Gabriel Marcel, Max Scheler, Paul Ricoeur, Martin Buber, Robert Spaemann, and Pope John Paul II.

It is far beyond the scope of this book to wade into this rich, dense, and fascinating thicket of debates. It will thus eschew the embrace of any of the panoply of isms that populate the landscape of these disputes, and it will certainly not seek to adjudicate the perennial arguments among these learned discussants. Instead, the analytic posture of this book is *inductive*. The goal is to understand and critique the regnant anthropology of American public bioethics by analyzing the law and policy (and the academic discourse that undergirds them) as they currently stand.

That said, the forms of individualism and expressivism described and analyzed by certain participants in the above debates—including especially Sandel, Taylor, and MacIntyre—are valuable for this inductive project. In different ways, they describe a vision of human identity and flourishing that strongly resembles the active, operative anthropology for American public bioethics that will emerge as foundational in the chapters that follow. As stated, this book takes no position on whether these thinkers (often referred to—mostly by others—as "communitarians") have accurately characterized and successfully critiqued their opposite numbers in these theoretical debates (often referred to by others as "individualists," "libertarians," "liberals," and the like). The particular accounts of individualism and expressivism offered by Sandel, Taylor, MacIntyre, and others are what come to the surface when one interrogates some of the key vital conflicts of American public bioethics, even though these thinkers have not deployed these concepts in their own reflections on matters of public bioethics; with the exception of Sandel, most of these thinkers have not addressed this domain at length. Accordingly, it is worthwhile to briefly discuss these accounts (and critiques) of individualism and expressivism before pressing ahead further.

INDIVIDUALISM

The term "individualism" is most often attributed to Alexis de Tocqueville in the nineteenth century (though Israeli historian Yehoshua Arieli notes that the word was used a few years before in both an American political magazine and in Michel Chevalier's *Lettres sur l'Amerique du Nord*).[12] In his travels in America, Tocqueville observed with distress the emergence of a new self-understanding that drew people away from their communal ties and sense of shared obligations into an isolated focus on a tight circle of family, friends, and their own limited interests. Individualism did not merely weaken the ties to the community and the sense of corporate responsibility for others, it also led people into the view that they "owe no man anything and hardly expect anything from anybody. They form the habit of thinking of themselves in isolation and imagine that their whole destiny is in their hands."[13] Tocqueville worried that this illusion of self-sufficiency and the abstraction of the individual would even lead people to "forget their ancestors" as well as their descendants. In the embrace of individualism, "each man is forever thrown back upon himself alone, and there is danger that he may be shut up in the solitude of his own heart."[14]

Robert Bellah drew upon these same concerns in his analysis of twentieth-century America. He traced the roots of the phenomenon identified by Tocqueville to a reaction to the hierarchies and roles imposed by monarchical, aristocratic, and feudal societies. Bellah, following many other thinkers, pointed to the Protestant Reformation as a reflection of a kind of incipient individualism—a rejection of the need for a mediator between a person and his god. And, with others, Bellah argued that in the seventeenth century, John Locke's image of pre-political man living in a state of nature offers an exemplar of what he calls "ontological individualism," namely, "a belief that the individual has a primary reality whereas society is a second-order, derived or artificial construct."[15] Machan, Long, and others point to Thomas Hobbes as earlier theorizing man as naturally and fundamentally atomized and alone, fearful and driven by desperation to survive a war of all against all. This vision of individualism served in part as Hobbes's rationale for the creation of a totalizing state that provided the only certain protection from lethal private violence. It was the sole entity capable of providing a peaceful coexistence among people.

Bellah described the individualism of Hobbes and Locke as utilitarian, in that it was driven by the desire to maximize self-interest in light of the hoped-for benefits (in the case of Locke) or the promise of protection from feared threats (in the case of Hobbes) that lead people to consent to form and join society. Tibor Machan calls Hobbes's approach "radical individualism," which understands human beings as "numerical separate bare particulars."[16] Subsequent thinkers, including Adam Smith, held that the aggregated pursuit of individual interests can serve the good of the general population, so long as the natural liberty of others is respected.[17]

However, with the advent of twentieth-century developments in politics, economics, novel corporate forms, and modern psychology, Bellah suggested that a new category of individualism emerged, with "the autonomous individual" at its center, "presumed able to choose the roles he will play and the commitments he will make, not on the basis of higher truths" (or, one might add, lower fears), "but according to the criterion of life-effectiveness as the individual judges it."[18] This is what he terms "expressive individualism."

In an influential essay entitled *Atomism*, Canadian philosopher Charles Taylor described (and criticized) a vision of society, rooted in seventeenth-century political theories such as those of Hobbes and Locke, composed of discrete individuals seeking to fulfill individual ends. As the name "atomism" suggests, this conception rests upon an understanding of human nature and the human condition as reductively and relentlessly individualistic.

On Taylor's account, it posits unconditional and inalienable individual rights and freedoms, but no corresponding obligations or "principle of belonging" to the community. Atomism rests on the premise of "the self- sufficiency of man alone, or if you prefer, of the individual."[19]

Atomized individualism defines human flourishing as the exercise of the freedom of the will. Taylor suggested that the proto-Atomist Hobbes rejected the notion of natural ends or perfections that determine in what human flourishing consists. Instead, he defined persons fundamentally as "agents of desire"— defined by the objects of their will: "Whatsoever is the object of any man's desire . . . that is it which he for his part calleth good."[20] Indeed, under this view, a human being's very attachment for life is driven by the "desire to go on being agents of desire."[21] In its modern form, Taylor argued, atomized individualism emphasizes the freedom to "choose life plans, to dispose of possessions, to form one's own convictions, and within reason to act on them, and so on."[22]

In his thoughtful taxonomy and genealogy of "individualisms," Roderick Long likewise identified "atomistic" individualism, which he associated with Hobbes and others, as a conception of human beings "as radically separate selves locked in a struggle for survival or power."[23] This individualistic vision of human identity only recognizes as binding those moral demands that cohere with the will, interests, and preferences of the individual. There are no "unchosen obligations" within this anthropology.

Political philosopher Michael Sandel likewise identified a conception of the person, which he termed "the unencumbered self," that closely resembled the atomized individualism flagged by Taylor and others. The occasion for Sandel's observation was his critique of John Rawls, whose late twentieth century political theory is arguably among the most influential in modern American politics, law, and public policy. In his essay entitled *The Procedural Republic and the Unencumbered Self,* Sandel takes Rawls to task for building his theory of justice and political liberalism on a vision of the person that is false and impoverished. According to Sandel, Rawls seeks to translate and adapt the moral theory of Immanuel Kant, who famously located the foundation of the moral law not in any discernible natural ends or externally manifest purposes of human life, but rather from within the human *subject* himself, capable of autonomous will—a "subject of ends." According to Kant, for the individual autonomous will that is the source of moral principles and judgment to be truly free, it must not be conditioned by or responsive to external influences. Thus, in Sandel's words, "the rational being must be made the ground for all maxims of action."[24] In this way, the acting subject—the self—is prior to the moral ends that he pursues.

Sandel suggested that Rawls sought to adapt this general principle, abstracted from Kant's complex philosophy of German Idealism, and translated it into a form palatable to modern American political sensibilities. Rawls posited that it was not appropriate to build a set of rules for the community based on conceptions of normative ends or "the good." Instead, for a pluralistic polity whose members strongly disagree about ultimate goals for and the meaning of life, the "right"—the operational regulative principles of justice that govern the community—must take precedence over and be prior to "the good." In Rawls's words, "We should therefore reverse the relation between the right and the good proposed by teleological doctrines, and view the right as prior."[25] Accordingly, Rawls argued that the rules adopted by a polity should not be rooted in a particular vision of the good life, but instead should merely provide background procedures and conditions that allow individuals to pursue their own purposes and plans. Rawls envisioned a procedural framework to provide equal liberty for all, admitting only those inequalities that would benefit the least advantaged members of the community.

Sandel noted that for Rawls's procedural vision to work, the individual self must be understood as prior to and not determined or defined by any purposes or ends (just as "the right is prior to the good").[26] Thus, the vision of human identity at the core of Rawls's political philosophy was an "unencumbered self." According to Sandel, Rawls's vision "ruled out *constitutive ends.* No project could be so essential that turning away from it would call into question the person I am."[27]

Having separated the person from defining ends and purposes, the essence of human identity for Rawls was not to be found in the object of one's choices, but rather in the capacity to choose itself. This is an anthropology of the solitary, free, and independent choosing self. And the realm of choice extends not only to pathways of action, but also the construction of ultimate meaning. "Freed from the dictates of nature and the sanction of social roles, the human subject is installed as sovereign, cast as the only author of moral meanings there are."[28] Rawls's person was, in Sandel's words, a "self-originating source of valid claims."[29]

This vision of the unencumbered self for whom no external purposes or relationships can be constitutive of identity causes severe problems for a coherent theory of moral obligation to the community and indebtedness to others, especially for those others to whom "more than justice is owed."

The anthropology grounding American public bioethics is not merely individualism, it is a relatively modern iteration of this conception of human identity, namely, *expressive* individualism. This vision of personhood understands human flourishing as the pursuit of projects of one's own invention and choosing— endeavors that express and define our true selves. To more fully grasp how expressive individualism animates the law and policy concerning bioethics in America, it is useful to turn once again to Bellah, Taylor, and briefly to Alasdair MacIntyre.

EXPRESSIVISM

As noted above, Bellah identified "expressive individualism" as a reaction to the more utilitarian version of individualism that placed a greater premium on the net social goods that emerge from the aggregated pursuit of self-interested individuals operating within a well-regulated system of laws. By contrast, expressive individualism "holds that each person has a unique core of feeling and intuition that should unfold or be expressed if individuality is to be realized."[30] Bellah connects this development in self-understanding to the Romantic literary movement of the eighteenth and nineteenth centuries as well as the evolution of psychotherapy combined with new managerial corporate practices and culture in the twentieth century. He pointed to American poet Walt Whitman as a pristine representative of expressive individualism whose "Leaves of Grass" is an anthem of sorts. Whitman wrote "I celebrate myself/I loaf and invite my soul" (lines 1 & 4). Whitman saw enormous promise in American freedom and viewed its highest use as facilitating the exploration and expression of the individual's inner self. Bellah likewise cites the work of Emerson, Thoreau, and Hawthorne as emphasizing the "deeper cultivation of the self" instead of individualism as a vehicle for maximizing utilitarian ends.[31]

In his *Journals*, Ralph Waldo Emerson clearly articulates this vision of an internally generated individual quest for self-expression:

> A man contains all that is needful to his government within himself. He is made a law unto himself. . . . Good or evil that can befall him must be from himself. . . . There is a correspondence in the human soul and everything that exists in the world; more properly, everything that is known to man. Instead of studying things without, the principles of them all may be penetrated into within him. . . . The purpose of life seems to be to acquaint a man with himself. . . . The highest revelation is that God is in every man.[32]

In its modern form, Bellah observed that expressive individualism reorients the moral life from honoring external normative obligations toward the quest for self-fulfillment. Bellah worried that this, in fact, leads to confusion and dislocation: "With the freedom to define oneself anew in a plethora of identities has also come an attenuation of those common under-standings that enable us to recognize the virtues of the other."[33] The freedom of the inward turn in expressive individualism, de-fining the self by its ability to choose rather than the object of its choice, can be disorienting.

Charles Taylor provided a fascinating intellectual genealogy, both literary and philosophical, that deepened and extended Bellah's reflections. Throughout multiple books, essays, and lec-tures, Taylor identified a profound reconfiguration of human self-understanding beginning in the eighteenth century.[34] Born out of a reaction to what Taylor described as an austere morality, in which people were obliged to behave in ways that conformed to rigid external standards of right and wrong, a new vision of human identity and flourishing emerged that turned inward to the interior self as a source of meaning and guidance. French philosopher Jean-Jacques Rousseau developed the notion of a voice of nature within—*le sentiment de l'existence*—that is the true source of moral authority, rather than the external stan-dards set or opinions held by others. Indeed, Rousseau worried that such dependence on the opinion of others was a primary source of confusion and error. Taylor noted that "in this first transposition of the morality of sentiment we're beginning to see emerge the modern form of individualism."[35] Taylor also drew attention to Rousseau's innovative conception of freedom, which though related is not identical to his conception of the inner voice as authoritative moral source. Rousseau's notion of "self-determining freedom," like the inner voice of sentiment, was an endogenous or internally generated quality.[36] In Taylor's words, self-determining freedom "is the idea that I'm free when

I determine the conditions of my own existence from out of myself."[37]

Rousseau's conception of an authoritative and self-defining inner voice was developed and extended further by writers and artists of the later eighteenth and nineteenth centuries such as Shelley, Byron, Wordsworth, and the other Romantic poets (including also non-Romantic literary figures such as Goethe) who rebelled against the classical emphasis on harmony, reason, and tradition as unduly confining strictures on artistic expression. But these artistic and literary developments added a new dimension, namely, the notion of "originality"—"the notion that each one of us, in listening to that voice within, is called on to lead a form of life, a way of being human, which is peculiar to himself or herself."[38]

Taylor held up German critic and writer Johann Herder (1744–1803) as a representative proponent of this new inward-turned truth-seeking, creativity, and originality. According to Herder, "each human being has his own measure, as it were an accord peculiar to him of all his feelings to each other."[39] In this way, expressivism constitutes a radical refinement to pre-Socratic philosopher Protagoras's assertion that "man is the measure of all things."[40] Here, every person constitutes *his own* measure. From the realization that one's unique truth is *inside*—that it must be discovered by searching the depths of one's inner feelings, and that the truths are original and unique to the subject—there emerges an imperative to live according to one's own originality. And living according to one's originality—following the path discovered by searching out one's own inner depths—frequently requires actions that conflict with the accepted standards and norms of one's community. This is what Taylor called the "ethic of authenticity."[41]

This striving for one's own internally generated goals and aspirations, over and above the norms and traditions of one's peers, is readily seen in the literature to which Taylor alluded. Goethe's Faust harnessed the dark powers of Mephistopheles and black magic to pursue his passion for Gretchen, rejecting and violating the religious standards of his community. Tirso de Molina's Don Juan (and later Mozart's Don Giovanni) imposed their wills on vulnerable others in pursuit of their own desires, against the mores of the time. Tennyson's Ulysses left the comfort (and boredom) of hearth and home in Ithaca to pursue adventure and glory once again ("Made weak by time and fate, but strong in will / To strive, to seek, to find, and not to yield").[42] The Byronic hero Manfred failed to harness dark supernatural powers to alleviate his own suffering at the loss of his beloved, and boldly embraced death rather than religious redemption ("'Tis not so difficult to die!").[43] This echoed the earlier boldness and individualism of John Milton's Satan from *Paradise Lost*, who defiantly denies his creaturely status before God and asserted that he and his fellow fallen angels were made by their own hands; the power they wield is their own:

> That we were formd then sais thou? And the work Of
> secondarie hands, by task transferd
> From Father to his Son? Strange point and new! When this
> creation was? Remembers thou

Thy making, while the Maker gave thee being? We know
no time when we were not as now; Know none before us,
self-begot, self-rais'd
By our own quickening power, when fatal course
Had circled his full Orbe, the birth mature Of this our
native Heaven, Etherial Sons.
Our puissance is our own, our own right hand Shall teach
us highest deeds, by proof to try Who is our equal.[44]

Taylor noted that this ethic and imperative of authenticity—
an individualism of self-fulfillment—not only requires searching
exploration of one's inner sentiments for the truth unique to the
subject, but also *expression* of the truths discovered in this process. To realize the truth of who we are (and to live it most fully)
it is necessary to express our inner voice and make it concrete.
This is a creative act of originality that makes manifest the
unique truths about ourselves and our purpose. This, in turn,
reveals the radical individuation of human beings: we are original and distinct, and the truth about us can only be fully known
by us and revealed through subsequent expressive actions. The
complete truth about the individual is inaccessible and opaque
to others, only made available by expression. Taylor wrote,
"What the voice of nature calls us to cannot be fully known outside of and prior to our articulation / definition of it. . . . If nature is an intrinsic source, then each of us has to follow what is
within; and this may be without precedent."[45]

Given its singular focus on excavating the inner depths of
the self to discover (through expression) the truth of who we are
and what constitutes our fulfillment, Taylor worried that this

culture of expressive individualism would lead to the erosion of social and familial ties, and render unintelligible obligations to others. Even relationships of marriage and family might be measured and embraced or abandoned strictly according to whether and how much they contribute to one's self-fulfillment. Taylor was also concerned about the possibility of a thoroughgoing relativism, wherein one does not feel authorized to criticize or even fully grasp the choices of others. Yet, at the same time, he identified a new category of harm that emerges in a culture of expressive individualism, namely, the *failure to receive, accept, and appreciate* the expression of others' inner depths. Taylor wrote, "the notion that everyone has a task to become their own person—the particular, original person that they are—complementing that is the belief that in order to do this they need the recognition of others."[46] To fail to recognize the expression of other selves is a violation and a harm to them.

Taylor noted that in the second half of the twentieth century, expressive individualism moved beyond the domain of writers and artists and was embraced by a substantial segment of the American (and broader Western) population at large. Sensuality and sexual fulfillment emerged in the latter part of the twentieth century as particularly important vehicles of self-realization. He noted the American sexual revolution and the Flower Generation of the 1960s as illustrative in this regard.

In his groundbreaking work *After Virtue*, philosopher Alasdair MacIntyre famously noticed a similar turn in modern moral philosophy, in the popularity and embrace of the theory of "emotivism," a philosophical doctrine that treats statements of moral judgment as merely expressions of the speaker's *own particular feelings of personal approval or disapproval.* For example, the expression "murder is wrong" would be read as "I personally disapprove of murder."[47]

MacIntyre likewise recognized the rise of an anthropology that closely resembles what here is termed expressive individualism more broadly, noting that proponents of this view declare that "I am what I myself choose to be."[48] MacIntyre noted that as far as moral authority is concerned, "the individual moral agent, freed from hierarchy and teleology, conceives of himself and is conceived of by moral philosophers as sovereign."[49]

THE ANTHROPOLOGY OF EXPRESSIVE INDIVIDUALISM

Aided by Bellah's, Taylor's, Sandel's, and MacIntyre's insights, the anthropology of expressive individualism comes into sharp relief. In its pristine form, expressive individualism takes the individual, atomized self to be the fundamental unit of human reality. This self is not defined by its attachments or network of relations, but rather by its capacity to choose a future pathway that is revealed by the investigation of its own inner depths of sentiment. No object of choice—whether property, a particular vocation, or even the creation of a family—is definitive and constitutive of the self. In Sandel's words, it is an "unencumbered self."[50] Because this self is defined by its capacity to choose, it is associated fundamentally with its will and not its body. The individual—the person—is thus understood to be identical with the exercise of this particular type of cognition. Therefore, expressive individualism is inevitably *dualistic*—privileging the mind while subordinating the body in defining the person.

Flourishing is achieved by turning inward to interrogate the self's own deepest sentiments to discern the wholly unique and original truths about its purpose and destiny. This inner voice is morally authoritative and defines the route forward to realizing the authentic self. The truth about the self is thus not determined externally, and sometimes must be pursued counter-culturally, over and above the mores of one's community. As noted previously, in Sandel's words, the expressive individual self is a "self-originating source of valid claims."[51]

Relatedly, as Long and Taylor point out, expressive individualism does not recognize unchosen obligations. The self is bound only to those commitments freely assumed. And the expressive individual self only accepts commitments that facilitate the overarching goal of pursuing its own, original, unique, and freely chosen quest for meaning.

This is the anthropology that will emerge from an inductive analysis of several of the vital conflicts of American public bioethics. Before proceeding to that analysis, however, it is important to examine some of the general criticisms leveled against expressive individualism, as well as some of the alternative virtues, goods, and practices that can correct the errors of this anthropology.

FORGETTING THE BODY

What, then, is problematic about the anthropology of expressive individualism and why might it be an ill-suited vision of human identity and flourishing for American public bioethics? To put it most succinctly, expressive individualism fails because it is, to borrow a phrase from Alasdair MacIntyre, "forgetful of the body."[52] Its vision of the human person does not reflect and thus cannot make sense of the full lived reality of human *embodiment*, with all that it entails. As mentioned previously, human beings experience themselves and one another *as living bodies*, not disembodied wills.

Because human beings live and negotiate the world *as bodies*, they are necessarily subject to vulnerability, dependence, and finitude common to all living embodied beings, with all of the attendant challenges and gifts that follow. Thus, the anthropology of the atomized, unencumbered, inward-directed self of expressive individualism falls short because it cannot render intelligible either the core human realities of embodiment or recognize the unchosen debts that accrue to all human beings throughout their life spans.

An inexorable reality of embodied human life is *dependence*. Most obviously, given the way human beings come into the world, from the very beginning they depend on the beneficence and support of others for their very lives. Among mammals, human beings in their infancy and youth have an unusually long period of dependence for basic survival—infants and babies require help with nutrition, hygiene, and general protection. Of course, this dependence on others for basic needs is not merely a transient feature limited to the beginnings of human life. There are, of course, those who spend their entire lives in conditions of radical dependency. But because all human beings exist as corruptible bodies, periods of serious illness, injury, and senescence create cycles of often-profound dependency throughout the life span for everyone. Consider, due to the very nature of living *as bodies*, in MacIntyre's words, all human beings exist on a "scale of disability."[53]

Given the role of dependence intrinsic to bodily existence, if human beings are to flourish, they must "receive and have an expectation of receiving the attentive care [we] need when [we are] very young, old and ill, or injured."[54] The care that human beings need must be unconditional and noncontingent. The weakest and most afflicted among the human community will, of course, require the most intensive and sustained care.

The paradigm for such caregiving—upon which nearly everyone relies in his early life—is provided by parents. MacIntyre argued that in its fullest expression, good parental care makes the object of concern *this child;* the commitment is unconditional and does not depend on the child's circumstances (such as disability), and the needs of the child are treated as paramount, over and above those of the parents. MacIntyre pointed to parents of disabled children as the pristine model of this form of care.[55] The same need for unconditional and noncontingent care arises again, of course, as human beings move towards the end of life's spectrum, if not before.

French philosopher Bertrand de Jouvenel similarly noticed the universal experience of human dependency. He also noted parental love and care are essential to development and flourishing. In his words, parents provide a "humanized cosmos" for the growing child who is welcomed and loved unconditionally.[56]

The anthropology of expressive individualism misses this basic feature of human life because it misses its lived realty; dependence is not part of the picture. Expressive individualism's image of the human person is one fully formed, at the height of his cognitive powers, turning inward to learn the truths that, when expressed, will form his identity and shape his life's course. Jouvenel criticized social contract theorists for similarly forgetting the dependence of life in its early stages of development: "These are the views of childless men who must have forgotten their childhood."[57] Like Milton's Satan and fallen angels, the expressive individual self "know[s] no time when [it was] not as now; Know none before [it], self-begot, self-rais'd / By [its] own quickening power."[58] A purely inward-looking and individualistic anthropology can give no intelligible or justified account of uncompensated, unconditional, and often self-sacrificial care of others. There is no warrant to give more than one could ever hope to receive. There is no imperative to give to those from whom nothing will ever be repaid in return.

The dependence of embodied human beings is not limited to relying on others for mere biological survival. The development of the capacities needed to negotiate and thrive in the world inexorably depend on the support of others. As Alasdair MacIntyre observed in his book *Dependent Rational Animals,* it requires the selfless and sustained work of countless others to build an individual's capacities for freedom and flourishing, such as the abilities to defer gratification, to imagine and choose from alternative futures, to obtain useful knowledge about the world, to cooperate with and care for others, and to come to know yourself. These are the qualities needed to become, in MacIntyre's words, an "independent practical reasoner."[59] Development toward this goal requires a family and a community of persons who are willing to make the good of others their own good. In this way, individuals can become the kind of people who are capable of making the good of others their own. Charles Taylor noted that even the traits required for thriving under the ambit of expressive individualism depend on social structures and conditions that nurture the development of such capacities.[60] Indeed, even a theory of the "autonomous self" requires a culture and civilization in which such an idea can emerge and be transmitted.

A single-minded focus on exploring and expressing the inner depths of the atomized self does not, within its own normative framework, include robust categories of community and cooperation for the sake of others. This is the grounding insight of Sandel's critique of Rawls: "What the difference principle requires but cannot provide is some way of identifying those among whom assets I bear are properly regarded as common, some way of seeing ourselves as mutually indebted and morally engaged to begin with."[61] An unencumbered self, without *constitutive* ties to others, does not recognize an imperative to share for the sake of the least advantaged when it is not in its own interest to do so.

Even the development and knowledge of one's own personal identity—the touchstone of expressive individualism—requires sustained support from others. MacIntyre argued that without a narrative context, the individual "story telling animal" is dislocated and disoriented.[62] In *After Virtue*, MacIntyre elaborated: "I can only answer the question 'What am I to do?' if I can answer the prior question 'Of what story or stories do I find myself a part?'"[63] Who we are is rendered intelligible by the narratives that form us—even if one chooses to rebel against the normative direction and embedded ends of the traditions and communities that have shaped this story. But the point is that one does not create his or her own narrative *ab initio*. Self-identity is in large part shaped by the inheritances, traditions, and cultures of others—family, community, civilization. Sandel puts it this way: "I move in a history I neither summon nor command, which carries consequences nonetheless for my choices and conduct."[64] And this history is the product of generations who have come before and will be sustained by those not yet born.

Moreover, human beings come to understand and refine their identities *in conversation* with others. Taylor called this the "dialogical" character of human life.[65] We understand ourselves not only by expressing ourselves, but by virtue of the reactions and responses of others—especially in genuine friendship with those whose goods we share. In collaboration with and in struggle against others, we give an account of ourselves as well as hold others to their own accounts. This results in a process of refinement and clarification that enhances and deepens self-understanding. Thus, the self-expression that is key to identity and flourishing in the anthropology of expressive individualism requires others for recognition and response. This, too, is a form of human dependence.

The anthropology of expressive individualism is monological and ahistorical. As MacIntyre wrote, "from the standpoint of individualism I am what I myself choose to be . . . a self that can have no history."[66] The unencumbered self is by definition incapable of constitutive relationships. It cannot genuinely make the good of another its own good.

Moreover, its good is not fully knowable by others; it is accessible only in full through self-interrogation and then expression. The unencumbered self is thus consigned to profound loneliness. Sandel captured this tragic circumstance in this arresting passage: "However much I might hope for the good of a friend and stand ready to advance it, only the friend himself can know what that good is. . . . Where deliberating about my good means no more than attending to wants and desires given directly to my awareness, I must do it on my own; it neither requires nor admits participation of others."[67]

It is clear that the life of embodied human beings is characterized by vulnerability and natural limits. Dependence is a central fact of human life. To live as a human is to incur debts— to our families and caregivers, our friends, our communities, and our civilization. In the words of the late British philosopher Roger Scruton:

> For us humans, who enter a world marked by the joys and sufferings of those who are making room for us, who enjoy protection in our early years and opportunities in our maturity, the field of obligation is wider than the field of choice. We are bound by ties we never chose, and our world contains values and challenges that intrude from beyond the comfortable arena of our agreements.[68]

An anthropology of expressive individualism lacks the resources to recognize, much less repay these debts. It cannot give an intelligible account of the debt owed to those who kept us alive and taught us what we needed to thrive in the world. It cannot explain the role played by and obligations incurred to others whose friendship and mutual calling to account led to the refinement and clarification of our own self-understanding. *A fortiori*, as a solely inward-looking anthropology, expressive individualism does not supply a justification for the payment of those debts in nonreciprocal and unconditional fashion to *others* who have nothing to offer us by way of recompense. It lacks a principle of belonging or moral obligation sufficient to build a community or civilization that will not serve one's interests beyond this life.

The failure of expressive individualism to respond to the reality of embodied human lives regarding their mutual dependence, integrated constitutive goods and histories, and shared *unchosen* obligations to one another is also associated with an array of social pathologies that are concerning in themselves, but also loom large for American public bioethics, as will be seen in the chapters that follow.

First, as Charles Taylor and Robert Bellah have observed (echoing related concerns raised by Alexis de Tocqueville), a purely inward-directed atomized self becomes untethered from social ties, including the most intimate family connections. The inner depths of the self which hold the sources of meaning and normative orientation are never fully transparent to others, raising the specter of a thoroughgoing relativism. At the same time, Bellah observes, the individual experiences alienation and dislocation, as he longs for community and shared values, but is isolated and enclosed within his own sentiments.

The conception of human relationships not as a web of mutual indebtedness and shared concern but rather as merely instrumental and transactional exacerbates existing inequalities and compromises the networks of support for the weakest and most vulnerable. Jouvenel colorfully refers to this as a "legalitarian fiction" that "results in a chartered libertarianism for the strong."[69]

The anthropology of expressive individualism, with its singular focus on the individual self as the sole source and summit of unique meaning, creates not only loneliness and alienation, but enhances the fear of death. In an address to the International Academy of Philosophy in Lichtenstein in 1992, Nobel Laureate novelist, poet, historian, and Russian dissident Aleksandr Solzhenitsyn elaborated:

> Man has lost the sense of himself as a limited point in the universe, albeit one possessed of free will. He began to deem himself the center of his surroundings, adapting not himself to the world but the world to himself. And then, of course, the thought of death becomes unbearable: It is the extinction of the entire universe at a stroke.[70]

This death-haunted existence looms large for the vital conflicts of public bioethics, as will be seen in subsequent chapters.

A thoroughgoing and singular commitment to expressive individualism may even result in a lessened commitment to human rights. In his 2016 book, *What is a Human?*, social scientist John Evans undertook a fascinating empirical study of the relationship between one's anthropological accounts of human identity and flourishing and attitudes toward "genocide, torture, experimenting on persons against their will, buying body organs from poor people, committing suicide to save money for families."[71] He found those who embraced a philosophical anthropology that privileges the cluster of traits and qualities most connected to expressive individualism (namely, the active cognitive capacities to invent and pursue future-directed plans) were "less supportive of human rights."[72]

Finally, the erosion of social ties noted by Bellah and Taylor (drawing again upon Tocqueville) could have deleterious consequences for self-government more generally. The so-called intermediate associations that comprise "civil society" are diminished as expressive individualism advances. People turn away from such shared enterprises, retreating into their own narrow circle of individual concerns. Without the buffer of civil society between the state and the individual, Bellah and his coauthors expressed grave worries of a resulting "mass society of mutually antagonistic individuals, easy prey to despotism."[73]

Given the failure of expressive individualism to account for fundamental realities of embodied human life, including especially its uniquely relational and interdependent features, and the potential individual and shared adverse social consequences that follow, what is to be done?

Here it is useful to turn again to the work of Alasdair MacIntyre for guidance.

AN ANTHROPOLOGY OF EMBODIMENT

Because the anthropology of expressive individualism is impoverished due to its forgetfulness—of the body, of human interdependence, of the consequent gifts received from and debts owed to others—the development of a fuller and truer vision of human identity and human flourishing can only be forged by a kind of *remembering*. In order to develop the virtues and practices necessary to participate and thrive in what Macintyre calls the "networks of giving and receiving," we must remember who we are and how we got here.[74] First, we must remember that we entered the world profoundly weak and vulnerable, dependent upon others for our very survival. We needed others to feed us, to protect us, to keep us clean and warm, and to nurse us back to health when we were sick. We needed others to teach us how to behave, the habits of forbearance and delayed gratification, the discipline to restrain our selfish animal impulses to put ourselves first, and the moral vision to see others as objects of respect and concern, with goods that we share in common. We needed others to react to our self-understanding and expression, to help us to define ourselves both in collaboration and competition with them. We needed a family, a community, and a civilization to transmit expectations, values, and standards, which shaped us as we accepted or rejected these sources of meaning in full or in part.

We need to remember the fact that even in a normal life trajectory, we will need this care and support again, in periods of illness and senescence. As MacIntyre writes, it matters "that those who are no longer children recognize in children what they once were, and those who are not yet disabled by age recognize in the old what they are moving towards becoming and that those who are not ill or injured recognize in the ill and injured what they often have been and will be and always may be."[75]

Those who cared for us and who will care for us in our moments of profound vulnerability, especially when we could not and will not offer anything by way of recompense, did and will do so unconditionally and noncontingently. Those who cared for us knew that these efforts would likely be vastly disproportionate to any reciprocal support that might be offered back in return in the future. They gave us care even when all we could do was passively receive it. This was and will be the care required to sustain and shape us, by virtue of our lives as embodied human beings.

Remembering who we are and where we came from in this way should awaken in us a profound sense of gratitude and a sense that a fitting response to such care is to become the kind of person who makes the goods of others her own—to become one who cares for others without condition or calculation. When one remembers how he came to be who he is, through this sustaining network of unconditional care and concern, he becomes alive to the fact that it is not possible to repay those who supported us; the only response is to extend the same care and concern to others in need, not because it satisfies a balanced owed, but because this is what it means to become one who is responsive to others solely because of their needs, without calculation or self-interest. We will be able to offer such care and concern because in having received it, we *become* people capable of extending it to others.

Within this framework, one's gaze is not fixed, limited to her inner self and its depths. One's attention instead turns outward, understanding that flourishing is becoming a participant and steward of the network of giving and receiving that sustains life as humanly lived. This outward-facing vision is augmented, strengthened, and sharpened by memory and moral imagination.

What goods, virtues, and practices are necessary, then, to participate in and contribute to the network of giving and receiving that is a response to the interdependence of embodied human life? They are what MacIntyre has called "the *virtues of acknowledged dependence.*"[76] It is through the cultivation and practice of these virtues that one becomes a person capable of the relationships of "uncalculated giving and graceful receiving" that characterize human flourishing.[77] The virtues of uncalculated giving include just generosity, hospitality, and "misericordia." Just generosity is manifest by acting in the aid of another merely on the grounds of her apparent need. It is *just* in the sense that it is fitting to return what we have received, and it is *generous* in the sense that is offered in genuine regard for the particular other in need. The measure of the response owed is proportionate to that need, and not a function of self-interest or rational calculation of likely return to the caregiver. Hospitality is the duty to render aid to the stranger simply because he or she is a stranger, ungrudgingly and without condition. Misericordia is the virtue of taking on the suffering of another as your own, which can oblige one to provide care and assistance, or if this is not possible, to accompany the other in his or her suffering.

The principal virtue of graceful receiving is the practice of *gratitude.* This is the fitting recognition and response to the care of others, past, present, and future who support us in our dependence. Again, the fruits of such gratitude include the desire and disposition to extend the virtues of uncalculated giving to those in need, because they are in need.

Another good that flows from both retrospective and anticipatory gratitude for the care and concern of others, as well as the giftedness of life more generally, is *humility*. As Michael Sandel pointed out, recognition that our life and talents are not of our own making can be a powerful counterweight to prideful self-regard. Moreover, it can temper a disposition toward rational mastery and a purely extractive attitude toward ourselves, others, and the natural world. If we did not create ourselves and depend upon others throughout our lives, the world and those in it are not simply materials for us to rationally order, harness, and exploit for our own projects. This "ethic of giftedness," as Sandel called it, awakens the felt need to share with others—including especially those who were not as fortunate in the natural distribution of gifts and benefits.[78] Embracing the gifts of one's life with gratitude and humility makes one especially alive to the least advantaged who have not received the gifts they need to flourish on their own. This might provide the principle of sharing that is missing from an anthropology of isolated individual wills seeking to realize their own self-invented dreams.

Moreover, gratitude and the humility that travels with it can give rise to what Sandel (quoting theologian William F. May) calls "*openness to the unbidden*."[79] This is a disposition of welcoming and hospitality towards others in all their uniqueness and particularity, a toleration of imperfection and difference. This is the opposite of raw choice, rational mastery, and control. Sandel notes that this virtue is most clearly demonstrated (and learned) in a parent's acceptance of her child as a gift, rather than a project or vessel into which a parent pours his own hopes and dreams. Openness to the unbidden is closely tied to MacIntyre's vision for "the paradigm of good motherhood and fatherhood" which is seen most clearly and beautifully in the parents of seriously disabled children.[80]

Gratitude for the gifts of others' support and life itself is also fertile ground for the cultivation of the sense of *solidarity*—extending one's field of concern to encompass those beyond his immediate circle of family, friends, and community, to encompass the wider circle of humanity. It grows from the recognition that dependence on the generosity and uncalculated giving of others is a universal condition of human beings, owing to their embodied existence.

Another fruit of gratitude and the acknowledgement of human interdependence is a sense of human *dignity*. While "dignity" is a famously contested concept, the sense here is one of the intrinsic equal worth of all human beings who are alike in vulnerability, neediness, and subject to natural limits. All human beings stand in the vast and particular networks of giving and receiving necessary for human flourishing. All human beings are created and embodied, unrepeatable, precious, and fundamentally equal. All are equidistant from Pascal's "two infinities" between which humankind is situated.[81] The equal dignity of all human beings in virtue of their humanity becomes clear once all of the tests and standards (mostly focused on cognition and active powers) devised by the strong to measure the ultimate worth of the weak, according to the former's interests, are stripped away and abandoned.

For these fruits to grow from gratitude and the insights that follow from it, it is necessary to cultivate and practice the virtue of *truthfulness*. It is necessary to be honest with and about oneself and his nature as an embodied and thus interdependent being. And one must be honest with others as the dialogical nature of our shared life unfolds.

Having considered the many virtues of acknowledged dependence, it is possible to see one overarching good under which all of these goods and practices necessary to the flourishing of the individual and shared lives of embodied beings might be situated. And that is the good of genuine *friendship*. Just generosity, hospitality, misericordia, gratitude, humility, openness to the unbidden, solidarity, dignity, and truthfulness, are all virtues and goods that cohere within the concept of friendship, understood as a relationship of persons who make one another's goods their own. Friendship, in this sense, is an essential good for the flourishing of embodied beings. One is supported and sustained throughout his life by those who make his good their own without calculation or expectation of return. And by receiving such support, one develops into the kind of person who can and wants to be just this sort of friend.

What kind of education of affections and inclinations is required to sustain these goods and practices of virtues of acknowledge dependence? To remember the body and its meaning for our lives and relationships, it is necessary to cultivate the moral imagination. One must learn to *see* himself in the dependent child, the disabled, and the elderly to remember his origins and his future. And to feel gratitude to those who have in the past and will in the future sustain his life and thriving. He must learn to *see* in those who need aid the people who provide the opportunity for him to *become* a friend through the practice of uncalculated and unconditional giving. These others become the occasion for the practice of generosity, hospitality, misericordia, humility, openness to the unbidden, solidarity, honesty, and respect for dignity.

Alongside these virtues and goods, an additional corrective to the idea of expressive individualism are practices that draw one's gaze from inside toward the outside. These are practices that take one outside of oneself, and that reveal the reality of interdependence and relationality of life as humanly lived. The paradigm for such a practice, which becomes directly relevant to the discussions that follow about public bioethics, is *parenthood*. Sandel describes parenthood as a "school of humility," in which we ideally accept children as gifts rather than products of rational control and place their needs and futures above our own.[82] The lived reality of dependence, relationality, and intersubjectivity comes into sharpest relief between parents and children. Becoming a parent makes it (sometimes painfully) clear that one's good is not entirely self-contained to the truth and goals found solely by interrogating one's inner depths.

The shift from an expressive individualist anthropology to one of embodiment owing to parenthood can occasionally be seen in popular culture. At the conclusion of his film *Close Encounters of the Third Kind,* Steven Spielberg's protagonist leaves his family to join the aliens on their spacecraft to pursue his lifelong dream and obsession. In a documentary on the making of the film, Spielberg observed that he wrote this ending before he became a parent and "would never have made *Close Encounters* the way I made it in '77, because I have a family that I would never leave."[83]

The radical reorientation of one's perspective as a parent is not limited to drawing his gaze outward only to his children, but it transforms how we view all other people, within the paradigm of parent and child. In the American sitcom "The Office," the lead character Pam Beesley captures this in her account of how she now views the creepy and villainous bondage slave known as "The Gimp" in Quentin Tarantino's dark but comic film *Pulp Fiction:* "I used to watch *Pulp Fiction* and laugh, and now I'm like, that poor gimp is somebody's child!"[84]

Other practices that can shift the inward gaze outward include participation in what Robert Bellah described as "communities of memory"—associations with their own stories and traditions that "can allow us to connect our aspirations for ourselves and those closest to us with the aspirations of a large whole and see our own efforts as being in part, contributions to the common good."[85]

When Taylor, MacIntyre, Sandel, Bellah, and others focused their critique of expressive individualism, primarily on the domains of academic philosophy and the social practices of modern Western culture, they did not focus on the institutions of the law. But as the subsequent chapters will illustrate, expressive individualism is manifest there as well. Legal icon and Dean of Harvard Law School Roscoe Pound (1916–1936) noted in his magisterial work *The Spirit of the Common Law* that American law is deeply animated by a conception of personhood akin to that identified by Sandel, Taylor, and others. Indeed, Pound described American law as "characterized by an extreme individualism," such that "the isolated individual is the center of many of its most significant legal doctrines," and features "an uncompromising insistence upon individual interests and individual property as the focal point of jurisprudence."[86] Pound sketched out a multilayered account of how this came to be, including the influences of eighteenth century political theories, Puritanism, and other factors. Harvard law professor and former U.S. Ambassador to the Holy See Mary Ann Glendon likewise observed (and critiqued) the individualism at the heart of much of American law which embraces as paradigmatic the "free, self-determining, and self-sufficient individual."[87]

Insights from this chapter about expressive individualism and the anthropological "corrective" of recalling our embodiment and its meaning will anchor the following analysis of three "vital conflicts" of American public bioethics—the vexed legal and policy disputes over abortion, assisted reproduction, and end-of-life matters. Expressive individualism is the underwriting anthropology of all of these domains. Because this account of human identity and flourishing omits the lived reality of human embodiment, with all the consequent gifts and challenges of dependence, vulnerability, and natural limits, it is not a suitable normative foundation for the law and policy in this field. It cannot make sense of or respond justly or humanely to those lives that are characterized by radical dependence, and who are historically the victims of exploitation and abuse, such as the victims identified by Beecher, the sharecroppers of Tuskegee, or the just-aborted newborns discussed in the Kennedy hearings. What is needed is a new vision and framework. In the chapters that follow I will explore how the virtues of acknowledged dependence might be integrated into the habits of thought and even the laws and policies of American public bioethics.

3

In Cases of Abortion

There is no more paradigmatic case in American public bioethics than *Roe v. Wade*. This case emerged at the beginning of public bioethics in America and has roiled law and politics ever since. Abortion involves complex questions about the meaning and value of human life in its earliest stages, questions of parenthood and procreation, the nature of killing and letting die, the ethics of medicine, the definition of "health," the contours of freedom and autonomy, the demands of justice and equality, and the concept of human dignity. It is the pristine exemplar of a "vital conflict"—a zero sum struggle involving literal life and death decisions. All of these questions unfold in the *sui generis* context of human pregnancy—a circumstance uniting and integrating the bodies and fates of living human beings like no other. And it remains the most bitterly contested public question in American life.

It is also ubiquitous; the issue of abortion hovers above and lurks below nearly every other vital conflict of public bioethics. The concepts of privacy, liberty, equality, and dignity as articulated in American abortion jurisprudence are raised in public matters of assisted reproduction. The notions of personhood underpinning abortion law and policy emerge in public conversations about the moral status of the living human embryos that are created in *in vitro* fertilization and destroyed in embryonic stem cell research. Judicial precedents of the U.S. Supreme Court on abortion have been invoked explicitly to justify a constitutional right to assisted suicide and euthanasia. No matter the public bioethical matter at issue, the reasoning in abortion law and policy is invariably invoked, and the question of how resolution of such vital conflicts might affect access to abortion is raised. Accordingly, abortion law is the first locus of inductive inquiry aimed at uncovering and critiquing the anthropological grounding of the vital conflicts of American public bioethics.

Before proceeding, it is important to be clear that the inductive analyses throughout this book focus on *the law* and its grounding conception of human identity and human flourishing. It is not meant as a diagnosis, commentary, or critique of the motives or anthropological premises held by the people responding to the law in their individual choices. It is not a sociological description of or normative judgment about why people do or do not seek or perform abortions. It is, of course, relevant to these reasons insofar as the law shapes and reflects the goods people hold dear or the evils that they seek to avoid. But it would be a mistake to read the discussion that follows as a direct assessment of decision-making at the level of individual persons. In the real world, people's reasons for action are complicated, messy, and spring from a wide variety of sometimes conflicting normative commitments, insofar as such choices are rooted in careful and conscientious reflection at all. People frequently make choices in response to intuition, social customs, internal or external circumstances, desires, pressures, and whims. In short, the following analysis and the conclusions that flow from it are one step removed from individual decision-making. The discussion concerns whether the law as presently constituted assumes a conception of persons and flourishing that captures the fullness of embodied human life, one that remembers the body.

The framework for analysis in this chapter is the model for all that follow. The primary question is: What vision of human identity and flourishing anchors the relevant legal doctrines and principles of enforcement? The law of abortion—like all law—exists to serve *persons*. What, then, is its grounding vision of persons, their needs, and their nature? As noted previously, my approach is *inductive*, aiming to evaluate the law *as it is*, both as written and as applied. Seminal philosophical or policy sources will be considered insofar as they illuminate the process and substance of the law. Once the core anthropological foundation is surfaced, it will be interrogated for its soundness and suitability to the human context it is meant to govern. Is it a vision of personhood that takes embodiment seriously and is thus fit for grounding law meant to protect and promote the flourishing of beings who live, die, and encounter one another *as bodies*? Is it a suitable anchoring conception of human identity for an area of law centrally concerned with the meaning and consequences of human embodiment, namely, vulnerability, dependence, and natural limits? Does it allow consideration of the public questions in all their complexity? Or does the underlying anthropological angle of vision prevent key dimensions from being seen? If the anthropological foundation is wanting in these ways, how can it be augmented and how might the law be improved to facilitate and promote the goods, practices, and virtues necessary to construct and sustain the networks of uncalculated giving and graceful receiving that are necessary for the survival and flourishing of embodied beings?

This analysis first offers an overview of the law of abortion in America. As will be explained, all legal and policy initiatives at the state and federal level relating to abortion must conform to the narrow framework set forth by the Supreme Court. Within these confined boundaries, the political branches can regulate abortion to a limited degree, focusing mainly on ancillary aspects of its practice. Accordingly, this section focuses its discussion primarily on this overarching structure as set forth by the relevant Court precedents, including the substantive and procedural doctrine, the explicit factual and conceptual premises on which the Justices have relied, the implicit or assumed axioms and postulates involved, the sources of constitutional authority invoked, and the normative principles that drive the Court's analysis and conclusions.

This inductive analysis of the Court's jurisprudence reveals that the conception of human identity and human flourishing anchoring the American law of abortion is that of expressive individualism, as described in the previous chapter. A similar anthropological exploration of the key seminal academic and philosophical works that reflect and inform the Court's decisions will offer further confirmation. I argue that because expressive individualism is "forgetful of the body," it cannot make sense of or offer a fitting response to the consequences of embodiment in the context of abortion, including matters relating to vulnerability, dependence, and natural limits. In light of this critique, I will then reflect on how the anthropology of American abortion law might be augmented and rendered more human by integrating the goods, virtues, and practices needed to support the individual and shared lives of embodied human beings.

AMERICAN ABORTION LAW

First, a descriptive account of the law of abortion in America. Because of its unique genesis in Supreme Court jurisprudence, this is a relatively straightforward task. The external boundaries of permissible abortion regulation have been narrowly fixed by the Supreme Court itself since 1973. Thus, to understand the law of abortion in America at its most fundamental level, there are six seminal sources of authority—all Supreme Court precedents—that must be grasped. They are *Roe v. Wade, Doe v. Bolton, Planned Parenthood v. Casey, Stenberg v. Carhart* (*Carhart I*), *Gonzales v. Carhart* (*Carhart II*), and *Whole Woman's Health v. Hellerstedt.* Each will be taken in turn with the ultimate goal of synthesizing a view of human identity and flourishing that animates the modern American law of abortion.

ROE V. WADE AND DOE V. BOLTON

In January of 1973, abortion was outlawed or subject to significant restrictions in the vast majority of U.S. states. Thirty states banned abortion except in those instances when the mother's life was at risk. Sixteen more states prohibited abortion, subject to various combinations of additional exceptions, such as when the woman's health (physical or mental) was endangered, cases where the pregnancy resulted from rape or incest, or when the child would likely be born with a physical or mental disability. Only four states took a broadly permissive approach to abortion, allowing it for any reason until later gestational stages.[1] But in the third week of that month, in a single opinion, the United States Supreme Court swept aside all of these laws and replaced them with a new rule and regulatory framework of its own making, thus fanning into life what remains to this day arguably the most controversial and bitterly contested issue in modern American law, politics, and policy.

The case arose in Texas, brought by three parties seeking to challenge that state's law, which banned abortion unless the mother's life was endangered by the pregnancy. The parties included a doctor who sought relief from state prosecution for performing unlawful abortions, a childless couple advised not to have biological children who had stopped using birth control, and "Jane Roe," a young single woman from a difficult and impoverished background seeking to terminate her pregnancy. Pursuant to a 1910 statute (the Three-Judge Court Act, repealed in 1976), the case was heard by a panel of three federal trial judges in 1970. In a unanimous *per curiam* opinion, the court found that the Texas law unconstitutionally abridged the parties' rights under the Ninth Amendment to the United State Constitution, which provides that "the enumeration in the Constitution of certain rights shall not be construed to deny or disparage others retained by the people."[2]

The Ninth Amendment had been widely viewed by courts and commentators as an obscure and largely inert source of authority until 1965, when Justice Goldberg controversially invoked it in his concurring opinion in *Griswold v. Connecticut*.[3] In that case, the Court struck down a law forbidding the use of contraception by married couples. The majority opinion written by Justice William O. Douglas famously identified an unwritten "right to privacy" in the Constitution, implied by the concrete language and logic of the First, Third, Fourth, and Ninth Amendments, that extended to protect the intimacy of marital relations.[4] Goldberg concurred separately to locate the right to privacy in the Ninth and Fourteenth Amendments.[5]

Despite finding the Texas law unconstitutional by extending *Griswold*'s newly identified right to privacy to the context of abortion, the court declined to enjoin its enforcement, under a doctrine of federal non-interference ("abstention") with state criminal prosecutions.[6] But by operation of the Three-Judge Court Act, the plaintiffs were permitted to appeal immediately and directly to the U.S. Supreme Court without the usual first step of seeking review of their claims in the U.S. Court of Appeals (the intermediate appellate court in the federal system, where 99 percent of cases are finally adjudicated).[7]

Because of the unique procedural posture of the case, there was no evidentiary hearing by the three-judge trial court. Instead, it was resolved by the lower court strictly as a matter of law.[8] Thus, when the case arrived at the U.S. Supreme Court, there were no findings of fact on which the Justices could rely. Every factual premise of the opinion in *Roe v. Wade*—historical, scientific, medical, or sociological—was the product of the

Justices' own private reflections, untested for reliability or accuracy by the adversarial process.

The Supreme Court heard oral arguments in the case twice (owing to Court vacancies) and issued its 7-2 opinion penned by Justice Blackmun on January 22, 1973.[9] It was a near-absolute victory for advocates of abortion rights. Put most succinctly, the Court held that there is an unenumerated fundamental right to privacy that included a right to abortion, arising from the Due Process Clause of the Fourteenth Amendment ("No person shall be deprived of life, liberty, or property without due process of law").[10]

The Constitution nowhere mentions the word "privacy," though there are several provisions that clearly protect the good of privacy. For example, the Fourth Amendment prohibits the government from conducting unreasonable searches and seizures of persons and their "houses, papers, and effects."[11] But unlike Justice Douglas, Justice Blackmun did not look to the "penumbras formed by emanations" of these enumerated rights to synthesize a broader right to privacy.[12] Nor did he, like Justice Goldberg or the three-judge district court below, look to the Ninth Amendment as its source of authority. Instead, he invoked the controversial doctrine of "substantive due process" to locate a right to privacy in the procedural guarantees of the Fourteenth Amendment.[13] The Supreme Court had previously invoked this doctrine at the dawn of the twentieth century in a case called *Lochner v. New York* to discover an unenumerated "freedom of contract" that it relied on to strike down a state law designed to protect laborers in bakeries from exploitation by their employers.[14] The doctrine holds that there are unstated substantive rights implied by the explicit procedural safeguards of the Fourteenth Amendment. The challenge and source of controversy is how such unstated rights are to be identified and applied. Some Justices have limited the range of possible unenumerated rights to those that are deeply rooted in the nation's law, history, and traditions. Others have drawn the boundary at those rights that are thought to be "implicit in the concept of ordered liberty" and essential to any just system of laws.[15] Despite these efforts at cabining the discretion of judges applying the doctrine of substantive due process, the theory has been intensely and broadly criticized as unbounded and without meaningful conceptual limiting principles. More deeply, the doctrine of substantive due process has been criticized as presenting an irresistible temptation to unelected and politically unaccountable federal judges to override laws duly enacted by the political branches of government, and to replace them with their own naked policy preferences under the false pretense of interpreting the Constitution.

Despite these concerns, Justice Blackmun and his six colleagues on the Court declared that the right to privacy was implicit in the Fourteenth Amendment and included those personal rights that are "fundamental" and "implicit in the concept of ordered liberty."[16] Citing prior Supreme Court precedents relating to marriage, procreation, contraception, family relationships, child-rearing, and education, Justice Blackmun sought to articulate the contours of the "zone of privacy" shielded from state action. He then concluded, without a great deal of argument, that the choice for abortion should be situated within this classification of fundamental privacy rights.[17]

"Fundamental Right"

What is a "fundamental right"? Once a right is declared "fundamental," it enjoys the strongest protection against state action available in American constitutional law. The mechanism of this protection is the "standard of review" applied by federal courts in evaluating state-imposed limitations on rights deemed fundamental. To survive a challenge to restrictions of fundamental rights, a state bears the burden of proving to the court that the constraint serves a "compelling interest"—a term of art denoting the most significant degree of concern a state can invoke. If the state satisfies this requirement, it must then prove to the court that the means chosen to vindicate this compelling interest are the "least restrictive" possible.

This standard of review is referred to as "strict scrutiny," and in practice nearly always results in the nullification of the challenged law by the court. All constitutional rights deemed "fundamental" enjoy this maximal protection by the federal courts. This is in contrast to rights designated as mere "liberty interests." Such liberty interests still receive protection of the courts, but not nearly to the same degree as fundamental rights. Instead of "strict scrutiny," courts review state restrictions on liberty interests under the highly deferential "rational basis" standard of evaluation. Under "rational basis," courts simply ask states to justify their restrictive laws by citing a "legitimate" state interest (as opposed to a "compelling" interest), pursued by means that are "rationally related" to that end (as opposed to "least restrictive"). In practice, states almost always prevail under rational basis review. Therefore, by declaring the right to abortion to be "fundamental" (under the aegis of the unenumerated right to privacy), the Court signaled that states would have virtually no latitude to restrict it.

It is worth pausing a moment to reflect on this. Commentators of all ideological stripes were struck by the extension of the right to privacy to the context of abortion. For one thing (as liberal icon Judge Henry Friendly of the U.S. Court of Appeals for the Second Circuit had observed in a pre-*Roe* opinion that was rendered moot and never published because of legislative action by the state of New York), the practice of abortion is not "private" in the same sense as marital intimacy, procreation, or child-rearing.[18] It involves multiple third parties—doctors, nurses, health care technicians, and staff of what are usually for-profit outpatient clinics. Moreover, abortion is distinguishable from the actions at the heart of the prior privacy precedents (including *Griswold*) in that it involves a process aimed at the intentional destruction of a developing human life *in utero*. This is, obviously, the primary source of controversy surrounding the practice, and the chief animating rationale for state laws restricting it.

Other commentators were (and remain) taken aback by the Court's discovering a right to abortion in the Fourteenth Amendment—a provision of the Constitution ratified in 1868 in the wake of the Civil War aimed at remediating and responding to the grave and shameful injustice of chattel slavery. Neither the framers of the Fourteenth Amendment, the states that ratified it, nor the American public more generally understood or intended for the Amendment to legalize abortion. To the contrary, in the year the Fourteenth Amendment was ratified, thirty of thirty-seven states explicitly criminalized abortion.[19] In fact, four months after ratifying the Fourteenth Amendment, the Ohio state legislature passed a law criminalizing abortion from the moment of conception. The rationale for the law, as reflected in a report of the Ohio Senate Committee on Criminal Abortion, was to prevent the intentional killing of the unborn "at any stage of its existence," which it equated with "child-murder."[20] There was no indication that the Ohio legislature (nor any state legislature) believed that this law or those like it conflicted with the Fourteenth Amendment's promises of due process or equal protection under law.

Thus, to find a fundamental right to abortion under the auspices of interpreting the Fourteenth Amendment as Justice Blackmun did, it is necessary to deploy a much more expansive, dynamic, and creative method of constitutional construction than the more conventional and limited focus on text, history, and American legal tradition. Many commentators (including those who support abortion rights) have expressed the view that Justice Blackmun's opinion did not do the necessary work to identify, explain, or defend such an alternative method of interpretation. This failure of explanation and argument was particularly concerning given the dramatic (one might even say radical, given the baselines of the day) change in the law and culture that the decision would abruptly compel. The controversy regarding Blackmun's opinion was further aggravated by the fact that none of his sociological, medical, or historical assertions were tested for accuracy or reliability by the adversarial process afforded by the usual trial-level evidentiary hearing. Instead, his arguments relied exclusively on appellate materials, such as amicus briefs and law review articles authored by individuals associated with advocacy organizations, as well as his own research.

CONFLICTING INTERESTS AND THE TRIMESTER FRAMEWORK

Be that as it may, Justice Blackmun and his six colleagues on the Court declared that the right to privacy announced in *Griswold* was broad enough to include a right to abortion. To ground the fundamental right, he specifically enumerated the burdens on women imposed by laws restricting abortion.[21] He first noted the possibility of medical harms associated with an unwanted pregnancy. But his list of burdens quickly moved on from the physical and psychic consequences of unwanted pregnancy, and expanded to the harms to women (and others) caused by unwanted *parenthood* following the child's birth, including "a distressful life and future," mental and physical health "taxed by childcare," "distress for all concerned associated with the unwanted child," the problem of bringing an additional child into a family unable or unwilling to care for it, and the "stigma of unwed motherhood."[22]

Having identified the protected interests grounded in a woman's fundamental right of "personal privacy," Justice Blackmun next sought to articulate the countervailing concerns of the state in restricting the practice. In this way, Blackmun framed the question before the Court as a conflict between the woman and the state's competing interests in "health and potential life."[23] Texas bore the burden of proving that the challenged abortion law was justified by a "compelling interest," and that the regulation at issue constituted the least restrictive means to this end.[24] This was the framework for "strict scrutiny"—the most exacting level of judicial review of state action, reserved for assessing limits on constitutional rights deemed by the Court to be "fundamental."

Texas's primary argument was that the protection of pre-natal human beings from lethal violence was a compelling interest sufficient to justify restricting abortion in all cases save for where the mother's life was endangered. Texas (and other *amici*) argued further that prenatal human beings were "persons" under the Fourteenth Amendment, thus enjoying the protections of due process and equal protection of the law. In a brief passage, Justice Blackmun dismissed this constitutional argument on the grounds that while "person" was not defined by the Constitution, in the handful of instances in which the term is used, it applies only postnatally. He thus concluded that the term "person" in the Fourteenth Amendment excludes human organisms *in utero*.[25]

Moving from the constitutional to the more general notion of "personhood" as a legal concept, Justice Blackmun turned to the state's general interest in regulating abortion for the "health of the mother or that of potential human life."[26] Regarding Texas's interest in protecting prenatal human life, Justice Blackmun observed that there is no consensus on the moral status of the unborn, and that the Court would not seek to adjudicate this question.[27] After offering a very brief historical narrative on the debate over "when life begins" and the moral and legal status of prenatal human life (none of which was presented or subject to evaluation at the trial phase), Justice Blackmun concluded that Texas was not entitled to embrace "one theory of life," and "override the rights of the pregnant woman that are at stake."[28] Thus, the Court declared implicitly that the question of the meaning and value of nascent human life was a matter for private judgment and private ordering. In the Court's judgment, the state's interest in shaping opinions about the meaning and value of human life in its earliest stages paled in contrast to a woman's interests in avoiding the burdens of an unwanted pregnancy and parenthood. (This proposition would return in an even more potent and explicit form nineteen years later in *Planned Parenthood v. Casey*.)

Justice Blackmun's evaluation of the state's interest in preserving a woman's health (as weighed against her interest in choosing abortion) took a somewhat different turn. Here, Justice Blackmun concluded that the state's interest might become compelling at the stage of pregnancy where the abortion procedure would be equally or more dangerous for the woman than continuing the pregnancy to term. Justice Blackmun asserted that it was a matter of proven medical fact that abortions in the first trimester are generally safer than carrying a pregnancy to term. Accordingly, he concluded that the state does not have a compelling interest in regulating abortion for the sake of women's health during these first twelve weeks. Thus, the first holding of *Roe v. Wade* is that the state may not limit the right to abortion for any reason during the first trimester.[29]

The Court held that in the second trimester of pregnancy the state's interest in regulating abortion for the sake of women's health becomes compelling, and therefore laws that are reasonably related to this goal are permissible. But this is the only legitimate grounds for abortion laws at this stage of pregnancy. No other state interest (including its interest in preserving prenatal life) is sufficiently weighty to warrant restricting access to abortion. Therefore, the Court held that the state may not limit abortion in the second trimester of pregnancy *except* for purposes of protecting women's health.[30]

As for the third trimester of pregnancy, the Court returned to the question of the state's interest in unborn life (referred to throughout the opinion as "potential life"). Justice Blackmun associated this stage of pregnancy with "viability," namely, the presumed capability of the child *in utero* for "meaningful life outside the mother's womb."[31] The Court held that at this gestational stage the state was free to ban abortion, so long as any restriction made exceptions when necessary to save a woman's life or to preserve her health.[32]

Thus emerged the famous and controversial trimester framework of *Roe v. Wade.* Interestingly, at no point in the briefs, oral arguments, or proceedings in the lower court had any party argued for a shifting legal standard according to stage of pregnancy. This was entirely an invention of Justice Blackmun as he drafted the opinion. The elaborate and detailed nature of the legal standard has struck many commentators as statute-like, amplifying the critique that the Court was acting more as a political branch of government, straying far from its limited role of judicial interpretation. It struck many observers as implausible that the Fourteenth Amendment required not just a right to abortion but prescribed this complex tripartite regulatory apparatus. Others have noted that Justice Blackmun's empirical claim about the relative risks of abortion and pregnancy that became an essential premise of the Court's reasoning was never presented, discussed, or evaluated as scientific evidence at trial. Still others on both sides of the abortion conflict have taken issue with the notion that either a woman's fundamental rights or the right to life of the unborn (the same organism throughout gestational development) should fluctuate with something as contingent and unstable as the concept of "viability"—which is a standard that changes with access to technology, skill of medical care, and even the race and sex of the fetus.

In sum, *Roe v. Wade* held that the Due Process Clause of the Fourteenth Amendment implied a fundamental right to privacy that includes the freedom of a woman to seek an abortion. Any proposed state restriction must satisfy "strict scrutiny," meaning that the law must serve a "compelling" interest, pursuant to the "least restrictive means." In the first trimester of pregnancy, there is no such state interest. In the second trimester of pregnancy, the only compelling state interest is the preservation of a pregnant woman's health. In the third trimester, the state's interest in prenatal life is sufficiently compelling that abortion can be proscribed, so long as the law provided an exception to preserve the life or health of the mother.

Doe v. Bolton *and the Meaning of "Health"*

Other than articulating the harms to women's well-being imposed by abortion restrictions, the Court in *Roe* did not specify what constitutes "health," nor what types of health interests would be sufficiently weighty to warrant an exception to a general law banning abortion in the third trimester. For this, it is necessary to consider the most important abortion case that most people have never heard of, decided on the same day as *Roe*. That case was *Doe v. Bolton*.[33]

Doe involved a challenge to a suite of abortion regulations in Georgia. The state law banned abortion except by licensed physicians whose "best clinical judgment" was that the pregnancy threatened the life or health of the mother, the "fetus would likely be born with a serious defect," or that the pregnancy resulted from rape.[34] Moreover, the challenged regulatory scheme required that abortions be performed only in accredited hospitals, that the procedure be approved by a hospital staff abortion committee, and that the abortion provider's judgment be confirmed by two independent physicians. Finally, the law limited abortions to Georgia residents.[35]

The Court struck the following down as unconstitutional: the hospital requirement (while noting that this rule might be permissible as applied to the second and third trimesters of pregnancy), the abortion committee approval provision, the two-physician confirmation rule, and the residency clause. The Court declared all of these provisions to be unduly restrictive of the fundamental right to abortion.[36]

For this discussion, the most important part of the *Doe* opinion is the meaning and legitimacy of the term "best medical judgment" as provided in the statute. The plaintiffs stated that the requirement for doctors to exercise judgment when evaluating the risks associated with carrying the pregnancy to term was unconstitutionally vague.[37] That is, they claimed that the law did not set forth its requirements with sufficient clarity and precision to put physicians on notice of what conduct was criminally prohibited, or to cabin the discretion of prosecutors.

The Court concluded that the phrase "best clinical judgment" was clear enough for constitutional standards of due process. To explain, the Court elaborated on the factors relevant to health, to be weighed and considered by the physician in determining if the abortion was warranted. Such factors included: "physical, emotional, psychological, familial, and the woman's age." All of these factors, according to the Court, related to the definition of "health."[38]

In this way, the Court made clear what had only been implied in *Roe v. Wade,* namely, that "health" is a capacious concept that incorporates all aspects of well-being. It is not limited to physical or even psychological health. It likewise relates to "familial" health. Perhaps this is what Justice Blackmun had in mind in *Roe,* when he declared that the fundamental right to privacy protects women from abortion limits that impose the burdens of unchosen *parenthood,* such as a distressful life and future "for all concerned" caused by the need to rear an unwanted child. By defining the meaning of health in such a broad fashion, the Court in *Doe v. Bolton* appeared to make it clear that the "health exception" that *Roe* mandated for all restrictions on abortion (even post-viability) could be invoked by the abortion provider in service of nearly any aspect of his patient's well-being. Critics of the opinion worried that this expansive notion of "health" could allow any abortion provider to circumvent any limit on abortion, simply by invoking such broadly framed interests (including "familial" concerns) to justify the procedure. (This worry would resurface in dramatic fashion twenty-seven years later in *Stenberg v. Carhart.*)

Unanswered Questions from Roe *and* Doe

Both the Court's opinions in *Roe* and *Doe* leave essential questions unaddressed, including who or what is destroyed in an abortion? Why should the stage of development of the human organism *in utero* matter to the scope of a woman's right to bodily autonomy, self-determination, and privacy? Why should the state be involved in this decision at all? In short, what is the Court's underlying normative theory justifying its decision? To explore these questions and consider answers, it is useful to turn briefly to highly influential contemporaneous philosophical work advocating for abortion rights. Without invoking this body of scholarship by name, the *Roe* and *Doe* opinions appear to echo the principles and arguments advanced therein.

In the early 1970s several prominent philosophy journals dedicated space to the discussion of the right to abortion. The publication of these volumes marked the birth of "public philosophy" as a field of inquiry and influence. In the articles therein, two primary philosophical justifications for the right to abortion emerged that persist to this day as the fundamental anchors of pro-choice public advocacy, deployed both singly and in combination. First, philosophers (and advocates) ground the right to abortion in the freedom to reject the unchosen and unwanted bodily burdens of pregnancy. This has been called the "bodily dependence" argument for abortion rights. The second philosophical justification for abortion rights—termed the "personhood" argument—argues that the prenatal human organism does not merit the legal protections against private lethal violence owed to post-natal human beings until he or she satisfies various predetermined criteria. Different criteria for personhood have been proposed, including cognition, self-awareness, the capacity to have desires, the development of a mature and familiar human morphology, and suchlike. Until it attains the moral status of "person," the interests of the fetus in avoiding destruction by abortion cannot override the right of the pregnant woman to choose the procedure. As will become evident in the discussion that follows, the bodily dependence and personhood arguments for abortion, while technically distinct, tend to depend on and intersect with one another, at least implicitly.

The most famous philosophical defense of the "bodily dependence" argument was advanced by Judith Jarvis Thomson in the first volume of the journal *Philosophy and Public Affairs* (Autumn 1971).[39] Her article, "A Defense of Abortion," is one of the most widely cited and republished pieces in all of academic philosophy. In it, she purports to assume for the sake of argument that the fetus is a person from the moment of conception, and proceeds to argue for the morality (and legality) of abortion nevertheless. (Thomson herself does not regard the fetus to be a person early in development, but suggests, without elaborating, that "we should probably have to agree that the fetus becomes a person well before birth."[40]) Thomson makes her argument by way of a series of colorful analogies involving the bodily impositions of one person upon another, in an effort to demonstrate that it is no injustice to reject such impositions, even when the other person will die as a result. She proffers a hypothetical case in which a woman is abducted by the "Society for Music Lovers," who sedate her, and surgically attach an unconscious famous violinist to her circulatory system. She is thus conscripted into the medical care of the violinist, whose blood her own kidneys will now clean for the nine months it takes for him to recover. The Director of the Hospital advises her that he is sorry for this imposition, but he cannot "unplug" her from the violinist, as this would result in his certain death.

Thomson's analogy is meant to appeal to the intuition that it is not murder or the violation of the violinist's right to life to disconnect from the violinist, even though it is sure to cause his death. This lethal action is justifiable because the violinist is not entitled to use the woman's body to survive without her consent: "[N]obody has any right to use your kidneys unless you give him such a right."[41]

Thomson deploys other similar analogies in an effort to justify rejection of nonconsensual bodily impositions including a woman trapped in a small house with a baby who is rapidly growing to fill the entirety of the home's interior, and two men fighting over a coat (belonging to one of them) to avoid freezing to death.

Of course, these analogies appear only to relate to the circumstances of forced impregnation, such as through rape. Thomson thus expands her argument to the context of unwanted pregnancy arising from consensual sex with further analogies. These involve the invasion of property interests by individuals despite the owner's best efforts to prevent them. A burglar who comes into one's home through an open window.[42] "People seeds" that take root inside one's home despite efforts by the owner to prevent this by installing fine mesh screens.[43] In each case, Thomson seeks to elicit the intuition that one is justified in evicting the unwanted intruder or parasite, even if their presence follows foreseeably from some consensual action, like leaving a window open or using potentially defective screens. These analogies are meant to persuade the reader that a woman is similarly justified to evict the unwanted fetus conceived due to contraceptive failure or unprotected sex, even if such actions cause its death.

As a concise summary of her core proposition, Thomson states: "I have been arguing that no person is morally required to make large sacrifices to sustain the life of another who has not the right to demand them, and this even where the sacrifices do not include life itself."[44]

She dismisses the notion that one's child has such a right to sacrificial care and support merely by virtue of her relationship to her mother or father. She elaborates that the only possible grounds for such an entitlement is the consent of the mother, which cannot be assumed simply by virtue of the relationship of parenthood. If parents "have taken all reasonable precautions against having a child, they do not simply by virtue of their biological relationship to the child who comes into existence have a special responsibility for it. They may wish to assume responsibility for it, or they may not wish to. And I am suggesting that if assuming responsibility for it would require large sacrifices, then they may refuse."[45]

Thomson concludes her essay with two clarifications. First, she suggests that some abortions later in pregnancy may not be justifiable, if pursued for what she regards to be frivolous reasons (she gives the example of an abortion in the seventh month of pregnancy for the sake of a vacation).[46] Second, she distinguishes the right to abortion from the right to ensure the demise of one's prenatal offspring. If it is possible to terminate a pregnancy without killing the fetus, she suggests that one should opt for this pathway.[47]

At roughly the same time that Thomson published her defense of abortion based on a woman's freedom to reject the fetus *in utero,* two other philosophers published articles defending abortion rights on "personhood" grounds. Michael Tooley published "Abortion and Infanticide" one year after Thomson's piece in the second volume of the same journal, *Philosophy and Public Affairs* (Autumn 1972).[48] A few months later, Mary Anne Warren published "On the Moral and Legal Status of Abortion" in *The Monist* (January 1973).[49] Whereas Thomson argued that abortion is a justifiable response to evict an unwanted bodily intruder (even where such eviction will result in her demise), Tooley and Warren both argue that the prenatal human organism is not a "person," and thus its interests are subordinate to those of a woman seeking an abortion.

Tooley asserted that a living being must satisfy specific criteria to be deemed a "person," with the attendant rights and interests, including especially the right to life. He begins with the proposition that a "right" is a claim "about the prima facie obligations of other individuals to act, or refrain from acting."[50] But the presence of a right is conditional on the desire of the bearer of that right. Tooley puts it this way: "'A has a right to X' is roughly synonymous with 'If A desires X, then others are under a prima facie obligation to refrain from actions that would deprive him of it.'"[51] Accordingly, there can be no right to life without someone capable of having the desire for life. To have such a desire, a being must "possess the concept of self as a continuing subject of experiences, and . . . believe that it is itself such an entity."[52] In other words, only those human beings who have self-awareness and desires have a right to life. Until and unless a human being's brain is sufficiently developed to support this form of cognition, she does not have a right to life. This, according to Tooley, is the case for the human organism at early stages of development, both *in utero* and even *ex utero*. That is, Tooley's definition of "person" excludes the preborn, the newly born, as well as human beings who irreversibly lose their capacity for self-awareness and desire formation. In other words, as the title of his article suggests, Tooley's principles lead to the acceptance of infanticide. Merely having the potential for self-awareness is not sufficient under Tooley's approach to qualify as a "person." (Interestingly, Tooley criticizes Thomson both for suggesting that the fetus becomes a person at some point before birth and for suggesting that bodily dependence alone can warrant the right to abortion of a being that qualifies as a person.[53])

In "On the Moral and Legal Status of Abortion," Mary Anne Warren undertakes a similar project. She begins with the observation that it is not possible to produce a persuasive defense of the right to abortion "without showing that a fetus is not a human being, in the morally relevant sense of that term."[54] Contra Thomson, Warren believes that if one grants the full moral personhood of the unborn child, it is not possible to establish conclusively that abortion is morally permissible. Like Tooley, she rejects Thomson's assertion that one has the moral right to expel an innocent person from her property (or body) when it will inexorably lead to his death. This echoes Justice Blackmun's statement in *Roe* that "if this suggestion of personhood [within the meaning of the 14th Amendment] could be established, the appellants' case, of course, collapses, for the fetus' right to life would then be guaranteed specifically by the Amendment."[55] Warren asserts that Thomson's analogy only holds for cases of coerced pregnancy such as rape.[56] Nevertheless, Warren believes that maximal abortion rights are justified morally and legally because the fetus is not a person at all.

In order to make the case for abortion rights, Warren proposes that even though the fetus is, biologically speaking, a living member of the human species, it is not a "person" entitled to full and equal moral rights. In her view, "it is personhood, not genetic humanity" that defines the boundaries of the moral and legal community.[57] The balance of the article is dedicated to demonstrating that "a fetus is not a person, hence not the sort of entity to which it is proper to ascribe full moral rights."[58]

Warren believes that the criteria for personhood and the grounds for moral rights are "perfectly obvious," and the article represents her effort to articulate such criteria in service of a defense of the moral and legal permissibility of abortion.[59]

Warren frames the question thus: "What sort of entity, exactly, has the inalienable right to life, liberty and the pursuit of happiness?" She then seeks to develop a set of criteria and a rough sense of how many must be satisfied for a being to qualify as a "person." One who satisfies the requisite number of criteria is a person, with human rights.

The five traits "most central to the concept of personhood" are: (1) consciousness and the capacity to feel pain; (2) reasoning ("the *developed* capacity to solve new and relatively complex problems"); (3) "self-motivated activity"; (4) the ability to communicate information "on indefinitely many possible topics"; and (5) "the presence of self-concepts, and self-awareness, either individual or racial, or both."[60]

Warren then seeks to discern how many of these elements must be present for a human being to warrant the status of personhood. She suggests that criteria (1) and (2) alone might be sufficient, and "quite probably (1)–(3)" if "activity" includes reasoning.[61] But, most importantly, she posits that a human being that has none of these traits does not have the status of personhood. Since the unborn child lacks all five traits, it is clear to Warren that human beings at this stage of development cannot reasonably be considered persons.

Warren thus observes that it is both overbroad and underinclusive to use the classification "human being" as a proxy for personhood. By her standard, she suggests that there are multiple types of human beings who are not persons, including men and women who have permanently lost their capacity for consciousness (no longer persons), "defective human beings" who never had the capacity for consciousness (these never were and never will be persons), and, of course, prenatal human beings *in utero* (not yet persons).[62] Moreover, in the future it may be discovered that intelligent alien life forms and perhaps even self-aware robots or computers possess a sufficient number of her criteria to count as persons.

Warren furthermore rejects the notion that as "potential persons," the unborn possess a right to life sufficient to outweigh a woman's right to abortion, since she is an actual person. Thus, Warren concludes that any restriction on abortion (absent "any overwhelming social need for every possible child") violates a woman's fundamental moral and constitutional rights.[63]

Unlike Tooley, however, Warren does not appear to be willing to embrace fully the practice of infanticide, even though her definition of personhood would rule out not only the unborn, but also newborns (as well as cognitively disabled children, adolescents, and adults). She resists endorsing infanticide in part because she believes that society appears to value the life of infants, and at the moment "can afford to provide care for infants which are unwanted or which have special needs."[64] Moreover, "the needless destruction of a viable infant inevitably deprives some person or persons of a source of great pleasure and satisfaction, perhaps severely impoverishing their lives."[65] She later points out, however, that she does not regard the killing of newborns as murder, because of their sub-personal status.

She likewise rejects restrictions on late term abortions, because the prenatal human beings involved may pose a risk to the mother's life or health. Warren does not address those cases where late term fetuses do not pose such a threat. But in any event, it is interesting to note that at the extremes of her argument, to avoid fully embracing infanticide, she must combine her argument from personhood with a discussion of the burdens of bodily dependence.

Thomson, Tooley, and Warren represent the philosophical defenses of abortion rights nested in arguments from bodily dependence and personhood. While there have been many other philosophers (such as David Boonin, Peter Singer, Alberto Giubilini, and Francesca Minerva) who have proposed variants and refinements of these arguments, both alone and in combination, the claims are quite similar: laws restricting abortion are unjustifiable because they improperly interfere with a woman's right to free herself from the burdens of unwanted pregnancy, and/or the fetus is not a being with the right to life sufficient to override the wishes of a woman seeking an abortion.[66]

While these philosophical principles are not outright mentioned in Justice Blackmun's opinions in *Roe* and *Doe,* they reflect his implicit reasoning. To justify the right to abortion (grounded in privacy), Justice Blackmun invokes the burdens of unwanted pregnancy. He includes, of course, the physical and emotional consequences of pregnancy, but seems to go even further than Thomson by invoking the burdens of unwanted *parenthood*—not just on the mother, but on the family and the community into which the unwanted child comes.

According to *Roe* and *Doe,* the fundamental right to abortion emerges from the unique bodily encumbrance that pregnancy represents, along with the impositions of postnatal childcare. Justice Blackmun does not raise the possibility that the woman might be obliged to endure the burdens of unwanted pregnancy and parenthood by virtue of her relationship of biological parenthood or the fact she is the only one capable of sustaining the life of the fetus, at least until viability. In all these ways, Blackmun's opinion follows implicitly the logic of Thomson's bodily dependence argument for abortion rights.

Blackmun also seems to have a personhood argument for abortion in mind as well. While he claims to be neutral and agnostic on the moral status of the fetus, he abandons this posture when he seeks to frame the state's interests that conflict with those of the woman seeking an abortion. His analysis of what the word "person" means as applied to the Due Process (and Equal Protection) clauses of the Fourteenth Amendment or in other areas of American law is cursory and truncated. He does not remand the case for factfinding on this question. He thus concludes that the dispute is between one who is without doubt both a moral and constitutional person (the pregnant woman) and the state's interest in protecting a constitutional nonperson, who is defined throughout much of the opinion as "potential life." This "potential life" has no meaningful interests that counterbalance those of the mother seeking an abortion until the third trimester of pregnancy. And even then, the mother's well-being, broadly defined to include interests such as "familial health" and the future burdens of rearing an unwanted child override any claim the fetus has to a right to life.

Most importantly, despite claims to neutrality, Justice Blackmun's opinion implicitly finds the human fetus to be subpersonal, when he declares its moral status to be strictly a matter for private decision-making. The Court in *Roe* explicitly forbade Texas from "adopting one theory of life" in its laws on abortion.[67] By contrast, after a human being is born, private individuals in Texas are not permitted to decide by their own lights whether she is a person under the state's criminal statutes. One of the hallmarks of personhood is that moral status and basic legal protections are not contingent upon the private opinions of others. By denying the state the capacity to extend such protected status to prenatal human beings, the Court effectively placed them outside the boundaries of the community of persons. This result closely tracks the reasoning of Tooley and Warren's defense of abortion in the name of a limited conception of "personhood."

Application of Roe *and* Doe

In the nearly two decades following *Roe* and *Doe,* the Court vigorously defended the fundamental right to abortion, and wielded the "strict scrutiny" standard of review to nullify a wide array of state laws meant to regulate and curtail the practice. From 1973 until 1992, under the auspices of applying *Roe* and *Doe,* the Court invalidated laws requiring second-trimester abortions to be performed only in hospitals, informed consent requirements (including a regulation requiring that only doctors convey such information), twenty-four hour waiting periods between informed consent and the abortion procedure itself, certain recordkeeping requirements regarding patient demographics and abortion procedures, and even parental notification laws. The Court also struck down as unconstitutional laws that sought to govern the determination of viability, and laws that required the use of an abortion technique most likely to preserve the life of the post-viable fetus. The Court nullified a law requiring the humane and sanitary disposition of fetal remains. The Court's persistent interventions invalidating state laws on abortion prompted Justice White in a 1986 dissent to complain that the Court was engaged in the "unrestrained imposition of its own extraconstitutional value preferences."[68] Few, if any, constraints on abortion rights were tolerated by the Court during this period.

The Anthropology of Roe *and* Doe

Before proceeding to consider the additional Supreme Court precedents that combine to constitute the law of abortion in America, we must discuss the anthropological premises that ground *Roe* and *Doe,* as written and as applied. The image of human identity and flourishing that emerges from the Court's reasoning (and the philosophical discourse it reflects) is that of the atomized individual, defined by the cognitive capacity for choice, striving to pursue, express, and live according to those original truths discovered from self-interrogation, unbound by unchosen obligations and relationships, natural limits, and the concept of natural ends. In short, the law's vision of the person undergirding *Roe* and *Doe* is that of expressive individualism.

We see this in the language about the source and substance of the right to abortion, the nature of prenatal human life, and the framing (and resolution) of the problem of unwanted pregnancy and parenthood. The overarching frame for these opinions is privacy—a good associated with solitude and separation, often described as a "right to be left alone." In this case, privacy is a value that extends to the right to shed unwanted burdens— to reject unchosen obligations to others, including those with whom one stands in the biological relation of parent. The burdens cited by Justice Blackmun go beyond the physical and psychological impositions of unwanted pregnancy and extend to the encumbrances of unwanted parenthood. In fact, the undeniable weight of these burdens is what convinces Justice Blackmun that a pregnant woman must have the freedom—the fundamental right—to seek relief through abortion, without serious constraints from the state.

Just as in the anthropology of expressive individualism, in *Roe* and *Doe,* there is no natural relationship, no claim arising from the maternal-fetal connection or any plea of kinship that can impose an obligation on the woman to carry her *in utero* offspring to term. For both Blackmun and Thomson, the fetus has no enforceable demands on her mother for continued life support. Rather, the fetus is an intruding stranger with no claims of sonship or daughterhood. It is an abstraction; merely "potential life." The maternal-fetal relationship instead is defined by will and choice, based on consent rather than unchosen duty. This is the case even after viability, when an abortion can be performed in the name of health, broadly understood to embrace all aspects of well-being, including "familial" concerns (*Doe*).

Expressive individualism is also evident as an anthropological grounding in Blackmun's discussion of prenatal life and personhood, which reflects, at least implicitly, the reasoning of Tooley and Warren. In *Roe,* the moral status of the unborn must remain a matter of private deliberation and judgment, according to one's own subjective values and beliefs.

By prohibiting the state from extending the protections of personhood to the unborn and declaring the moral status of the fetus to be a question proper only to private reflection, Justice Blackmun implicitly decided the matter of prenatal personhood in the negative. If the state cannot protect unborn children as persons, and their moral status is left up to each individual to decide, then it follows inexorably that they are not persons in the eyes of the law.

Blackmun never explains why Texas is forbidden from treating the matter of abortion as a highly complex, even *sui generis* case involving a parent and child whose interests apparently conflict. As noted above, even though Blackmun's explicit arguments sound in bodily dependence, he seems to be relying on a normative theory to justify his refusal to recognize the legal personhood of the fetus. (To be clear, the question of legal personhood is distinct from the narrower question of the word "person" as used in the Fourteenth Amendment.) The most prominent theories of personhood of the day as applied to abortion were, as noted above, well represented by the views of Tooley and Warren.

Tooley and Warren's conceptions of personhood only include those capable of flourishing as dictated by expressive individualism. They both equate the person with the exercise of the will and include in the class of persons only those with the active capacity for self-awareness, self-motivation, and the generation and pursuit of desires. Tooley goes so far as to say only those capable of desire and an awareness of the self as a continuing subject of experiences are "persons" endowed with a right to life. Similarly, Warren privileges self-consciousness, reason, and expression as the *sine qua non* of personhood. In other words, only those with the currently active capacity to interrogate their innermost selves to discover, express, and pursue their originality are properly members of the community of persons, with all the attendant basic legal protections and moral concerns. Only those currently capable of thriving when viewed through the lens of expressive individualism are persons. Those, like the human fetus, without such capacities do not qualify as persons.

Finally, by framing the abortion dispute as essentially a clash of raw interests between strangers—a person and nonperson—Justice Blackmun embraces the narrative of expressive individualism: a universe of lonely atomized wills each seeking their own self-invented destinies, encountering other wills as transactional collaborators or adversaries to be overcome. For Blackmun, the interests of the fetus do not even rise to the interests of a person, but rather a sub-personal being whose interests must necessarily give way when they conflict with those of a bona fide person. This clash of interests bears little relation to the reality of human procreation and pregnancy, in which the *dramatis personae* include a woman and her biological offspring literally joined in body, one inside the other, utterly dependent on the other, with lives integrated and intertwined to a degree like no other human relationship. They are, biologically speaking, mother and child.

They are not homeowner and burglar, host and parasite, or violinist and unwilling conjoined kidney donor. This is not a dispute over private property. Moreover, there is no mere "unplugging" to undo this relationship—modern methods of abortion involve the direct killing and removal of the fetus through highly invasive and violent means. Blackmun's narrative of conflict is simplistic, foreign, and forgetful of the body.

PLANNED PARENTHOOD V. CASEY: THE MODERN RULE

By 1992, the cultural and political movement to overturn *Roe v. Wade* and restore meaningful protections for prenatal human life appeared to have achieved some of its key political aspirations. Presidents Ronald Reagan and George H. W. Bush had made multiple appointments to the Supreme Court thought to be hostile to *Roe,* namely, Justices Antonin Scalia, Sandra Day O'Connor, Anthony Kennedy, David Souter, and Clarence Thomas. With the original dissenters in *Roe,* Chief Justice William Rehnquist and Justice Byron White, still on the Court, observers believed that *Roe* would be reversed. The opportunity appeared to present itself in 1989 with the passage of the Pennsylvania Abortion Control Act, signed into law by Governor Bob Casey, Sr., a prominent Democrat who was famously opposed to abortion.[69]

The Pennsylvania law included measures regulating the manner in which abortion was provided, some of which had been previously struck down by the U.S. Supreme Court as unconstitutional, including a mandatory informed consent provision, followed by a twenty-four-hour waiting period, a parental consent requirement (with a judicial bypass provision for exceptional cases), a spousal consent provision (with judicial bypass), and certain reporting requirements for facilities that provide abortions.[70]

On June 29, 1992, to the great surprise of many, the Court announced its decision (decided by a margin of 5–4) reaffirming what it termed the "essential holding of *Roe*" in a joint plurality opinion written by Justices Kennedy, O'Connor, and Souter.[71] The announcement shocked pro-life and pro-choice communities alike, to the great despair of the former and to the elated relief of the latter. But on reading the decision closely, it quickly became clear to both sides that despite the opinion's claim that it had reaffirmed *Roe,* American abortion jurisprudence had been formally, if not functionally, significantly altered.

The Court shifted the normative grounding for the right to abortion from privacy to "liberty."[72] This change closely mirrored Justice Kennedy's strong libertarian judicial philosophy, and the passages of the plurality opinion expounding on the good of liberty are commonly attributed to his authorship. The opinion renewed a commitment to substantive due process, noting that the procedural protections of the Fourteenth Amendment preclude certain government actions "regardless of the fairness of the procedures used to implement them."[73] The plurality sought to articulate a zone of liberty into which the state may not intrude, including "a person's most basic decisions about family and parenthood, as well as bodily integrity."[74] The Court framed the question before it as regarding *the freedom to make choices* about the meaning and value of prenatal life, procreation, parenting, social roles, and family. "The underlying constitutional issue is whether the State can resolve these philosophic questions in such a definitive way that a woman lacks all choice in the matter, except perhaps in those rare circumstances in which a pregnancy is itself a danger to her own life or health, or is the result of rape or incest."[75]

The plurality answered this question in the negative, reaffirming *Roe*'s holding that these are matters for *private* decisionmaking, and thus the state cannot impose its own normative vision. In an oft-quoted passage, the Court wrote:

> These matters, involving the most intimate and personal choices a person may make in a lifetime, choices central

to personal dignity and autonomy, are central to the liberty protected by the Fourteenth Amendment. At the heart of liberty is the right to define one's own concept of existence, of meaning, of the universe, and of the mystery of human life. Beliefs about these matters could not define the attributes of personhood were they formed under compulsion of the State.[76]

Despite the shift from privacy to liberty, the Court emphasized the burdens that uniquely and exclusively fall on women facing unwanted pregnancy as a core rationale for the right to abortion. And it expressed a concern that by enforcing one conception of fetal personhood and pregnancy the state was trading in an outmoded "vision of the woman's role" in society.[77] In this way, the Court's reasoning echoed the defense of abortion as a mechanism of liberation for women from patriarchal structures and enforced limits on sex-roles that inhibit their capacity to define their futures by their own lights, on an equal footing with men. The Court put it this way: "The destiny of the woman must be shaped to a large extent on her own conception of her spiritual imperatives and her place in society."[78]

In addition to these normative justifications for reaffirming *Roe,* the plurality opinion was quite candid in its opinion that there were additional prudential reasons that convinced the Justices not to reverse the precedent even if they would not have voted with the majority had they been on the Court in 1973. First, the opinion invoked the doctrine of *stare decisis,* a principle of judicial prudence in common law systems that invites (though does not require) a court to consider the practical and social consequences of reversing a prior precedent, even though it was wrongly decided in the first instance.[79] Second, the Court invoked the need to preserve its reputation and legitimacy as grounds for sustaining *Roe*, lest they be seen as capitulating to political pressure.[80]

In applying the principles of *stare decisis*, the Court concluded that the rule announced in *Roe* had not proven to be unworkable, nor had it been eroded by subsequent legal decisions, or undermined by new factual developments. But the plurality asserted that overturning *Roe* would disrupt reliance on abortion access as a guarantor of self-definition through sexual choices and women's equal participation in the economic and social life of the nation. "[F]or two decades of economic and social developments, people have organized intimate relationships and made choices that define their views of themselves and their places in society, in reliance on the availability of abortion in the event that contraception should fail."[81]

For all the foregoing reasons, the plurality decided to reaffirm *Roe*'s "core holding," albeit rooted in the good of liberty—the freedom of a woman to make decisions essential for self-definition and "to retain the ultimate control over her destiny."[82] But when the plurality finally specified what it meant by "essential holding," it bore only a passing resemblance to the rule announced in *Roe*.

First, in *Casey* the Court downgraded the right to abortion from "fundamental" to a "protected liberty interest."[83] The plurality suggested that *Roe*'s approach was too demanding and did not provide sufficient latitude for states to express their strong respect for prenatal life (from the moment of conception) and to seek to persuade women to choose childbirth over abortion. Accordingly, the Court replaced the nearly insurmountable "strict scrutiny" standard of review for state limits on abortion with a new, seemingly more lenient "undue burden" standard.

Under the new "undue burden" standard, the state was not permitted to adopt a measure "if its purpose or effect is to place a substantial obstacle in the path of a woman seeking an abortion before the fetus attains viability."[84] The Court did not define "undue burden" with specificity but seemed to suggest that measures would be invalidated that prevented a woman from making the "ultimate decision to terminate her pregnancy before viability."[85] However, legal measures designed to persuade a woman to choose to carry her pregnancy to term, to convey medically accurate information, or to otherwise signal the state's profound interest in prenatal human life would be permissible, even if they had the incidental effect of making abortion more difficult or expensive to obtain. After viability, the state could regulate or proscribe abortion, so long as such laws included an exception for the preservation of the life or health of mother. By adopting this pre- versus post-viability framework, the plurality opinion abandoned another key aspect of *Roe*, namely, the trimester framework.

While the Court's explanation of "undue burden" was not entirely clear, it became slightly more so as the plurality opinion applied it to the challenged Pennsylvania law. The Court affirmed the constitutionality of all the legal provisions at issue, save one—spousal notification. But every other aspect of the law was upheld, including several that had been struck down in previous Supreme Court opinions as unconstitutional under *Roe*. According to the plurality, neither the informed consent requirement, the twenty-four-hour waiting period, the parental notification provision, nor the reporting requirements constituted "undue burdens" to women seeking abortions in Pennsylvania. The prior Supreme Court precedents that had invalidated similar provisions in the past were thus overruled.

At first glance, it seemed that *Casey* had cleared the way for much greater regulation of abortion prior to viability than had been possible under *Roe,* and perhaps its proscription after viability. But on closer examination, the Court had left unaltered an essential element of the previous regime of abortion jurisprudence, namely, the broad scope of "health" to encompass all aspects of well-being (including "familial" interests) as defined in *Doe v. Bolton.* By extension, the "health exception" that *Casey* required as an adjunct to any limit on abortion—including after viability—appeared to remain so broad as to swallow any state rule, so long as the abortion provider could warrant that some aspect of the woman's well-being would be advanced by the procedure.

ANTHROPOLOGY OF *CASEY*

As was the case in *Roe,* the underlying assumptions regarding human identity and thriving that emerge from the plurality's decision in *Casey* reflect the anthropology of expressive individualism. This is evident in the opinion's framing of the legal conflict at issue and its treatment of the state's interest in prenatal life. But the influence of the anthropology of expressive individualism is most striking in the plurality's discussion of the normative grounding of the right to abortion, including the ostensible goods it secures and the harms it protects against.

Just as in *Roe*, the *Casey* plurality styles the legal question at issue as involving a conflict of interests between atomized individuals—one being a person and the other something less than a person. There is no serious consideration of their integrated and intertwined bodies and futures. There is no acknowledgement of their relationship—they are treated as strangers rather than mother and offspring. The Court's theory of "personhood" remains mysterious, but it is essential to the opinion (as it was in *Roe*) that the moral status of prenatal life remain strictly a matter of private judgment, to be decided by each individual according to her own values and interests. In other words, *Casey* forbids the state from offering the protections to the fetus that are afforded to a legal person, whose moral status cannot be relegated to the domain of private opinion. Whether the developing human organism *in utero* is deemed to be a nonperson because of its bodily dependence on the mother or because it fails to meet predetermined criteria of active capacities remains unclear. In *Casey*, the Court opens the door to more state protections for prenatal life after viability, justified by its assertion that this is the point at which "the independent existence of the second life can in reason and all fairness be the object of state protection that now overrides the rights of the woman."[86] But it does not explain why this developmental moment is significant, beyond suggesting without a developed argument that it is a "workable" line and that "a woman who fails to act before viability has consented to the State's intervention on behalf of the developing child."[87] But, again, given *Casey's* retention of *Doe v. Bolton's* broad conception of "health," and, by extension, the open-ended "health exception" that must accompany any restriction on abortion, the Court in *Casey* stops far short of declaring the viable unborn human being to be a "person" with a right to life.

In these ways, *Casey* follows *Roe*'s implicit embrace of expressive individualism. But it goes far beyond *Roe* in this regard when the opinion discusses the justification for and the nature of the right to abortion. The opinion is a paean to *liberty* of a very particular sort. It is the freedom of the unencumbered atomized will—the self-originating source of valid claims—to define and express its originality over and above outmoded social conventions and to pursue a destiny of its own choosing. The right to abortion springs from the freedom "to define one's own concept of existence, of meaning, of the universe, and of the mystery of human life."[88] The right to abortion frees a woman to make choices based on "her own conception of her spiritual imperatives and her place in society," and to break away from outmoded and repressive norms regarding appropriate social roles.[89] It is the freedom to live authentically in a way that may be transgressive of conventional mores. And the right to abortion guarantees the continuing freedom for women to "organize intimate relationships and ma[ke] choices that define their views of themselves and their places in society" in the event that efforts at birth control fail.[90] In this way, the right to abortion serves as an indispensable mechanism to allow women to pursue the same forms of sexual expression available to men, without being unequally burdened in charting their own destinies socially and economically. In short, the plurality in *Casey* defends the right to abortion as derived from and in service of the liberty to pursue the aspirations of expressive individualism.

This is likewise evident in what the *Casey* plurality does not discuss. There is no serious discussion of the possible meaning of the singular bodily integration and intertwining of mother and child presented in human pregnancy. There is no exploration of the significance of the bonds of kinship. There is no reflection on the fact that sexual intercourse is the means by which a new human life comes into being—emerging already embedded in a relationship with mother, father, and family. The Court does not consider that the womb is the locus of this event and the first place of belonging for the unborn child. There is no wrestling with the complexity and risks of dividing the world of living human organisms into "persons" who bear human rights and "nonpersons" who live at the sufferance of others, based on their interests and desires. The opinion does not grapple with the possibility that in the networks of uncalculated giving and graceful receiving that are required to protect and promote the flourishing of a community of embodied beings, the vulnerability and dependence of a woman facing an unplanned pregnancy constitutes a summons for aid that must be answered by all those able to render it. It is a world of strife and conflict among atomized strangers, without unchosen obligations. It is a place where "natural givens" are not used as an aid to interpret the world of physical reality. The opinion makes no mention of the virtues of just generosity, hospitality, misericordia, gratitude, solidarity, openness to the unbidden, tolerance of imperfection, or friendship. The opinion does not serve as an aid to the moral imagination; its reasoning and logic do not reveal the hidden faces or voices of others who have claims on us, to whom we owe an obligation of care in proportion to their needs, regardless of how it might benefit us in return. The opinion is, as evidenced by the foregoing, forgetful of the body.

The foregoing analysis of American abortion jurisprudence reveals the anthropology of expressive individualism at work. It animates and undergirds a legal framework that reflects a fatally partial and limited vision of human identity and flourishing. As a result, the law is not responsive to the complexity of embodied life in its fullness, and leaves both mother and child unprotected and exposed. But before exploring this notion further, it is important to complete the picture of American abortion jurisprudence, which requires a brief discussion of three more judicial precedents that comprise the current law of abortion in the United States.

STENBERG V. CARHART (CARHART I) AND GONZALES V. CARHART (CARHART II): THE PARTIAL BIRTH ABORTION CASES

STENBERG V. CARHART (CARHART I)

A short article by Dr. Martin Haskell entitled "Second Trimester D&X, 20 Weeks and Beyond," published in the proceedings of a 1992 conference of the National Abortion Federation, set off a fifteen-year firestorm of controversy leading to nearly thirty state statutes, federal legislation (including multiple presidential vetoes and attempted Senate overrides) and two Supreme Court decisions.[91] In this article, Haskell described, in a step-by-step manner, a method of abortion that many found shocking and gruesome. The procedure involves the intentional "delivery" (Haskell's words) of much of the fetal body—trunk and extremities—feet first into the vagina.[92] With the fetal head in the cervix, the abortion provider pierces the skull with forceps, suctions out the skull contents, crushes the head, and the removes the fetal remains intact. Haskell noted that he "routinely performed this procedure on all patients 20 through 24 weeks" of gestation.[93] Because the procedure involves a process much akin to a live birth delivery and may even involve some of the lower extremities of the living fetus becoming visible outside of the mother's body, opponents of the procedure describe it as a "partial birth abortion."

The response? As one could expect, much of the American public reacted in horror, including many elected officials who self-identified as pro-choice. Senator Daniel Patrick Moynihan (D-NY), himself a longtime abortion rights supporter, famously said in response to the procedure, "It is as close to infanticide as anything I have come upon in our judiciary."[94] Public debate ensued, with dramatic moments that included Ron Fitzsimmons, Executive Director of the National Coalition of Abortion Providers, admitting to an American Medical News reporter that he had "lied through [his] teeth" on national television in a previous interview when he asserted that such procedures were rare and only used to preserve women's health.[95] To the contrary, he estimated that the procedure was performed 3,000–5,000 times annually on "a healthy mother with a healthy fetus that is 20 weeks or more along."[96]

Efforts at legislation quickly followed. In the 1990s, the U.S. Congress passed bans on the procedure on more than one occasion, but President Clinton vetoed each effort. Nearly thirty state legislatures passed laws banning intact dilation and extraction. It was in response to these measures that the dispute moved into the United States courts.

The battle to ban "partial birth abortions" at the state level culminated in 2000 with the U.S. Supreme Court decision *Stenberg v. Carhart* (*Carhart I*), which focused on a Nebraska law that mirrored those in dozens of other states.[97]

In a 5–4 decision, the Supreme Court struck down all of the challenged laws on the grounds that they were unconstitutionally vague in describing the prohibited procedure, and because they did not include a "health exception," allowing an abortion provider discretionary judgment to perform this form of abortion.[98] State legislatures had declined to include such an exception because they maintained that there were no known actual cases involving women with conditions that required this procedure to preserve their physical health or life. (This argument was echoed in a 1997 letter from the American Medical Association to Congress in support of the federal ban.[99]) Moreover, they worried that given the capacious nature of "health" as defined by *Doe v. Bolton*, inclusion of a health exception would be tantamount to providing what some referred to as an "abortionist's veto."[100] For support, they cited the public statement of late term abortion practitioner Warren Hern, M.D., who was quoted in *USA Today* on May 15, 1997 as saying "I will certify that any pregnancy is a threat to a woman's life and could cause 'grievous injury' to her 'physical health.'"[101]

Opponents of the laws countered that there may be hypothetical medical circumstances in which the procedure might be the safest option for women.[102]

Justice Breyer and four colleagues in the majority concluded that in the face of this disagreement among distinguished experts, the Court must defer to the "significant body of medical opinion" suggesting that in certain circumstances this procedure might afford the safest option for patients.[103] Justice O'Connor concurred separately to underscore the proposition that post-viability restrictions must always include a health exception, as per *Casey*.[104] Thus, the majority struck down as unconstitutional every state law in the nation banning so-called partial birth abortions.

Two of the three Justices from the *Casey* plurality joined the majority opinion in *Carhart I*. However, Justice Anthony Kennedy wrote a blistering dissent, all but accusing his *Casey* plurality colleagues—Justices Souter and O'Connor—of betrayal. He had intended for *Casey* to be a statesmanlike compromise on the issue of abortion, allowing states greater latitude to regulate the practice and signal respect for prenatal human life. But in this case, his colleagues in the majority had cast aside substantial medical authority that this procedure was not necessary to avert any serious health risks to a pregnant woman and deferred instead to the medical judgment of the plaintiffs' experts and Dr. LeRoy Carhart who admitted to using the technique "for every patient in every procedure, regardless of indications, after 15 weeks' gestation."[105] Echoing prior critics of the "health exception" jurisprudence of *Roe* and *Doe*, Justice Kennedy lamented that the inclusion of a health exception "which depends on the appropriate medical judgment of

Dr. Carhart is no ban at all."[106] He noted that both the American Medical Association (who had officially expressed supported for a federal ban in 1997) and the American College of Obstetricians and Gynecologists (who opposed the ban) "could identify no circumstances under which [partial birth abortion] would be the only option to save the life or preserve the health of the woman."[107] He observed that "no expert called by Dr. Carhart, and no expert testifying in favor of the procedure, had in fact performed a partial birth abortion in his or her medical practice."[108] Regarding the question of relative safety, he wrote that "[t]he most to be said for the D&X is it may present an unquantified lower risk of complication for a particular patient but that other proven safe procedures remain available even for this patient."[109] In short, Justice Kennedy was convinced that "substantial evidence supports Nebraska's conclusion that its law denies no woman a safe abortion."[110]

Kennedy concluded that Nebraska's interests in preserving the integrity of the medical profession, preventing the coarsening of society's moral sense, and promoting respect for life more generally were all important goods served by the challenged law, and that the state was well within its discretion to accept the opinion of those substantial medical authorities who found that there was no medical reason to include a health exception in the law. But his arguments failed to muster five votes among his colleagues. Until seven years later.

GONZALES V. CARHART (CARHART II)

Between 2000 and 2007 several things occurred that resulted in a significant shift in the law regarding intact dilation and extraction abortions. First, a president was elected who supported the proposed federal bans on partial birth abortion that his predecessor had vetoed. Second, two new Justices were appointed to the Court, John Roberts and Samuel Alito, the second of whom replaced a Justice (O'Connor) who had been in the majority in *Carhart I*. Third, the U.S. Congress passed the Partial Birth Abortion Ban Act of 2003, which more carefully specified the prohibited procedure than the state laws at issue in *Carhart I*.[111] The law banned abortions in which defined anatomical parts of a living fetus were intentionally delivered outside of the woman's body prior to "performing an overt act that the person knows will kill the partially delivered fetus."[112] But like the laws struck down as unconstitutional in *Carhart I*, the federal ban did not include a health exception.

Nebraska abortion provider LeRoy Carhart sued again along with plaintiffs in several other U.S. district courts including San Francisco and New York, and the federal law was enjoined as unconstitutional, following *Carhart I*. The Court granted certiorari and in a 5–4 decision authored by Justice Kennedy affirmed the law as constitutional on its face.[113]

Justice Kennedy began his opinion by describing in exacting and graphic detail how the prohibited procedure is performed, including the testimony of a nurse witness who recounted her own adverse emotional reaction to observing the effects of the technique on a living fetus when she had assisted in an intact dilation and extraction abortion.

Justice Kennedy next acknowledged that some of his colleagues in the majority (Justices Scalia and Thomas) had expressed opposition to the reasoning and result in *Planned*

Parenthood v. Casey, but asserted that, rightly understood, the rule from that precedent supported affirming the federal Partial Birth Abortion Ban Act as constitutional. Justice Kennedy's analysis proceeded from the assumption that *Casey* governed the case, without explicitly reaffirming it. Because the law applied both pre-viability and post-viability, the question presented was whether it constituted an "undue burden" as defined by *Casey*. In noting what he took to be the correct framework for analysis, Kennedy observed that "by common understanding and scientific terminology, the fetus is a living organism while within the womb, whether or not it is viable outside the womb."[114]

In Kennedy's view, *Casey* created sufficient latitude for state legislatures to ban controversial abortion methods that threatened the integrity of the medical profession, led to a diminished respect for life generally, and a reduced valuation of the life of the unborn specifically. He found the federal law not to be unconstitutionally vague—distinguishing it from the state laws at issue in *Carhart I* (which he did not overrule, despite the close similarities shared by the laws at issue in that case and the federal Partial Birth Abortion Ban Act). The federal law specified precisely what was prohibited, had a robust intent requirement for prosecution, and did not sweep into its ambit any other more common abortion procedures used around the same gestational stage.

Turning to the absence of the health exception, for the same reasons he cited in his dissent in *Carhart I*, he found that there were several safe alternative methods of abortion available such that the categorical ban on intact dilation and extraction abortions did not constitute an undue burden. One way to avoid the strictures of the ban, for example, would be to induce fetal demise prior to delivery of any portion of the intact fetal remains. Justice Kennedy concluded by affirming that even in areas where there is medical uncertainty and disagreement among experts, the state and federal governments enjoy wide discretion to enact laws.

Justice Kennedy noted that his decision did not preclude future so-called "as-applied" challenges to the federal Partial Birth Abortion Ban Act's absence of a health exception, meaning cases brought by actual patients whose health was threatened by the prohibition of the technique. As of the time of this publication, no such claim has ever been raised, nor have there been any reports in the media of injuries suffered as a result of the federal Partial Birth Abortion Ban Act.

Justice Ginsburg wrote a scorching dissent, joined by three other colleagues, that is crucial to understand not simply because it fell only one vote shy of commanding a majority, but because it seems to represent an important shift in the normative justification for abortion from the previous grounds of privacy (in *Roe*) and liberty (in *Casey*). Justice Ginsburg grounds the right to abortion in the good of *equality*. That is, in her dissent she is emphatic that the right to abortion is central to a woman's "dignity and autonomy, her personhood and destiny . . . her place in society."[115] She notes that it is an essential mechanism by which a woman can free herself from outmoded patriarchal norms that have historically prevented women from pursuing their economic and social ambitions on an equal footing with men. As suggested in *Casey*, men are free to embrace forms of sexual expression and behavior without the bodily burdens of unwanted pregnancy. A right to abortion levels the playing field for women in the event of contraceptive failure or unprotected sex. Thus, Justice Ginsburg emphasized that challenges to restrictions on abortion are not about an abstract commitment to privacy, but rather "center on a woman's autonomy to determine her life's course, and thus to enjoy equal citizenship stature."[116]

Justice Ginsburg took umbrage at Justice Kennedy's rhetoric in the majority decision in which he expressed worries that women might not receive full information regarding the nature of the challenged procedure and come to regret their abortions when these details later came to light. Justice Kennedy was reacting to a brief filed by Sandra Cano (the plaintiff "Mary Doe" in *Doe v. Bolton* who later became a pro-life advocate, as did Norma McCorvey, the plaintiff "Jane Roe" in *Roe v. Wade*) signed by 180 women who reported that they were injured physically and psychologically by their abortions.[117] He opined that the federal Partial Birth Abortion Ban Act would shape public understanding and encourage women to carry their pregnancies to term rather than seek late term abortions. Justice Ginsburg vigorously objected to this line of argument and condemned the notion that a ban on the procedure was an appropriate tool toward this end. Moreover, she argued that Justice Kennedy was indulging "ancient notions about women's place in the family and under the Constitution" that had long been "discredited."[118] Justice Ginsburg was particularly critical of Justice Kennedy's comment that "[r]espect for life finds an ultimate expression in the bond of love the mother has for her child."[119] She likewise objected to his use of the phrase "abortion doctor" (which she took to be pejorative), as well as his references to a fetus as an "unborn child" and a "baby."[120]

Justice Ginsburg's dissent in *Carhart II* is an excellent representative of current thinking among abortion rights advocates, scholars, and at least four Supreme Court Justices regarding the justification for abortion rights and the anthropological premises that undergird it.

For nearly ten years after *Carhart II*, the Supreme Court was largely dormant in its development of the jurisprudence of abortion. That all changed in the summer of 2016 when the Court issued its most recent decision in this perennially vexed domain.

WHOLE WOMAN'S HEALTH V. HELLERSTEDT

Forty years after the Supreme Court struck down Texas's abortion law in *Roe v. Wade*, the same state legislature passed a suite of abortion regulations following a special session characterized by high drama, acrimony, and a thirteen-hour filibuster that drew national attention. The law, HB-2, contained several provisions, including a ban on abortions after twenty weeks post-fertilization (twenty-two weeks measured from the last menstrual period or "LMP," the most common method for dating pregnancies). But two provisions in particular became the basis for the Court's most recent pronouncement in its nearly fifty-year period of governing the practice of abortion. First, HB-2 required physicians providing abortions to have admitting privileges at a hospital within a thirty-mile radius of the site of the procedure. Second, the law mandated that abortion facilities meet the stringent requirements of "ambulatory surgical centers," as defined by the Texas Health and Safety Code, including operations standards, fire and safety guidelines, and physical plant criteria. These new laws replaced previous regulations requiring abortion providers to have a "working arrangement" with nearby hospitals and a less exacting regime of safety and inspections. These provisions were proposed in response to the high-profile prosecution of Dr. Kermit Gosnell in Philadelphia, who was later convicted and sentenced to three life terms in prison for murdering three newborns who had survived their attempted late term abortions, and manslaughter for the death of patient Karnamaya Mongar, who died of an overdose of sedatives in his clinic.[121] Gosnell's clinic had operated for years without oversight despite deplorable and unsafe conditions and illegal practices.[122] Texas justified the new regulations on the grounds that they would make abortion safer for women and raise the quality of care at abortion facilities.

Plaintiffs immediately sued to enjoin these two provisions as unconstitutional "undue burdens" on the right to abortion. The federal trial court agreed, but was reversed in part by the U.S. Court of Appeals, which found that the plaintiffs had failed to demonstrate that the challenged laws imposed an unconstitutional undue burden, except as applied to one plaintiff physician in McAllen, Texas, who was the sole abortion provider for women in the Rio Grande Valley.[123]

The Supreme Court granted certiorari and in June 2016, in a 5–3 decision (Justice Scalia had died earlier that year, leaving a vacancy on the Court) struck down the laws as unconstitutional.[124] In doing so, Justice Breyer, writing for the majority, announced a new standard for determining the constitutionality of abortion regulations aimed at promoting health and safety. Such laws will be deemed an unconstitutional "undue burden" when the judicial branch finds that they do not confer sufficient medical benefits to warrant the limits on abortion access that they impose.[125]

Two aspects of Justice Breyer's approach seem to stand in tension with the Court's prior decisions, though the Court did not overrule any earlier precedents. First, by emphasizing the independent role of the judiciary in evaluating the facts relevant to burdens/benefits analysis of challenged health and safety regulations, Justice Breyer appeared to limit the authority accorded by *Carhart II* to state and federal legislatures to enact laws in the face of scientific uncertainty and divided expert authority. Second, in a very odd passage, Breyer misstates the *Casey* standard altogether when he writes that "we now use viability as the relevant point at which a State may begin limiting women's access to abortion for reasons unrelated to maternal health."[126] To the contrary, both *Casey* and *Carhart II* specified that a state may restrict abortions prior to viability in the name of a wide array of other interests, including its desire to signal its high regard for prenatal life, to promote respect for life generally, or to safeguard the integrity of the medical profession, so long as such limitations do not constitute an "undue burden." The Federal Partial Birth Abortion Ban Act of 2003, affirmed as constitutional, was itself a pre-viability restriction adopted to advance these purposes; it was not enacted for the purpose of maternal health and safety.

Justice Breyer and his colleagues concluded that neither the admitting privileges requirement nor the ambulatory surgical center standards offered any material benefits for health and safety, but taken together would result in a substantial burden on access in the form of massive closures of abortion facilities across Texas. The number of facilities that could comply with both standards totaled seven or eight. Prior to the case, there were forty abortion clinics across Texas. The majority inferred that this reduction in available facilities would result in increased travel time and dramatic overcrowding of the remaining facilities.[127]

Justices Thomas and Alito (who was joined by Chief Justice Roberts) filed separate dissents, objecting to the new benefits/burdens standard and the application of the new rule in the absence of concrete evidence regarding the causes of clinic closures and the number of women affected as a result. Justice Thomas lamented that the new burdens-benefits standard marked a return to *Roe*'s discarded strict scrutiny standard of review, as it invited the judicial branch to conduct an independent searching interrogation of the efficacy of challenged laws rather than simply evaluate their burdensome effects. He criticized the majority's "embrace of a jurisprudence of rights-specific exceptions and balancing tests" and, quoting a law review article by the late Justice Scalia, declared it to be "a regrettable concession of defeat—an acknowledgment that we have passed the point where 'law,' properly speaking, has any further application."[128]

Justice Alito complained that the Court had failed to hold the plaintiffs to their burden of marshalling empirical proof based on hard data, and instead simply indulged "crude inferences" about the causes and effects of the clinic closures.[129] He noted that even if only seven or eight clinics remained open, 95 percent of women of reproductive age in Texas would live within 150 miles of an abortion provider. This travel distance was deemed not to constitute an "undue burden" in *Casey*. He further objected that there had been no rigorous factfinding regarding the capacity of these remaining clinics to provide abortions to the population of women that might seek them.

Thus, the two challenged provisions were nullified as unconstitutional, with Justice Kennedy curiously silent, having written no concurring opinion. He retired from the bench two years later.

THE LAW OF ABORTION IN AMERICA

These six Supreme Court precedents constitute the fundamental law regarding abortion in the United States. A fair summary would be that a bare majority of the Court has found a liberty interest implicit in the Due Process Clause of the Fourteenth Amendment that includes a right to abortion. The liberty interest becomes manifest in light of the unique burdens of unplanned or unwanted pregnancy and parenthood that fall exclusively on women, threatening their self-conception, self-determination, and capacity to pursue their chosen social and economic aspirations. To free herself from these burdens, a woman must be at liberty first, to define the meaning and value of prenatal human life. The state is forbidden from imposing its own judgment on this question, especially when its law is rooted in what the Court takes to be outmoded premises about gender and social roles. Next, the woman must be free to act on her belief—to seek an abortion in the event of contraceptive failure or unprotected sex.

This ultimate liberty is unfettered until fetal viability, after which an abortion may be obtained when the provider can cite some aspect of a woman's well-being, broadly understood (including "familial interests"), that would be served by the procedure. At no point prior to birth is the human organism a legal or constitutional "person" with a right to life (its moral status is always a matter for private judgment), but the Court has recognized the state's interest in what it has variously described as "potential life," "prenatal life," and even an "unborn child."

Operationally, this is translated as a judicial restraint on the state to "unduly burden" access to abortion pre-viability (*Casey*), and the obligation for the state to include a very broad "health exception" to any bans on abortion post-viability (*Casey* taken together with *Doe v. Bolton*). Under the U.S. Supreme Court framework, no state has ever been permitted to ban abortion *as such* either pre- or post-viability. Instead, only ancillary side constraints on the manner in which abortion is provided have been affirmed as constitutional. Such measures include waiting periods, informed consent provisions, parental involvement laws, and bans on particularly controversial abortion techniques (for example, the Partial Birth Abortion Ban Act of 2003). Abortion rights advocates strenuously object to such laws as improper and unjustified restraints on access to abortion. Where a state seeks to regulate abortion for the sake of women's health and safety, it must satisfy the Supreme Court that the purported benefits of such laws are great enough to warrant the limits on abortion access that they impose.

There have been many recent efforts to curtail abortion both in part and altogether by states including Texas, Missouri, Ohio,

Georgia, Indiana, Kentucky, and Alabama. These include bans after twenty weeks post-conception (premised on the unborn child's capacity to experience pain), bans on "live dismemberment" of fetuses in the second trimester or later, bans on abortions solely for purposes of genetic, racial, or sex discrimination (for example, to prevent the birth of children with Down Syndrome), bans on abortion after a fetal heartbeat becomes detectable, and straightforward prohibitions on abortion except in cases where a woman's life or health is threatened, or in case of fetal abnormality. All laws of these sorts have been enjoined as unconstitutional by the lower federal courts under the *Roe/Casey* framework.

Yet, there is nothing in Supreme Court jurisprudence of abortion that forbids states from actively promoting abortion rights, even after fetal viability.

Recently, several states have moved to sweep away all preexisting limits on the practice and to require that abortion be funded by taxpayer dollars. New York, for example, recently passed a state law explicitly permitting abortion as of right up to twenty-four weeks of pregnancy, in the "absence of fetal viability," or at any point in gestation if "necessary to protect the patient's life or health."[130] "Health" in this instance, is left broadly open-ended, as the sponsors and supporters of the law regard abortion to be a "fundamental component of a woman's health, privacy, and equality."[131] The New York law also repealed prior limits on abortion in state law, including a provision that specified that abortion is only permissible with a woman's consent, a law allowing for charges of manslaughter for causing a woman's death during an abortion, and a law requiring care for newborns who survive an attempted abortion. Other states have followed suit.

Illinois likewise passed a law codifying abortion as a "fundamental right," repealing its state law banning partial birth abortions, eliminating preexisting conscience exemptions for health care providers, requiring abortion coverage in insurance plans, and explicitly declaring that "the fertilized egg, embryo, or fetus does not have independent rights under the law."[132] This last provision shows that current American abortion jurisprudence allows a state to deny prenatal human organisms the legal status of persons but forbids them from extending the protections of personhood. It is, to borrow a phrase from American constitutional law, a "one-way ratchet."[133]

American abortion law under U.S. Supreme Court precedent likewise permits state supreme courts to recognize robust rights to abortion (beyond those identified in *Roe* and *Casey*) in construing their own states' constitutions. A handful of state Supreme Courts have done so, most following the same reasoning as *Roe* and *Casey*. Most recently, the Supreme Court of Kansas declared that there is a right to abortion under that state's constitutional guarantee that "all men are possessed of the equal and inalienable natural rights, among which are life, liberty, and the pursuit of happiness."[134] The case, *Hodes & Nauser MDs v. Schmidt,* involved a challenge to a Kansas state law that banned "dismemberment abortions," defined as "knowingly dismembering a living unborn child and extracting such unborn child one piece at a time from the uterus. . . ."[135] The majority opinion included an extended exegesis of the scope of "natural rights," drawing upon a variety of classical sources of political theory, including the thought of John Locke.

Locke, the Court observed, wrote that "every Man has a Property in his own Person."[136] It concluded that "at the heart of a natural rights philosophy is the principle that individuals should be free to make choices about how to conduct their own lives, or, in other words, to exercise personal autonomy."[137] The Court extended this conception of bodily autonomy to include a fundamental right to abortion, adopted a strict scrutiny standard of review for state limits on the right, and struck the law down as unconstitutionally burdensome.

Since *Hellerstedt,* there has been a significant change in the Court's composition, with two Republican appointees, Justices Neil Gorsuch and Brett Kavanaugh, assuming the seats vacated by Justices Antonin Scalia and Anthony Kennedy, respectively. It is possible that Justice Kavanaugh disagrees with his predecessor (for whom he clerked) regarding the existence and scope of a right to abortion under the U.S. Constitution, and the application of principles of *stare decisis* to the Court's abortion precedents. If this is so, and four other Justices concur, then perhaps the Court will overturn the *Roe/Casey* line of cases and return the regulation of abortion to the political branches of the states and federal government. This possibility may be what has motivated state legislatures such as New York and Illinois and courts such as the Kansas Supreme Court to proactively ensure that their state laws protect abortion access. Perhaps this is also the reason that states such as Alabama, Missouri, Kentucky, Georgia, Indiana, and Ohio have passed laws that appear designed to call the question of *Roe* and *Casey*'s continuing vitality. Only time will tell.

ANTHROPOLOGY OF AMERICAN ABORTION LAW

The foregoing survey of the nearly fifty years of the Supreme Court's abortion jurisprudence and the legal framework that it has created reveals that its animating foundation of human identity and flourishing is expressive individualism. The law proceeds from the assumption that the core unit of reality is the atomized and isolated self, lacking any unchosen constitutive attachments, along with the obligations and benefits that might flow from them. It reduces the person to a lonely agent of desire, defined by the will and the capacity to make choices, whose highest thriving is self-definition and the pursuit of economic and social aspirations.

Given these suppositions about what it means to be a person, it is not surprising that the Court discovered a constitutional right to self-determination—under the variable and shifting auspices of privacy, liberty, and equality—to exercise "self-help" in the form of abortion so as to overcome the burdens and obstacles to pursuing one's chosen destiny, whether they be imposed by others, the state, or perhaps even nature itself.

It is also not surprising that viewing human identity through the lens of expressive individualism as it does, the Court excludes from the community of legal persons those living human organisms not yet capable of actively discerning, inventing, and pursuing the projects essential to self-definition. To be clear, this is not simply a matter of the Court's narrow interpretation of the word "person" in the Fourteenth Amendment, but results from its categorical prohibition on the state from extending the protections of any form of legal personhood to prenatal life in the context of abortion. The Court explicitly empowers private citizens to judge for themselves the moral status of the unborn, without interference from the state. Which is to say that the Court implicitly judges the human being *in utero* to be something far less than a legal person for reasons that it never explains.

Finally, the anthropological assumptions of the Court obscure from view the networks of relationships in which the parties are embedded—relationships of family (including, but not limited to maternal-fetal biological kinship), community, and polity—that could and should be responsive to the basic human needs that arise from unwanted or unplanned pregnancy. Accordingly, the narrow right the Court identifies as crucial to human flourishing is simply the entitlement to terminate the unwanted pregnancy and the life of the prenatal being *in utero*. There is a brute logic to the recognition of this right given the Court's background assumptions about the nature of human life, humanly lived. In a world of atomized wills locked in conflict with one another (and other sub-personal beings), the right of private force is essential to preserving the fundamental right to express one's identity and to pursue one's chosen destiny. And this right is particularly weighty when balanced against the interests of *nonpersons*.

Viewed in this light, the Court's rendering of the constitutional right to abortion is best understood as the liberty to protect and vindicate the most important goods at the heart of expressive individualism. It is the liberty to define for oneself the meaning of procreation and prenatal life without interference or imposition by the state, and the freedom to act on this choice by terminating a pregnancy prior to viability as a matter of right, and even after viability, in the name of a wide array of additional goods relating to well-being (including "familial heath"), by operation of *Doe v. Bolton*'s health exception. The right to abortion thus conceived is not simply about responding in justice and compassion to the bodily and psychic burdens imposed on women by unwanted pregnancy, but rather, in the Court's words, to protect the freedom to "organize intimate relationships and ma[ke] choices that define [women's] views of themselves and their places in society."[138]

I believe it is true that persons are free, particular, and individuated beings, and that interrogating and then expressing the truths discovered in one's inner depths can be a fruitful and dynamic source of meaning. Indeed, such expression can be a crucial catalyst for promoting justice and resistance to conventional but repressive ideologies. It is true that freedom of conscience is important to human flourishing, and that many—perhaps most—important questions are rightly left to private judgment and private ordering. Each person is, in deep and important ways, associated with his or her will, judgment, rationality, and cognition. What's more, women deserve to be free and equal to men in the eyes of the law and should not be held hostage to discredited patriarchal conceptions of social roles imposed by the state, or anyone else for that matter. They should indeed be free, as the Supreme Court has written, to shape their own destinies, in accordance with their self-understanding and their spiritual imperatives, as they understand them. They should be free and uncoerced in matters of procreation and parenthood.

The problem for American abortion law is that this is not the *whole* truth about human beings, and these are not the only goods at stake or evils to be avoided in this most vexed and bitterly contested realm of public bioethics. What is missing? A serious consideration of *embodiment* and its meaning and consequences. This "forgetfulness of the body" distorts and stunts the Court's understanding of the full human dimensions at issue. Specifically, the Court is blind to the reality of vulnerability, dependence, and natural limits that necessarily attend any problem or conflict involving embodied beings.

Because the Court fails to consider embodiment as an indispensable aspect of human reality, it misses goods, practices, and virtues that are essential to the thriving of the individual and shared lives of beings who live, die, and encounter themselves and one another as bodies. Most gravely, the Court fails to consider the networks of uncalculated giving and graceful receiving that are necessary for the survival of embodied beings, as well as vital to their development into the kind of people who can sustain such life-giving networks of relationships. The virtues and practices essential to building and maintaining these networks—generosity, hospitality, misericordia, gratitude, humility, openness to the unbidden, solidarity, dignity, and honesty—help one to learn how to make the good of another one's own good—to be a friend in the truest sense. Alongside the development of these practices and virtues, the cultivation of moral imagination—to see the other who has a claim on our attention and support—and the pursuit of practices that take us "outside of ourselves" is essential to the project of building, sustaining, and learning from these networks of giving and receiving.

The Supreme Court jurisprudence of abortion is blind to all of this because the law it constructs is not true to lived human reality, which depends on unearned privileges and unchosen obligations, and is populated by vulnerable, dependent, and disabled human beings with claims on our care and concern by virtue of their relationship to us and not our consent. Therefore, the Court's prescriptive framework is gravely misguided, and indeed, *inhuman*.

The primary relationship that is invisible to expressive individualism, and by extension, the Court's abortion jurisprudence, is that of parents and children. Focusing as it does on the atomized individual will seeking to express and live out its internally discovered truths in an authentic way, expressive individualism cannot make sense of the connection between parent and child. Parent and child are, instead, conceived as competitors over scarce resources necessary to pursue their own individual interests. This is precisely how the Court frames the conflict of abortion—a clash of strangers each seeking its own advantage. Indeed, this is how it understands human pregnancy itself.

But this description of procreation, pregnancy, and parenthood does not do justice to the lived, embodied human reality of these experiences.[139] Analogies to disputes with trespassers to property, bodily invasions by parasites, or being kidnapped and conscripted into supporting an unconscious violinist are not apt. Psychologist and feminist Sidney Callahan puts it thus:

> The abortion dilemma is caused by the fact that 266 days following a conception in one body, another body will

emerge. One's own body no longer exists as a single unit but is engendering another organism's life. This dynamic passage from conception to birth is genetically ordered and universally found in the human species. Pregnancy is not like the growth of cancer or infestation by a biological parasite; it is the way every human being enters the world.[140]

It is not simply that the womb is the locus of gestation, growth, and birth of every human being, but in every case in which a woman seeks an abortion, the relationship involved is, biologically speaking, that of *mother* and *child*. They are not strangers.

But the Court's reasoning, limited by the anthropology of expressive individualism, misses this relationship and, in doing so, the opportunity to reflect on the fact that the parental relationship is not the transactional domain of consent, but is the pristine case of uncalculated giving and graceful receiving. It is the singular experience that "takes one outside of him or herself," and transforms him or her from an "I" to a "we." A child does not and need not earn the privilege of her parent's care. The parent does not contract to take on such obligations. Being a parent means being responsible for the neediness of one who is utterly dependent and vulnerable, regardless of what one might receive in return. A parent takes on this duty by virtue of an embodied, biological relationship. Human beings begin their lives *in utero* already embedded in the relationship of children to parents. (Of course, biological parents may discharge their obligations by making an adoption plan, facilitating the construction of a new family—a genuine place of belonging for the child in need, with real and new bonds of parenthood. In adoption, as Gil Meilaender has written, love and shared history transcend biological kinship, and create a genuine family for all involved.[141])

But despite the fact that the life *in utero* is a distinct living human organism of the species *homo sapiens,* genetically related to the woman seeking the abortion (in precisely the same way that all children and parents are), the maternal-child relationship is effectively invisible in the Court's reasoning. The Court, following the rubrics of expressive individualism, turns away from the embodied givens of human procreation, and treats the unborn human being as an isolated individual. But perhaps because the fetus cannot yet actively participate in the behaviors that expressive individualism recognizes as proper to persons—higher cognition, self-awareness, reflection, and expression of desires—she is relegated to the domain of legal *nonpersons,* where her status is to be determined by those who are capable of these actions.

Thus, by virtue of its embrace of expressive individualism, the Court is not able to take full account of the biological relationship of mother and child, nor can it even offer a description of the individual life *in utero* that corresponds to lived embodied reality. The relationship is that of strangers, and the fetus is a mere abstraction.

Similarly, the discussion of the burdens of unwanted or unplanned pregnancy and parenthood are incomplete. Of course, these burdens are real and can be crushing. In some cases, pregnancy can pose grave threats to a woman's health or even life.

Unchosen parenthood can create overwhelming stresses and burdens, both economic and emotional. But because the Court atomizes the woman, it both abstracts from the meaningful context of parenthood and isolates her in her suffering, abandoning her to struggle alone as a disembodied self in a world of contending wills, lacking any unchosen obligations or duties of care that might be owed to her by her family, community, state, or nation. Because it is rooted in expressive individualism, the American jurisprudence of abortion cannot respond fully to a pregnant woman's dependence and vulnerability, as it ignores key avenues of aid and support to which she is entitled as a member of the human community.

Because of its implicit embrace of expressive individualism, the Court likewise misses the fact that parents and children are together embedded in a wider network of others who, by virtue of their relationship as extended family members, neighbors, fellow citizens, and polity members, owe them obligations of just generosity, hospitality, misericordia, solidarity, honesty, and respect for their intrinsic equal dignity. Parents and children both depend on these networks, and through their participation in them, become the kind of people who can contribute to their continued sustainability, namely, the sort of people who are able to make the good of others' their own.

But the Court conceives of pregnancy and parenthood as a clash of strangers, "clad in the armor of their rights" (to borrow a phrase from Carl Schneider's more general critique of the overemphasis of autonomy in bioethics).[142] Thus, the Court's chosen anthropology transforms medicine into a tool that is wielded to eliminate unwanted burdens and the beings whose lives are burdensome in an act of "self"-defense. In fact, by emphasizing the sole authority of women to seek abortion in the name of securing her future on an equal footing, the Court lends support to a man who chooses to abandon a pregnant woman in need, since she alone decides whether or not to carry the baby to term. In doing so, the Court embraces an anthropology that weakens the ties between parents and children by ignoring the biological and genetic relationship of mother (and father) and prenatal child. It further weakens the ties of extended family, neighbors, fellow citizens, and the government to the pregnant woman because it isolates her in her suffering and vulnerability and ignores the obligations *of everyone* to come to the aid of women and families in crisis.

Through the frame of expressive individualism, and by ignoring embodiment and the goods, virtues, and practices necessary to responding to its challenges, the Court is left with only one option to respond—the freedom to use force to terminate the prenatal life that constitutes a threat to the individual woman's future.

PROVISIONAL WAY FORWARD: AN ANTHROPOLOGY OF HUMAN EMBODIMENT IN ABORTION LAW AND POLICY

The Supreme Court in *Roe* and *Casey* erred by grounding the law of abortion in an impoverished anthropology that conceals the essential reality of the very human context it seeks to govern, and thus prevents the law from responding to the full range of human needs at issue. Whether constructed by the Supreme Court under the auspices of a maximally unbounded theory of substantive due process, or established through more conventional procedures by a state legislature or the U.S. Congress, what would a legal framework for abortion that remembers the body look like?

Given the intricacies and complexities of making and administering law and public policy in a federalist regime as large and diverse as the United States, it will only be possible here to outline some broad concepts. But as will become clear momentarily, even framed at a high level of abstraction, the principles for the law and policy of abortion rooted in an anthropology of human embodiment do not fit neatly within the left-right or Republican-Democrat paradigm of modern-day America. All sides of the current American political divide may find the following suggestions challenging and provocative to the familiar and preferred legal and normative categories, as expressive individualism runs deep in American law and politics.

To start, we must remember that the law exists to protect and promote the flourishing of persons by regulating conduct, but also to teach and shape the public's understanding of the demands of justice, freedom, and equality. A legal and political regime that takes embodiment seriously would be especially mindful of its concrete human entailments, namely, vulnerability, dependence, and natural limits. Taking account of the "virtues of acknowledged dependence" necessary for the survival and flourishing of embodied human beings, law and public policy would promote the construction and strengthening of the human networks of uncalculated giving and graceful receiving upon which human beings depend both for their very survival and to realize their potential.[143] It would encourage and reward the practices of just generosity, hospitality, and accompaniment of others in suffering (misericordia). It would likewise seek to inculcate the practices of gratitude, humility, openness to the unbidden (and tolerance of imperfection), solidarity, truthfulness, and respect for dignity. Law and public policy animated by an anthropology of embodiment would seek to strengthen the familial and social ties that serve these ends, including institutions of civil society that help to combat a purely inward-looking and individualistic perspective and encourage a sense of belonging. Finally, the law would serve to cultivate the moral imagination, helping persons to see more clearly those other members of the community to whom they owe duties of care, and of whom they can make claims of assistance for themselves and their families.

Where incentives and inducements fall short, and people find themselves without the support and security of the networks of giving and receiving essential to life as humanly lived, the law must step in directly to offer protection and render aid. This could, of course, entail a very robust role for government.

In the context of abortion, an approach to governance grounded in an anthropology of embodiment looks very different from the regime established by the Court in *Roe, Casey,* and their judicial progeny. First, the framing of this issue would not by styled, as under current law, as a clash of atomized interests—a woman's interest in defining for herself the meaning of procreation, prenatal life, avoiding the physical and psychic burdens of unwanted pregnancy and parenthood, and pursuing her chosen future on an equal footing with men, versus the state's interest in "potential life." Rather, it would build from the biological reality of pregnancy and *par-*

enthood, from which several principles and points of decision would follow.

But first, why *parenthood*? Because an anthropology of embodiment takes seriously the process by which human beings come to be, how they survive and thrive, and the web of relationships in which they are embedded as they come into the world. The Supreme Court implicitly followed Tooley and Warren by drawing a bright line distinguishing biological genetic humanity—living members of the species *homo sapiens*—from the narrower classification of "persons." But whereas Tooley and Warren drew the line at the acquisition of certain cognitive capacities connected to self-understanding and expression, the Supreme Court drew the line at birth as the moment that the state may extend the full legal protections of personhood to a new human life.[144]

A legal approach to the question of abortion grounded in the anthropology of embodiment would be very skeptical of a framework for the legal protection of living human beings that either depends on the acquisition of capacities or waxes and wanes based on conditions and degrees of dependence, or the interests and opinions of others (even those of the human subject's parents). The anthropology of embodiment as set forth above regards frailty, weakness, dependence, vulnerability and even disability as part and parcel of the human condition. It does not privilege the capacities of cognition and will. It does not reward the powerful with greater legal protection and withhold the benefits of the law from the weak, because of their weakness. An anthropology of embodiment would follow Hans Jonas's injunction that "utter helplessness demands utter protection."

As a matter of basic embryology, the life of the human organism begins as a biological matter with fertilization, from which emerges a distinct, self-directing, genetically unique embryo, which moves (if all goes well) along a species-specific continuum of development, to fetus, newborn, adolescent, adult, and so forth. From the beginning, the new human being is, of course, radically dependent upon her mother to nurture and bear her in her womb. "Personhood" theory seeks to differentiate the moral status of the organism based on specified capacities or circumstances. Unlike expressive individualism, which dictates that the criteria for personhood are those that enable self-reflection, expression, and pursuit of one's destiny according to the endogenous truths of the inner self, an anthropology of embodiment would regard any living member of the species *homo sapiens* as entitled to the respect owed to persons, regardless of her location (*in utero* or *ex utero*), age, size, state of dependence, active capacities for cognition or desire, her circumstances, and perhaps most of all, regardless of the opinions of others.

In an anthropology of embodiment, there are no pre- or post-personal human beings. Being human is the only criterion for membership in the community of persons.[145]

Thus, an anthropology of embodiment would reject the Supreme Court's rule that in American abortion law the definition of fetal personhood must remain relative and subjective—to be determined by every pregnant woman for herself without imposition of the state. In this view, all human beings are persons and must be recognized as such in the law.

Importantly, the anthropology of embodiment does not simply regard the fetus as just any person. She is the *child* of the woman seeking the abortion. This, of course, means that the woman seeking the abortion is not a stranger to the fetus. She is her *mother*. The relationship, as understood through the anthropology of embodiment, is one of *parenthood*—the most fundamental network of uncalculated giving and graceful receiving essential to life as humanly lived. The question of abortion is thus best understood as a matter involving a mother and her child.[146]

Law and policy animated by an anthropology of embodiment would view the mother as a vulnerable, dependent member of the community, who is entitled to the protections and support of the network of uncalculated giving and graceful receiving that must exist for any human being to survive and flourish. Her neediness is a summons to everyone who is able to come to her aid and extend the same gestures of just generosity, hospitality, and accompaniment in suffering (misericordia) on which they have depended and from which they have benefited in their own lives as vulnerable dependent beings. This applies with special force to the male who is the *father* of the child she carries. It likewise applies to her immediate and extended family members, her neighbors, her community, and her polity (including the government). To be fully human—to practice the virtues necessary to sustaining life as humanly lived—they *must* come to her aid, simply by virtue of and in proportion to her neediness. This is an unchosen obligation that binds everyone who can to respond to her vulnerability and need. In turn, the law must encourage and reward such care and assistance. It must create space for individuals and civil society to respond in charity to the mother in crisis. And if there are no family members, neighbors, or voluntary associations that come forward to help, or they are inadequate to or unworthy of the task, then the government itself must do so directly and indirectly.

And to be clear, these unchosen obligations do not end with the birth of the child. The networks of uncalculated giving and graceful receiving are necessary throughout the human life span; we all exist on a "scale of disability" for our entire lives, so long as we are embodied. Concretely, this means the law must facilitate and catalyze support for mothers and fathers, their extended family, and the broader community to care for children in difficult circumstances. Of course, sometimes parents care best for their children by making an adoption plan, so that a genuine family might be formed with those who do not share biological kinship but will assume the role of parents by welcoming a child as their own.

Law and policy infused by the anthropology of embodiment would view the living human being *in utero* as a *child*, whose dependence and vulnerability likewise call others to render aid. The presumed incapacities of the unborn child to actively engage in self-reflection and expression do not disqualify her from membership in the community of persons. Nor does her state of radical dependence. She is therefore entitled to the moral concern and care of her parents, her extended family, and her community. They owe to her the just generosity, hospitality, and accompaniment that sustained them in their dependence. But the unborn child is also entitled to recognition by the law as a *person*. Thus, she should be protected by the law against the unjustified and unexcused actions of others intending to do her harm. This is not to say, of course, that clinicians may not pursue methods aimed to help the mother that bear significant indirect risks to the child, including termination of the pregnancy by preterm delivery, followed by best efforts to preserve the newborn child's life.

In those tragic circumstances where the continued pregnancy constitutes a grave and proportionate risk to the mother, the law should deploy the familiar legal concepts developed to govern the use of potentially lethal force against innocent persons who pose threats to others. More specifically, the matter should be framed as a conflict between mother and child. Working out how the American legal doctrines of justification, excuse, necessity, and such related concepts as "proportionality," "unjust aggression," and the like would apply to the wholly unique context of pregnancy would require a great deal of fact-intensive analysis and reflection to answer responsibly. Such an inquiry is beyond the scope of this book but must be undertaken in the future to flesh out the concrete entailments of a public bioethics rooted in an anthropology of embodiment. The fundamental point here is that the crisis of unplanned or unwanted pregnancy should be viewed through the normative categories of *mother, child, father, family, community,* and *polity* (including the government).

In short, law and policy driven by the anthropology of embodiment would respond to the question of abortion in a way that is quite distinct from the current American abortion jurisprudence. But it is also important to note that it is not a purely "fetus-centered framework" rooted in a desire "to compel women who are resisting motherhood to perform the work of bearing and rearing children," out of fidelity to an ancient patriarchal and repressive gender-based vision of social roles.[147] It is, instead, a *family* and *community-centered* framework, oriented toward the construction and development of the networks of giving and receiving that are essential to the survival and success of all human beings in their embodied vulnerability and interdependence. This mode of law and policy embraces the humanity of all individuals involved, understood according to their relationships to one another in such networks. It would hold people to account to take responsibility for one another, and in those circumstances where no such aid is forthcoming, would step into the breach directly and provide protection and support.

Such law and policy would also seek to make room for, encourage, and facilitate the practice of gratitude by the beneficiaries of the sustaining networks of care and aid, including the mothers, children, parents, and communities whose lives are touched by unplanned and unwanted pregnancy. The fitting response to selfless giving is graceful receiving, and the related virtues of openness to the unbidden, tolerance of imperfection, and humility.

How the law might be concretely designed and implemented to facilitate the construction and tending of these networks of giving and receiving, along with the goods, virtues, and practices necessary to sustain them is, to be sure, a very complicated and difficult question. It involves myriad considerations of how American law can contribute to these ends using its numerous and fine-grained mechanisms for shaping behavior ranging from passive suasion to direct compulsion, and many measures in between. In broad strokes, a legal regime for abortion rooted in the anthropology of embodiment would extend legal protections to unborn children from the moment they are conceived, forbidding others from intentionally harming them and providing for their care. It would, at the same time, offer maximal support for their mothers, providing for their health care and other needs, both during and after the pregnancy. It would likewise incentivize family members (including the child's father), employers, the community, and the state to construct the vast networks of giving and receiving required to support the flourishing of all involved. In those rare circumstances where continued pregnancy constitutes a serious threat to the mother, the law will draw upon existing doctrines and principles governing circumstances where the vital interests of innocent persons conflict, keeping in mind that this is a case involving a mother and her child. The question of concrete implementation of such a legal framework, and whether it operates through private ordering within the organs of civil society or by direct governmental intervention and oversight is for another time. It will suffice for present purposes to have articulated the broad normative and anthropological foundation on which more particular legal structures might be erected.

4

Assisted Reproduction

[Reproductive technologies] are means to achieve or avoid the
reproductive experiences that are central to personal conceptions of meaning and identity.

—PROF. JOHN A. ROBERTSON, *Children of Choice*, 4 (1994)

Reproductive medicine is helping prospective parents to realize
their own dreams for a disease free legacy.

—DR. GERALD SCHATTEN, TESTIMONY BEFORE THE
PRESIDENT'S COUNCIL ON BIOETHICS (DECEMBER 13, 2002)

In 1969, British researchers Robert G. Edwards and Patrick G.
Steptoe achieved a feat that changed the world forever. As described in the *Nature* article entitled "Early Stages of Fertilization *in vitro* of Human Oocytes Matured *in vitro*," their research
team conceived a living human embryo by combining ova and
sperm in a glass dish (literally "in vitro").[1] Steptoe and Edwards
were thus able to hold and observe the human organism at the
earliest stage of development outside the body. In natural re-

production, the embryo emerges from sperm-egg fusion in the fallopian tube but is not detectable by modern techniques of pregnancy testing until days later. Steptoe and Edwards were able to bring out into the light what had long been shrouded in mystery.

Of course, there were major transformations in human pro-creation before and after Edwards and Steptoe developed *in vitro* fertilization (IVF). Nine years earlier the FDA's approval of an oral contraceptive pill—Enovid 10 (known colloquially as "The Pill")—had created the possibility of reliably severing sexual intercourse from pregnancy.[2] Four years after the publication of their article in *Nature*, the Supreme Court's decision in *Roe v. Wade* recognized a constitutional right to abortion—the freedom to break the necessary connection between pregnancy and birth.[3] But IVF was altogether different. IVF promised not only a possible avenue for infertile people to conceive biologically-related children, it fractured almost entirely the previously integrated component parts of human reproduction—fertilization, gestation, and raising children. For the first time, it was possible to create a human being whose genetic parents (providers of egg and sperm), gestational mother, and rearing parents were five different people, not including the practitioner and staff who prepared and cultured the gametes and performed the fertilization itself.

In 1978, Edwards and Steptoe's research moved from bench to bedside with the birth in England of Louise Brown, the first "test tube baby," as she was described in the press.[4] And, three years later, in 1981, Elizabeth Jordan Carr became the first such baby born in America.[5] Along with the relief promised to the infertile through this revolution in medicine, IVF presented new and radical challenges to seemingly stable conceptions—the nature and meaning of human procreation; the identity, worth, and definitional boundaries of human persons; the substance and contours of parenthood and obligations to children; the fitting ends and means of biomedical science; what it means to be a "patient"; conceptions of health and wholeness; and norms against commodification of the body and its parts.

To date, more than one million babies conceived by IVF have been born in the United States.[6] According to the Centers for Disease Control in 2016 (the last year for which such numbers are available), 76,897 infants were born in the United States following IVF, representing 1.9 percent of all babies born that year (3,941,109).[7] From 2007 to 2016, the number of assisted reproductive technology (ART) cycles performed in America had increased 39 percent.[8] To be sure, these children represent the fulfilments of the hopes and dreams of a vast array of loving parents, and relief from the suffering caused by infertility.

But, as with all paradigm shifts in humankind's enhanced power over nature, there is another side to this reproductive revolution. In the United States alone there are reports of one million human embryos frozen in cryostorage.[9] Their existence stokes a constant and growing demand for their use and destruction in biomedical research (for example, for the derivation and the study of human embryonic stem cells), even though surveys have shown that the vast majority of these embryos have not been designated for donation to researchers.[10]

There is a growing market for gametes, including nationwide advertising campaigns soliciting highly intelligent, athletic, and accomplished female college students to sell their ova, sometimes for tens of thousands of dollars in compensation. One for-profit enterprise, California Conceptions, procures sperm and ova and creates "batches" of embryos which it then sells to patients for implantation (to initiate a pregnancy) at a fraction of the cost of conventional IVF, including a money-back guarantee.[11] The firm typically conceives multiple embryos from a single donor of ova and sells the embryonic siblings to different clients. Prospective patients can browse the catalogue of gamete donors in the hopes of having a baby with preferred traits. An earlier iteration of this business model was the "Repository for Germinal Choice," a sperm bank that purported to make available the sperm of Nobel Prize winners and, when that proved to be too difficult, other "Renaissance Men" of great achievement and quality.[12] Only three Nobel Laureates, including avowed eugenicist William Shockley, actually donated sperm, but no ova were fertilized with their seed. Most of the sperm donors, it turned out, were perfectly ordinary people. It closed its doors in 1999.

Embryo screening for sex selection has become a common feature of IVF practice; 73 percent of clinics in the United States offer this testing.[13] There are patients who use genetic screening to identify and initiate pregnancies with embryos who are immunocompatible to an older sibling who needs an umbilical cord blood stem cell transplant (harvested upon birth of the newborn). Babies born from this process are sometimes called "savior siblings." The *Guardian* has reported that an American biotech company named "Genomic Prediction" goes beyond testing for single-gene mutations or chromosomal abnormalities to aggregating data to develop "polygenic risk scores" that indicate an increased probability of having a child with a variety of health difficulties, but also tests embryos for probable "low IQ."[14] According to the *Guardian*, "the company projects that once high-quality genetic and academic achievement data from a million individuals becomes available, expected to be within five to ten years, it will be able to predict IQ to within about 10 points."[15]

As will be developed further below, all of the foregoing is perfectly legal and essentially unregulated beyond the usual laws governing the practice of medicine, the use of human tissues, cells, and tissue and cell-based products, and the general civil and criminal laws of the separate states.

It is this second domain of public bioethics—assisted reproduction—to which this inquiry now turns.

Whereas the public questions of abortion involve the termination of pregnancy, the avoidance of parenthood, and the ending of nascent human life, the domain of inquiry of this chapter—assisted reproduction—concerns the initiation of pregnancy, the pursuit of parenthood, and the creation of new human life. Both contexts are also distinguished by understandably profound and overwhelming emotional counterpoints—on the one hand, dread and panic at the prospect of the burdens and disruptions of unwanted pregnancy and parenthood, and on the other, desperate sadness and longing for a child of one's own flesh. But normatively, anthropologically, and legally speaking, these vital conflicts of American public bioethics are deeply linked to one another. Unlike American abortion law, which is shaped by nearly fifty years of jurisprudence, the realm of assisted reproduction is notable for the *absence* of law governing it. Even though this is the case, assisted reproduction is squarely rooted in the anthropology of expressive individualism.

United States law defines ART as "all treatments or procedures which include the handling of human oocytes or embryos" for the purpose of establishing a pregnancy.[16] This includes *in vitro* fertilization and its variants, egg or embryo cryopreservation and donation, and gestational surrogacy. It does not include artificial insemination (injection of sperm into the uterus) by a donor or from a woman's partner. For the sake of brevity, our discussion will not engage in depth with the important questions of determining legal parentage (which varies from state to state), insurance coverage, the patchwork landscape of state laws governing surrogacy, and the novel and projected techniques of ART that are on the more distant horizon, such as deriving sperm and egg from stem cells or aborted fetuses, artificial wombs, creation of live born animal-human hybrids or chimeras, genetic engineering of children (for example, by cloning or gene "editing"), or gestating babies in machines or nonhuman animal surrogates. These important questions will be reserved for a future analysis, which will depend, of course, on the more fundamental anthropological analysis to be set forth in the pages that follow. The discussion here focuses primarily on IVF and the closely-related techniques in current use.

IVF: A PRIMER

As conventionally practiced, IVF involves five steps: (i) collection and preparation of gametes; (ii) fertilization; (iii) screening and transfer of the resulting embryos to the gestational mother's uterus and disposition of non-transferred embryos, if any; (iv) pregnancy; and (v) birth. Each stage involves distinct interventions and possible adjunct techniques and entails various risks to mother and child-to-be.

Sperm is most often obtained directly from the prospective father; less frequently it is procured from a donor. Obtaining ova is significantly more difficult, painful, and costly. The ova provider is most often also the prospective gestational and rearing mother. The process usually involves the chemical stimulation of her ovaries to produce many more mature ova than the single egg released during a typical menstrual cycle. This is called "superovulation." One possible complication from this procedure is "Ovarian Hyperstimulation Syndrome," which involves severe enlargement of the ovaries and fluid imbalances that in extreme circumstances cause serious health risks, including death. Such severe cases of the disorder are rare, with a clinical incidence of 0.5–5 percent.[17]

The clinician tests the patient's blood and monitors the ova maturation. Once mature, the ova are harvested, most often by ultrasound-guided transvaginal aspiration. Using ultrasound to visualize the procedure, the clinician inserts a needle into the wall of the vagina and withdraws the ova from the ovarian follicles. Complications from this procedure are rare but can include accidental perforation of nearby organs and the typical risks associated with outpatient surgery.

Once the ova are removed they are placed in a culture medium. Sperm are modified—seminal fluid is removed and replaced with a synthetic medium. Sometimes sperm are sorted for motility.

Conception is attempted *in vitro* by combining the gametes in a dish, in hopes that a sperm fuses with the egg, from which arises a new, genetically distinct living human organism, the embryo. The traditional method of attempting fertilization is simply to collocate ova and sperm and wait for fertilization to occur as it might in the fallopian tube. There are other methods, including Gamete Intrafallopian Transfer (GIFT), in which the gametes are inserted into the patient's fallopian tube in hopes that fertilization will occur.[18] But an increasingly common fertilization technique is called Intracytoplasmic Sperm Injection (ICSI), which involves the direct injection of one sperm into the ovum.[19] ICSI was discovered by accident (when Belgian researchers mistakenly injected a sperm into an ovum) but was later developed as a method of fertilization for men suffering from male factor infertility. Its rate of use has increased dramatically even for cases not involving this condition. From 2007 to 2016, the total percentage of cycles involving ICSI increased from 72 percent to 81 percent.[20] Among cycles *without* male factor infertility, ICSI use increased from 15.4 percent in 1996 to 66.9 percent in 2012.[21] The reason for this increase is not clear. According to the CDC, the "use of ICSI did not improve reproductive outcomes, regardless of whether male factor infertility was present."[22] While instances of fertilization may have improved, the rate of live births has not. "For cycles without male factor infertility, ICSI use was associated with decreased rates of implantation, pregnancy, live birth, and multiple live births compared with conventional IVF."[23] Some have speculated that the inefficacy of ICSI may be connected to the circumvention of the usual competition among sperm to penetrate the egg, allowing "unfit" sperm that would not have survived this natural process to fertilize the egg.

If fertilization is successful, the embryos are placed in a culture medium and evaluated for qualities that are associated with enhanced likelihood of implantation (though according to clinicians this is an inexact "science").

Some embryos are evaluated using preimplantation genetic diagnosis (PGD) to test for a variety of conditions, not all of which relate to the physical health of the resulting child. A 2018 study found that among all ART clinics in the United States, 92 percent offer PGD.[24] In this process, the early embryo is "biopsied," and cells are removed for analysis. Clinicians can perform the biopsy on the polar bodies just after fertilization, on embryos three days following conception at the six-to-eight cell stage of development ("cleavage stage" or "blastomere" biopsy), or on day five or six at the blastocyst stage of development ("blastocyst" biopsy), when the embryo is comprised of approximately one hundred twenty cells.[25] PGD is almost always combined with ICSI to make embryo biopsy a cleaner and easier process. Two-cell biopsy has been associated with a decline in successful implantation compared with single-cell biopsy. Some have raised concerns about the long-term health effects on children born following embryo biopsy—which, in the case of blastomere biopsy, can involve removal of a significant percentage of the embryo's cells prior to implantation. The biopsied cells are evaluated for specific genetic or chromosomal conditions. Those embryos that meet the predetermined criteria are transferred to the patient or surrogate's uterus or are frozen for future reproductive purposes. Those embryos that fall short of the criteria are discarded and destroyed.

PGD is commonly used to screen embryos for chromosomal abnormalities associated with implantation failure and various disorders, including Down Syndrome. It is also used to detect single-gene disorders such as cystic fibrosis, Tay Sachs, and sickle cell disorder. (At present, more than 1,000 single gene disorders have been identified.) PGD can also be used to test for a heightened risk for some single-gene late onset diseases and conditions such as certain forms of ovarian and breast cancer, Huntington Disease, and Alzheimer's Disease.[26] PGD can even be used to identify embryos that are immunocompatible with a sick older sibling. Such embryos are transferred to a woman's uterus to initiate a pregnancy, and once such children are born, stem cells are harvested from their umbilical cord blood and transplanted to the elder sibling. This procedure has been used to treat children with Fanconi anemia.[27]

But PGD is also used for nonmedical purposes. Chromosomal analysis in PGD can be used to determine the sex of the embryo. As of 2018, 73 percent of American IVF clinics offered PGD for sex selection.[28] Of these clinics, 94 percent offered sex selection for "family balancing" (for example, choosing the sex of one's offspring in light of current family composition), and 81 percent offered it regardless of the patient's rationale.[29] Moreover, 84 percent of clinics offered PGD for family balancing and 75 percent offered it for purely elective sex selection for patients not suffering from infertility, who could conceive and bear children without assistance.[30] Jeffrey Steinberg, a clinician in

California, advertised screening not just for sex selection, but to choose skin, eye, and hair color. After public outrage, he discontinued screening for skin color, but continues to offer it to choose eye color, a test with a reported success rate of 60 percent.[31]

Once the screening and evaluation is complete, the selected embryo or embryos are transferred to the woman's uterus in order to initiate a pregnancy.[32] Less often, the embryo is transferred to the patient's fallopian tube in a process called Zygote Intrafallopian Transfer (ZIFT).

The number of embryos transferred depends on a variety of factors, including the patient's age. Overall for cycles involving newly-conceived (not frozen) nondonor embryos, 40 percent involved single embryo transfer, 49 percent two embryo transfer, 9 percent three embryo transfer, 2 percent four embryo transfer, and 1 percent five or more embryo transfer.[33]

According to the CDC, the average number of embryos transferred per patient has decreased dramatically over the past several years. The percentage of elective single-embryo transfers has simultaneously increased; from 2007 to 2016 the rate tripled from 12 percent to 40 percent of all cycles.[34] During this time period, the percentage has jumped from 5 percent to 43 percent for women under the age of 35, and from 3 percent to 25 percent for women 35–37 years old. At the same time, the percentage of transfers of three embryos has dropped from 26 percent to 9 percent.[35] As will be seen in the passages that follow, the number of embryos transferred has a significant impact on the health and well-being of mothers and children, and is thus crucial to any reflection on the regulation of assisted reproductive technology.

Embryos not transferred or discarded due to failed screening are cryopreserved in freezers. Studies suggest that the vast majority of these embryos are designated for use in future reproductive cycles. Very few (as a percentage) are discarded, donated to other patients, or to researchers. Most remain in cryostorage indefinitely. It has been estimated that one million human embryos are stored in freezers in the United States.[36]

There have been several high-profile court cases involving custody disputes over frozen embryos, usually featuring the ex-spouses who conceived them. Most often, one ex-spouse seeks to implant the embryos and bring them to term (either herself or by donation to another fertility patient), whereas the other wants the embryos destroyed in order to prevent the birth of children with whom he or she would have a biological relationship.

In IVF, embryos are most commonly transferred to the recipient's uterus to initiate a clinical pregnancy, marked by implantation of the embryo in the uterine lining.

Pregnancies are monitored closely, and women frequently receive treatments, including progesterone, to maintain the health of the child-to-be. In 2016, 27 percent of IVF cycles (and 44 percent of embryo transfers) resulted in a clinical pregnancy.[37] A significant percentage were multi-fetal pregnancies (21 percent). Among the cycles involving newly-conceived non-donor embryos, 20 percent of the pregnancies involved twins, and 1.1 percent triplets or more; 73 percent of the pregnancies were singleton.[38]

Multiple gestation pregnancies, attributable in large part to the practice of multiple embryo transfer described above, pose greater health risks to women. As reported by the President's

Council on Bioethics in its 2004 report *Reproduction and Responsibility: The Regulation of New Biotechnologies,* potential complications associated with multiple gestation pregnancies include high blood pressure, anemia, preeclampsia, uterine rupture, placenta previa, or abruption. Multiple gestation pregnancies are also more likely to aggravate preexisting health conditions than a singleton pregnancy.[39]

According to the CDC's most recent analysis, 22 percent of IVF cycles (and 36 percent of embryo transfers) involving newly-conceived nondonor embryos resulted in a live born child.[40] Of the all pregnancies initiated via IVF, 81 percent resulted in live births. Of these births, 19.4 percent involved multiple newborns (18.8 percent twins) and 81 percent singleton babies.[41] By way of comparison, the *overall* birth rate of twins in the U.S. during the same period was 3 percent (one third of which is attributed to fertility treatments).[42] Seventy-seven percent of higher order multiple births in the U.S. are attributed to ART.[43] However, statistics compiled by the CDC indicate that there is a downward trend in these numbers due to improvements in IVF and the increased incidence of single-embryo transfer. "From 2007 through 2016, the percentage of multiple-infant live births decreased from 35 percent to 20 percent for women younger than age 35, from 30 percent to 21 percent for women aged 35–37, from 24 percent to 18 percent for women aged 38–40, and from 15 percent to 13 percent for women aged 41–42."[44]

IVF is associated with preterm births (defined as birth before thirty-seven weeks of pregnancy) and low birthweight (5.5 pounds or less). A recent study found that IVF increases the risk of preterm birth by 80 percent. The study set the rate of pre-term birth from natural pregnancy at 5.5 percent.[45] According to the CDC, in 2016 the percentage of cycles resulting in pre-term births for single infants from singleton pregnancies was 11.1 percent (16.7 percent for single babies born after multiple gestation pregnancies). For twins and higher order multiple newborns, the rates of preterm birth and low birthweight increase dramatically. The CDC reports that for twins, 57.6 percent of cycles resulted in preterm birth and 54.4 percent of cycles involved low birthweight. For triplets or more, the percentages of preterm birth and low birthweight jump, respectively, to 97.2 percent and 87.8 percent.[46]

Preterm birth and low birthweight are associated with a host of adverse health outcomes for children. According to the CDC, such children are "at a greater risk of death in the first year of life, as well as other poor health outcomes, including visual and hearing problems, intellectual and learning disabilities, and behavioral and emotional problems throughout life."[47]

There has been some concern raised that the use of IVF increases the incidence of birth defects among children conceived with its aid. The CDC recently conducted a study of four million infants and found that "singleton infants conceived using ART were 40 percent more likely to have a nonchromosomal birth defect (such as cleft lip and/or palate or a congenital heart defect) compared with all other singleton births."[48] But the authors of the study caution that more investigation is required, as the researchers did not control for "some factors related to infertility" that might account for the increased rate of birth defects.[49]

Despite the enhanced risks, the rate of birth defects overall is relatively low. A 2012 study in the *New England Journal of Medicine* found that the rate of birth defects for children conceived by ART was 8.3 percent versus 5.8 percent for those conceived naturally.[50]

The CDC likewise reports that "overall, children conceived using ART were about two times more likely to be diagnosed with ASD [autism spectrum disorder] compared to children conceived without ART." The reason for this higher rate appears to be linked to increased rate of adverse ART pregnancy and delivery outcomes that seem to correlate with an ASD diagnosis, including being born a twin or higher order multiple, preterm birth, and low birthweight. The CDC has called for more study of the issue.[51]

The use of ICSI, which appears to be increasing every year, including among male patients without male-factor infertility, has been associated with possible adverse outcomes. A diagnosis of ASD is more common for children conceived using ICSI than conventional IVF. The CDC reports, "Findings from some but not all studies suggest that ICSI is associated with an increased risk of chromosomal abnormalities, autism, intellectual disabilities, and birth defects compared with conventional IVF."[52] However, the report cautioned that these risks "may also be due to the effects of subfertility."[53] For example, if a man who suffers from a particular form of male factor infertility (associated with low sperm count and a particular Y-chromosome deletion) is able to successfully fertilize an ovum via ICSI, he risks passing this chromosomal abnormality on to the child, who, if male, will likewise be infertile.

SURROGACY

While the issue of surrogacy is vast and complex, and largely beyond the scope of this chapter, a few brief comments are in order. The CDC reports that the overall use of gestational surrogates is rare (around 3 percent), but the incidence has more than doubled over the past decade and a half.[54] Between 1999 and 2013, the agency reports that ART cycles involving gestational surrogates resulted in 13,380 deliveries and the birth of 18,400 babies.[55] Intended parents who use gestational carriers are generally older than those who do not. The majority of gestational carriers are younger than 35.[56] ART cycles involving gestational carriers had higher rates of success than cycles where the intended mother carried the baby, measured by pregnancies and live births. However, due to the transfer of a greater number of embryos per cycle (two or more), gestational carrier cycles had higher rates of multiple births and preterm delivery.[57]

LEGAL LANDSCAPE

Assisted reproductive techniques are subject to the federal laws regulating the safety and efficacy of drugs, devices, and biological products, and preventing the spread of communicable disease. The physicians who work in ART must be licensed and certified to practice medicine, and are, like all doctors, subject to the incentives and deterrents of medical malpractice law and the more general civil and criminal laws of the jurisdictions where they reside. But as such, the legal landscape of ART is famously and controversially sparse. The absence of specific and meaningful regulation of ART in the United States is quite surprising, especially to foreign observers, given that it is the only medical intervention that ostensibly results in the creation and birth of a new human being. Moreover, ART is singular in the world of medicine because it frequently does not aim at curing the patient's underlying pathology, but rather at circumventing it. IVF does not cure infertility, it works around it. Be that as it may, there is simply not much law dedicated to regulating ART *qua* ART in the United States.

The only federal statute specifically dedicated to ART, the Fertility Clinic Success Rate and Certification Act of 1992 (FCSRCA), is a weak consumer protection law.[58] It does two things. First, it creates a model program for the certification of embryo laboratories that clinicians are free to adopt voluntarily if they wish. There is no evidence that this has had any perceptible effect; in its analysis the President's Council on Bioethics reported that not a single embryo laboratory in America had adopted the model framework offered by the statute.[59]

The second function of the FCSRCA is to mandate that all clinics in the United States practicing ART report annually to the CDC certain data relevant to success rates. CDC contracts with the Society for Assisted Reproductive Technology (SART)—an ART professional organization comprised of most clinics in the nation—to validate the information provided. SART conducts an audit of a small sample of clinics each year to confirm data reported. The CDC analyzes the data and issues publicly available reports that include some (though not all) of the information gathered. It reports success rates (reported both per "cycle," defined as a process that starts "when a woman begins taking fertility drugs or having her ovaries monitored for follicle production," and per embryo transfer), type of ART performed, and patient diagnoses of infertility.

The CDC does not, however, report information of crucial relevance to prospective patients. It includes no information on the types or rate of adverse health outcomes to mother or child (beyond noting the percentage of term, normal weight, and singleton births). It does not include any information regarding the costs of procedures. It does not include information on the number of human embryos created, frozen, or destroyed.

Some clinicians reported to the President's Council on Bioethics that "success rate" as a reporting metric is highly manipulable by unscrupulous clinics.[60] For example, the numbers could be artificially inflated by accepting only the most promising patients, by terminating and reclassifying unsuccessful cycles rather than reporting them, and by other similar tactics.

Most worrisome to critics of the CDC surveillance regime established by FCSRCA is that there are no serious penalties for noncompliance other than the publication of the offending clinic's name in the report itself. Beyond the listing of these names on the CDC's website, the FCSRCA has no enforcement mechanism.

There is an additional federal law that has an incidental effect on ART research. In 1996, Congress, via an appropriations "rider" (a spending restriction appended to the annual federal statute that appropriates funding to government agencies), prohibited federal funding for "the creation of a human embryo or embryos for research purposes" as well as for research "in which a human embryo or embryos are destroyed, discarded, or knowingly subjected to risk of injury or death greater than that allowed for research on fetuses *in utero* under" relevant federal regulations on human subjects protections.[61] This law, known as the "Dickey-Wicker" amendment (named after sponsors Jay Dickey and Roger Wicker) does not limit the practice of ART, though it does prevent federal funding of ART research that runs afoul of its criteria.

For the most part, ART is regulated just as any other branch of medicine, primarily at the state level. The law touches medicine mostly at the front end, at the point of licensure and certification to practice. The primary legal tool to regulate the ongoing practice of medicine is the private law of malpractice. The legal standard for malpractice liability is conduct that falls below the "standard of care"—the type and level of care of an ordinary prudent physician, with the same training and experience, under the same circumstances. The standard is established through expert testimony regarding the practices of the specialty in question. Plaintiffs can also sue doctors in tort for misconduct associated with the failure to obtain proper informed consent. But malpractice litigation is a reactive and ad hoc form of governance.

There is no systematic mechanism for ongoing regulation and oversight of the practice of medicine. There is not, for example, any administrative agency charged with this responsibility. The FDA regulates the drugs, devices, and biological products used by ART physicians for safety and efficacy, but does not regulate the practice of medicine itself. It does administer a statutory framework (established by the Public Health Services Act) for preventing the spread of communicable diseases. Under these auspices it promulgates regulations for the screening and use of "Human Cells, Tissues, and Cellular and Tissue-Based Products." But FDA has, at the urging of the ART professional societies and "individuals who facilitate embryo donation," carved out very broad exemptions for sperm, egg, and embryos used in IVF.[62]

There have been a few notable exceptions to the FDA's general practice of non-interference with ART. In 1998, Associate Commissioner of the FDA Stuart Nightingale issued a "Dear Colleague" letter asserting that the agency had jurisdiction over any experiment involving cloning to produce a live born child, presumably under its authority to regulate gene transfer research. The letter advised researchers that the agency would not approve such practices, given safety concerns.[63] Later in 2001, Kathryn Zoon, a former head of the agency's Center for Biologics Evaluation and Research (CBER), which oversees human gene therapy research[64] speculated that if such concerns over safety and efficacy were resolved, proposed research on cloning to produce children would be approved.[65] FDA's announcement was criticized as exceeding the agency's authority under the statutes it was created to administer. After the 2001 Zoon statement, the FDA has not reasserted similar claims of authority. Some commentators have speculated that the earlier statements by the agency were meant as a bluff to deter unscrupulous researchers from proceeding; others have suggested that they were meant to discourage Congress from adopting overly restrictive legislation disfavored by the scientific community by assuring members that the agency was in control of the situation.

More recently, Congress adopted an appropriations rider forbidding the FDA from approving "research in which a human embryo is intentionally created or modified to include a heritable genetic modification."[66] The "Aderholt Amendment" (named for its Congressional sponsor Robert Aderholt) effectively forbids gene editing of embryos as part of IVF treatment, because such changes would be "heritable" to the future generations of genetic descendants of the adults these embryos would later become. The Aderholt Amendment also forbids the various methods of mitochondrial disease treatment that involve the creation and transfer of an embryo with the mitochondrial DNA from two women (usually from a donor and the mother), and the nuclear DNA of the mother and father. Such embryos are sometimes called "Three Parent Embryos." Because mitochondrial DNA is maternally inherited, any female offspring conceived with the aid of these techniques will likewise pass along the donor mitochondrial DNA to her genetic children. All female descendants in this line will likewise pass the genetic change to their offspring.[67] The Aderholt Amendment has been renewed every year since its adoption in 2015.

Putting aside these very atypical examples of FDA involvement in the practice of medicine, ART proceeds largely unregulated by any administrative agency. Physicians are thus left free to practice medicine with a creativity and dynamism that might not be possible with a more cumbersome, comprehensive regime of ongoing oversight. The deference to physicians in the law signals the well-earned respect and esteem in which the profession of medicine is held in American culture. But as applied to ART, which is *sui generis* in both its means and ends, this largely *laissez faire* framework has been a source of consternation. Novel practices such as ICSI and PGD move from bench to bedside very rapidly and become routine in short order. This passage from the President's Council on Bioethics report is arresting:

> IVF itself was performed on at least 1,200 women before it was reported to have been performed on chimps, although it had been extensively investigated in rabbits, hamsters, and mice. The same is true for ICSI. The reproductive use of ICSI was first introduced by Belgian researchers in 1992. Two years later, relying on a two-study review of safety and efficacy, ASRM [the American Society for Reproductive Medicine] declared ICSI to be a "clinical" rather than "experimental" procedure. Yet the first non-human primate conceived was born only in 1997 and the first successful ICSI procedure in mice was reported in 1995.[68]

Whereas creativity, dynamism, and an entrepreneurial spirit are highly valued when medical practice simply aims to restore a patient to health, the calculus is quite different when the "cure" involves the creation of a new human being. The background facts of IVF's exorbitant cost, the market pressures on clinics to show greater "success" than their competitors, and the human desperation and vulnerability understandably caused by infertility all combine to create strong temptations for everyone involved to push the envelope of innovation when more caution is in order.

STATE COURTS AND ART

The handful of state supreme court opinions dealing directly with ART involve custody disputes over frozen embryos, usually between former spouses. There are divergent approaches, with some state supreme courts (New York, Washington, Colorado, and Tennessee) signaling a willingness to treat such disputes as straightforward contract cases, applying the terms of any valid prior agreement that sets forth the procedures for embryo disposition under the circumstances.[69] Other state courts of last resort, such as Massachusetts, have refused to enforce such agreements, at least when they appear to require transfer, gestation, and birth against the wishes of one of the parties.[70] Still other state supreme courts, like New Jersey and Iowa, have refused to enforce prior agreements when parties change their minds about embryo custody and disposition.[71]

Despite the disagreement in framing, there are some commonalities among the decisions of these courts of last resort. First, none of them have permitted one partner to implant embryos, gestate, and deliver a baby over the objections of the other.[72] Second, none have treated the frozen embryos as legal persons or children, despite entreaties by one of the parties or the decision of the lower court. Instead, such courts have either deemed frozen embryos to have some "intermediate status" between persons and things, or simply treated them as marital property. Some state courts have explicitly invoked the U.S. Supreme Court's abortion jurisprudence to support their conclusion that the human embryos at issue are not "persons," despite the absence of the unique burdens present in pregnancy. Finally, the state supreme courts have drawn deeply upon the principles of reproductive liberty, autonomy, and privacy of American abortion jurisprudence as the touchstone for analysis, and all but one have evinced a strong presumption for enforcing the wishes of the party seeking to "avoid procreation" and the unchosen familial relationship with child born as a result.[73]

In the context of surrogacy, there have been some recent high-profile examples of disputes between gestational carriers and intended parents. Two recent instances involved intended parents demanding that the surrogate abort her pregnancy because the child-to-be was diagnosed *in utero* with an adverse but treatable medical condition. In one case, Andrea Ott-Dahl agreed to be a gestational carrier (and an egg donor) for a lesbian couple unable to conceive using ART. When a twelve-week ultrasound revealed that the child-to-be likely had Down Syndrome, the intended parents demanded that Ott-Dahl terminate the pregnancy. Ott-Dahl refused and informed the intended parents that she and her wife Keston planned to keep the baby. The intended parents threatened to sue to try to compel the termination or seek damages, but ultimately did not.[74] In another case, two intended parents demanded that a surrogate terminate her pregnancy when the child-to-be was diagnosed *in utero* with a severe heart defect—Hypoplastic Left Heart Syndrome (HLHS). HLHS is fatal if untreated. However, with a surgical intervention it has a survival rate of 70 percent, though patients may require continued monitoring and care throughout their lives. The surrogate refused to terminate the pregnancy but reported a great deal of anxiety when she learned that the intended parents intended to opt against life-sustaining measures and let the baby die once they assumed custody of the baby following its birth. In a newspaper interview, the surrogate reported with relief that the intended parents changed their minds and sought treatment for the baby.[75]

There have been other recent cases in which the intended parent or parents directed the surrogate to abort ("reduce") one of the multiple fetuses she was carrying. California resident Melissa Cook contracted to be a gestational carrier for a fifty-year old deaf and mute single man from Georgia who lived alone with his elderly parents. When he discovered that she was carrying triplets, he demanded that she selectively abort one of them to avoid the costs of raising three children. She refused, and he sued. Her parental rights were terminated upon birth and custody was awarded to him. She unsuccessfully sought relief in the California courts and the United States Supreme Court.[76]

Gestational carrier (and California resident) Brandyrose Torres read about the dispute involving Melissa Cook and came forward to tell her story to the press. She was directed by the intended parents to abort one of the triplets she was carrying, even though the pregnancy was healthy and none of the children-to-be were in distress. Torres refused and the intended parents threatened suit for breach of contract. Ultimately, Torres gave birth to the triplets and conveyed custody to the intended parents.[77]

LEGAL OVERSIGHT OF ART *QUA* ART

The findings of the President's Council on Bioethics in 2004 regarding the legal landscape for ART *qua* ART remain effectively unchanged. To wit, "there is no uniform, comprehensive, and enforceable system of data collection, monitoring or oversight for the biotechnologies affecting human reproduction."[78] Direct governmental regulation of ART is minimal. The FCSRCA remains a very weak consumer protection law. Most worrisome to the Council was the absence of a legal framework for comprehensive research or regulation focused on the possible effects of ART on the health and well-being of children conceived with its aid, gestational mothers, and egg donors.[79] The Council further observed that in the absence of such regulation, "novel technologies and practices that are successful move from the experimental context to clinical practice with relatively little oversight or deliberation."[80] It noted that PGD is essentially unregulated, with no comprehensive data gathering on the health impact on children born following its use, and no limits on its specific applications, including screening for non-medical criteria such as sex, intelligence, or eye color. The Council observed that there is no comprehensive, uniform legal framework or information gathering system regarding the creation, use, and disposition of human embryos in ART.[81] It further noted that "there is no comprehensive mechanism for regulation of commerce in gametes, embryos, and assisted reproductive technology services."[82]

All of these observations remain true today.

In the absence of comprehensive governmental regulation, the practice standards and ethical guidelines governing ART doctors are promulgated by the profession itself—through professional associations and practitioner societies. Thus, self-regulation is the primary mode of governance for ART. The primary professional societies who set these standards, the

American Society for Reproductive Medicine and the Society for Assisted Reproductive Technologies, have been criticized in some quarters (including by the patient advocacy community) for being too permissive. Supporters of these organizations retort that the purpose is not to police members and that a lighter self-regulatory touch is more likely to keep members aligned with the values of the professional societies. It is very clear that the core animating normative goods driving the prescriptive pronouncements of ASRM (which promulgates ethics and practice guidelines) are patient autonomy and reproductive liberty.

THE ANTHROPOLOGY OF AMERICAN ART LAW

Like the American jurisprudence of abortion, the anthropology of the legal landscape for ART is expressive individualism. The vision of identity and flourishing assumed by ART law becomes clear when one considers the type of liberty that emerges from the absence of meaningful regulation. From this absence of law arises a very particular kind of freedom, perfectly suited for the atomized individual will seeking to express the originality discovered within itself, and to pursue the life plan of its own authentic design. It is the singular freedom of the unencumbered self, lacking constitutive attachments and unchosen obligations, for whom relationships are either transactional or adversarial, but always instrumental. It does not take embodiment into account, and as anyone who has ever suffered from or has loved someone suffering from infertility understands, it not the kind of freedom that responds fully to the pain of those longing for a child, who feel betrayed by their bodies. Whereas the American law of abortion responds to the complex crisis of unplanned pregnancy by conferring the simple and brute liberty to eliminate the nascent human life *in utero,* the American law of ART responds to the vulnerability and suffering of infertility by conferring the freedom to create new life by nearly any means necessary. These are rules and remedies designed for persons understood through the imperfect lens of expressive individualism.

A fruitful point of entry into the anthropology of American ART law is through the writings of the man who was arguably the intellectual godfather of the United States framework, the late Professor John Robertson. Robertson, a prolific scholar of the law, was an iconic figure in American public bioethics for decades, serving on numerous influential governmental and private sector advisory committees, including an extended term as Chairman of the American Society for Reproductive Medicine's Ethics Committee. Perhaps more than any single person, Robertson's thought and work is reflected in the modern American legal framework for ART. To understand the anthropology of the law of ART, it is important to explore briefly his conception of human identity and flourishing. Robertson published numerous essays and scholarly articles until his untimely death in 2017, but the most useful and comprehensive source for understanding his vision and the current legal landscape is his 1994 book, aptly titled *Children of Choice.* The themes and concepts he developed in this work recur throughout his whole body of scholarship and advocacy, and have become core animating principles of the current legal paradigm for ART in America.

Robertson's normative framework is squarely anchored in the primacy of "procreative liberty," which in his words is "first and foremost an individual interest."[83] He defines procreative liberty as simply "the freedom to decide whether or not to have offspring."[84] It can often be difficult to determine when Robertson is describing current law and policy or making a moral argument, but this difficulty springs in part from the fact that the law as it currently exists (or, more precisely, the absence of law) broadly mirrors Robertson's approach. He roots the right to procreative liberty explicitly in the Supreme Court jurisprudence of contraception and abortion, styled as the right to avoid procreation.

From this he infers the converse aspect of procreative liberty, namely, the freedom to pursue procreation, both coitally and noncoitally. For Robertson, the right to procreation is a negative right, meaning the government cannot interfere with its exercise. But it is not a positive right; the government is not obliged to facilitate its practice.

Procreative liberty is essential to human flourishing according to Robertson, because it is necessary for self-defining experiences that people greatly value. Maximal freedom to use reproductive technologies is thus crucial because "they are the means to achieve or avoid the reproductive experiences that are central to personal conceptions of meaning and identity."[85] Restrictions on the freedom to avoid procreation unjustly "determine one's self-definition in its most basic sense," whereas limits on the pursuit of procreation through one's chosen means "prevents one from an experience that is central to individual identity and meaning in life."[86] Accordingly, the rights of procreative liberty should be jealously guarded and walled off from state interference except for the most compelling reasons, which Robertson suggests are "seldom" present.[87]

Framed as an operational legal standard to govern conflicts in this domain, Robertson argues that "procreative liberty should enjoy presumptive primacy when conflicts about its exercise arise because control over whether one reproduces or not is central to personal identity, to dignity, and to the meaning of one's life."[88] Those who would restrict procreative liberty always bear the burden of demonstrating that it is necessary to prevent "substantial harms to the tangible interests of others."[89]

But what kinds of practices fall within the scope of procreative liberty? Here again, Robertson defines the field of protected activities according to their subjective value to the individual involved. "A person's capacity to find significance in reproduction should determine whether one holds the presumptive right."[90]

Even the discrete, isolated actions of gamete donation or gestation without any intent to parent the child born can offer highly valuable and meaningful experiences to donors and gestational carriers. Accordingly, they should be protected from state interference.

When presented with a particular application of reproductive technology, Robertson asks whether the activity is "so central to an individual's procreative identity or life plan" that it deserves protection under the aegis of procreative liberty.[91]

What about screening embryos for preferred traits or conditions? According to Robertson, "Some degree of quality control would seem logically to fall within the realm of procreative liberty."[92] At points in his writings, Robertson seems to entertain the possibility that certain practices that fall outside the mainstream and to which most people would not ascribe value (for example, genetic enhancement) might lie beyond the scope of procreative liberty, but he always stops short of categorically ruling them out. It is difficult to see how his larger normative framework of maximal procreative liberty would allow such restrictions in the absence of serious harms to others.

What kinds of harms are sufficient for Robertson to curtail procreative freedom? Use and destruction of *in vitro embryos* do not constitute sufficient harms to restrict procreative liberty. Robertson rules out the possibility that they are "persons," but seems to suggest that they should be respected insofar as they have the potential to become a person (if they are transferred, gestated and born), and because of the "symbolic meaning" they hold for "many people."[93] But these interests are easily outweighed in the face of an individual's desire to procreate. Robertson also holds that the fetus *in utero* is likewise not a person, and therefore may be destroyed to vindicate the right of a pregnant woman not to procreate. He states explicitly that in his view, no one has the right to be born.[94]

What about harms to children later born who are injured by the ART techniques from which they are conceived? Or harms to such children caused by their genetic parents' underlying pathologies that required the use of ART to conceive in the first place? For Robertson, it turns out that in almost every instance, such harms are also not sufficient to justify restrictions on procreative liberty. In fact, he does not recognize injuries caused by IVF and adjunct techniques to be a "harm," rightly understood. In support of this proposition, Robertson invokes philosopher Derek Parfit's "non-identity problem," which holds that if a person is harmed by the very intervention that made his existence possible (such as ICSI), and the only way to prevent such harms is not to use this intervention at all, then such a restriction is not a benefit to the person, because he would not otherwise exist.[95] Moreover, because his life in the injured state is not worse than nonexistence, the use of the harmful technique is, in fact, a benefit to him. Following this reasoning, Robertson concludes that for children harmed by such techniques, "ARTs to enable their birth does not harm them and does not justify restriction on those grounds."[96]

Turning to concrete cases, Robertson applies this principle to the risk of birth defects from ICSI and concludes that children born with these afflictions would not be "harmed," because the alternative future for them is nonexistence.[97] Thus, restrictions on ICSI to prevent birth defects in children are not justifiable restrictions on procreative liberty. For the same reasons, Robertson expresses opposition to bans on the transfer of multiple embryos to prevent harms associated with preterm birth and low birthweight. He likewise opposes bans on novel forms of procreation including the use of gametes derived from stem cells or fetuses, genetic manipulation of embryos, or even cloning to produce a live born child, if the reason for such bans is to protect the well-being of the child born as a result. He does not regard such harm as cognizable. If the freedom to pursue these modes of producing children is to be limited, it must be justified on other grounds. Robertson is doubtful that alternative rationales for bans or restrictions would be compelling.

Robertson does allow the possibility that some intentions of parents, if they do not entail the desire to rear the child, might put the enterprise outside the domain of "procreative liberty." And he notes that state interests (other than preventing harm to children—which he does not recognize) "*might*" warrant regulation when parents' aims are far afield of "traditional reproductive goals."[98] But in making this allowance, it is once again not clear if Robertson is describing the law as it is or as it should be. Moreover, it is difficult to reconcile this solicitude for "traditional reproductive goals" in light of the almost unalloyed libertarian orientation of Robertson's approach.

Surveying the current American legal landscape for ART, it is more or less John Robertson's world. His views have not been constitutionalized by the Supreme Court, but the absence of meaningful, comprehensive regulation and oversight of ART creates conditions that closely approximate his vision of "procreative liberty." There are no legal limitations specific to ART meant to protect the health and well-being of children born with its aid. There are no legal restrictions on techniques that are routinely used that result in a massive increase in risk of preterm births and low birthweight, with associated adverse health consequences for such children. There is no regulation or even federally sponsored longitudinal study of commonly used interventions that appear to increase the risk of birth defects, autism, and other maladies. Parents, *including those who are not infertile,* freely use PGD to select the sex of their children by transferring preferred embryos and discarding others. Parents use PGD to screen and discard those embryos who have a higher probability of contracting treatable diseases that do not appear until later in life. Organizations advertise predictive testing for low intelligence, with the promise of developing tests for predicting high intelligence in the near term. People screen embryos for eye and hair color. People buy and sell sperm, eggs, and even "batches" of embryos. Intended parents who contract with gestational carriers sometimes demand the abortion of children-to-be with adverse but treatable medical conditions, threatening lawsuits and the withdrawal of financial support. There are a million human embryos stored in freezers as a result of the absence of comprehensive and uniform laws governing their creation, use, and disposition.

All of these practices are legal and unrestricted, creating a domain of free choice and private ordering that replicates Robertson's vison of procreative liberty. And, with Robertson's work as an interpretive guide, it is clear that this particular conception of liberty is firmly rooted in the anthropology of expressive individualism. As Robertson states explicitly, this liberty is meant to serve *individuals* in their quest to pursue reproductive experiences that they highly value as meaningful and essential to self-definition. Human bodies at all stages from embryonic to adult are recruited as instrumentalities of these personal projects. In some cases, the body and its parts are explicitly reduced to articles of commerce. People enter and exit intimate procreative relationships marked by contract and bargained-for exchange. Parental relationships, be they genetic or gestational, are created, avoided, and dissolved through will, choice, and rational ordering. Procreative liberty thus understood alters the role of physician from servant of health and wholeness to a skilled technician enabling the projects of the will. Thus "health" itself is transformed from a concept connected to the natural functioning of the organism to one nested in will and desire.

This notion of procreative liberty, following its anthropological foundation of expressive individualism, reorients the purposes of reproduction from the aim of bringing about the birth of *one's child* to the satisfaction the self-defining goals of the individuals involved. This transformation of purpose was evident in the 2002 comment of Dr. Gerald Schatten in his testimony to the President's Council on Bioethics: "Reproductive medicine is helping prospective parents realize their own dreams for a disease free legacy."[99] But the version of procreative liberty nested in expressive individualism that arises from the American legal landscape of ART encompasses dreams of more than just a disease-free legacy. It includes a legacy free from a much broader array of imperfection, including even the presence of children of a disfavored sex.

And like all legal frameworks built upon expressive individualism, the current regime is blind to the vulnerability, dependence, and fragility that inexorably attends an embodied life. The American law of ART does not consider the vulnerable and dependent child-to-be in the calculus of interests to be protected and harms to be avoided. Along with John Robertson, American law does not count prevention of harms to children caused by the ART interventions by which they were conceived as grounds for restricting procreative liberty. The law is designed to serve the desires of those seeking to reproduce, despite the risks to the health of the child-to-be discussed above. It likewise fails to adequately protect the health and well-being of the genetic or gestational mothers.

Even evaluated according to the metrics of the law's own aspiration for consumer protection, it does not sufficiently protect ART patients (clients?)—men and women who are profoundly vulnerable by virtue of the deep sadness, exhaustion, and desperation caused by infertility, along with the potentially ruinous financial costs of pursuing treatment for it. The law does nothing to aid their moral imagination—nothing to help them to see the child-to-be at every step of the process as a gift to be treasured and protected. It does nothing to protect them from themselves and the temptation to undertake serious risks to their future child's health and well-being, not to mention their own. The law does not protect patients from making dehumanizing and discriminatory choices like sex selection in bringing their children into the world. The law indulges intolerance of imperfection by allowing unfettered screening for all manner of "flaws." The law fails to teach against the destructive notion that the parent-child relationship is defined by will, control, and mastery rather than unconditional love and gratitude.

And the law as presently constituted does nothing to prevent the community from coarsening and coming to see the entire enterprise not as medically-aided conception and birth of children to be welcomed and loved unconditionally, but rather as a form of manufacture of products subject to quality assurance, and accepted or rejected according to their conformity with the preferences and desires of the "customer" who paid for it.

Here again, the perils of a public bioethics rooted in expressive individualism become apparent. The law is blind to the weak, vulnerable, fragile, and dependent, and all interests and concerns are crowded out by the law's focus on the desires of the individual will seeking its own way.

But the law's vision of procreative liberty is not the freedom that patients seeking infertility treatment in the real world want or need. They are not unencumbered selves, but people who are desperately seeking to embrace a role that is defined by a relationship; they want to be a *parent*. And there is no such thing as a parent without *a child*. Despite the weariness, sadness, and even bitterness that comes with experiencing infertility as a betrayal by one's own body, they do not pursue ART to realize any dream of a particular legacy or to assert their atomized will, but to be a mother or a father.

Accordingly, for the public bioethics of ART to respond to their neediness, promote their flourishing, and to protect them and their children from harm (even arising from their own choices), it must begin with the meaning and consequences of embodiment.

Accordingly, just as in the context of abortion, the task for the law is to support, protect, and sustain the networks of uncalculated giving and graceful receiving necessary to respond to the neediness of the vulnerable and dependent, and through which embodied beings come to realize their potential as the kind of persons who are able to make the goods of others their own. By virtue of our individual and shared lives as *embodied* beings, human flourishing is most profoundly achieved through love and friendship. Of course, where such networks of shared sacrifice and support are missing or become frayed, the law must step in to protect the vulnerable, weak, and marginalized.

More concretely, just as in the context of abortion, the normative paradigm most fitting to the public bioethics of assisted reproduction is *parenthood*. Assisted reproduction, like all reproduction, involves parents and children. The complexity that arises from advances in the medicine and biotechnology of ART does not change this fact, even as it fractures the previously integrated dimensions of procreation. Because of IVF and related techniques and practices, there is the potential for *many* mothers and fathers—genetic, gestational, and rearing. But all are mothers and fathers just the same, albeit in different respects. They are made so by the fact that they are engaged in the business of making and raising *babies*.

Thus understood, the networks of giving and receiving to which the law should respond are those proper to parenthood, which includes, of course, parents and children, but radiates outward to the physicians and health care providers who serve them, extended family members, neighbors, community, and polity (including the government itself), all of whom are reciprocally obliged and entitled to render and receive mutual aid.

An anthropology of embodiment and laws built upon it recognizes that the most vulnerable protagonist of procreation is the child. She depends on the uncalculated giving of her parents—of every sort—who will make her good their own as they engage in whatever role they might play in her life. By virtue of their relationship to her, the genetic, gestational, and rearing parents must act in her best interests, and must make every effort to protect her from harm, at every stage of her development from conception forward. More deeply, her parents—all of them—must understand that she is a gift, a person who has been conceived, not a product manufactured to serve the desires of another. The proper disposition toward a gift is gratitude and humility, not mastery and exploitation. She was not selected to meet anyone's specifications but emerged from a procreative process possessed of intrinsic and equal dignity. Her "imperfections" or "flaws" are of no consequence, except insofar as they are occasions for unconditional care and support. Doubtless, to see her as she is at every stage of her life from conception forward requires moral imagination. And to honor unchosen obligations to her requires restraint, discipline, and sacrifice. But such is the relationship of parent to child.

Parenting thus requires the virtues of uncalculated giving—just generosity, hospitality, and, when necessary, accompanying the child in suffering as if it were one's own (misericordia). This means subordinating one's desires for the sake of one's child—giving without concern for receiving, in proportion to neediness. It also requires the virtue of gracefully receiving the child who is a gift. This includes gratitude for the child, humility (rather than the hubris of rational mastery), and openness to the unbidden and tolerance of imperfection (rather than the drive to weed out flaws).

The law, then, must support and sustain parents, regardless of type, in discharging these obligations. It must facilitate the understanding and practice of these virtues of parenthood. How and by what means the law might most successfully enable this mindset and the goods and virtues that follow from it are highly complicated questions requiring consideration of factors well beyond the current inquiry. There are many means—passive and active—that could be deployed to this end. But the law must begin by expanding its anthropological foundation to encompass the meaning and consequences of embodiment. Concretely, the law must offer support, directly and indirectly, for parents of all sorts in fulfilling their duties to children, whom they have a role in conceiving, gestating, and rearing.

Where parents and others fail to meet their obligations to the children, the law must intervene to protect them directly. Again, what this might mean concretely is a large question for another time, but at a minimum, certain principles are clear enough. The law must closely regulate or perhaps even prohibit medical interventions that foreseeably endanger the health and well-being of children conceived with the aid of ARTs. To this end, the government must conduct rigorous longitudinal studies on the impact of ARTs on the flourishing of children, broadly understood. Whether the harm to children is caused by the ART itself, or by the underlying pathology of the infertile parent, the ultimate focus of the law should be on protecting the health and flourishing of children.

Obvious areas of concern are practices that contribute to low birthweight and preterm birth, increased rate of birth defects, as well as the harms wrought by discriminatory and dehumanizing practices such as sex selection, screening for disfavored traits, intolerance of the imperfect and disabled, and the commodification of the body and its parts.[100] States could consider moratoria or bans on practices shown to be harmful.

Moreover, the law must be devised to secure the intrinsic equal dignity of children conceived by ART, and to avoid the risk that others will regard them as unequal and inferior to their "creators" because of how and why they came into the world. They are not creatures devised in a lab to fulfill the dreams of others. They are, in the words of Gil Meilaender, "begotten and not made."[101]

And it may go without saying, but the most fundamental goal of the law in this domain is to ensure that every child born with the aid of ART is received and raised as a son or daughter in a loving family: the network of uncalculated giving and graceful receiving *par excellence.*

Reorienting the purposes of ART regulation toward the well-being of the child will likewise have consequences for how medicine is practiced. From the outset, measures taken must account for the downstream effects on the child-to-be's health and flourishing. In fact, given that the successful culmination of the enterprise is the birth of a child, practitioners would do well to think of the child-to-be *as a patient* in her own right, and make choices with this in mind, even during the preconception stages of the process. Again, how the law might contribute to shaping and directing these behaviors is a complex question for another time.

Vulnerability and exploitation are possible at all stages of the ART process. It is the obligation of the community and the polity to protect these individuals, perhaps even from their own self-destructive decisions or misguided choices that harm the children who are born with their assistance. Areas of concern include the exploitation of gamete donors and gestational surrogates, the commodification of the body and its parts, and the use of IVF techniques and interventions that bear significant risks for the women involved. Developing concrete legal structures responsive to these concerns will, of course, require careful study, reflection, and prudence across a wide spectrum of factors. But the goals, at least, are clear.

The networks of giving and receiving necessary to support the dependent and vulnerable in this context do not merely encompass the parents, children, and health care providers involved, but radiate outward to extended family, community, and polity. The law must have a role in strengthening these bonds and promoting the reciprocal rendering and receiving of care.

It is important to address yet another vulnerable and dependent population that is centrally involved in and affected by the lack of meaningful regulation of ART as such in America, namely, the living human embryos who are conceived, cultured, screened, transferred, intentionally destroyed, donated to other patients, sold in "batches," given to scientists for use and destruction in research, or most often, frozen indefinitely. The moral status of the human embryo is a central question of public bioethics and has been since its inception. The public question has been addressed by government advisory commissions, state legislatures, state courts, administrative agencies, Congress, multiple presidents, and several different intergovernmental bodies including the United Nations, UNESCO, and the Council of Europe.

For present purposes, the narrow question is what (or who), exactly, is the embryo in the context of ART? For commentators like John Robertson and like-minded advocates of maximal procreative liberty, they are not persons, despite their biological status as living organisms of the human species. For some, they are simply raw biological materials to be used and discarded with impunity; for others they have an "intermediate status" warranting "special respect," which precludes their use and destruction except in compelling circumstances (though this turns out to be a very broad category in practice).

The arguments against the personhood of the living human embryo track the abortion debate somewhat, though the context is distinguishable, as there are no burdens of unplanned pregnancy at issue. Some argue (like Tooley and Warren) that embryos are not persons because they are not yet capable of preferred capacities such as cognition, self-awareness, the formulation of desires, and the creation of future directed plans.[102]

Others argue that embryos that are slated for destruction or indefinite cryostorage are not persons because they will never develop these preferred capacities as they will never enter an environment (namely, the womb) that would support such development. Still others argue that all IVF embryos are not persons based on the assertion that they are incredibly fragile and that most will die of natural causes ("natural embryo loss") before they develop the preferred capacities of personhood. Some argue that they are not persons because they are very small—"a tiny clump of cells no bigger than the period at the end of this sentence."[103] Others assert that they are not yet persons because they are not, in fact, human beings at all but merely "an undifferentiated ball of cells."[104] Finally, there are those who argue that IVF embryos are not persons prior to the formation of the "primitive streak"—a biological structure that appears around 14 days of development that is the precursor to the nervous system, after which the phenomenon of monozygotic "twinning" is thought to be no longer possible. For such advocates, the primitive streak signals the rudiments of the brain and spinal cord—essential to the cognitive functioning associated with their conception of personhood—and guarantees that the human organism is a stable individual who will not divide into multiple individuals. These arguments are sometimes made individually, sometimes in combination.

As discussed in the previous chapter, an anthropology of embodiment construes the biological origins, structure, and function of the embryo differently. It begins with a posture of great skepticism toward arguments that make "personhood" contingent upon a being's achievement of certain milestones established by others relating to size, strength, cognition, and dependence. This skepticism grows when those setting forth such criteria for personhood are strongly motivated by the desire to use or destroy the being whose moral status they seek to evaluate. Such decisionmakers have a vested interest in a finding of non-personhood; if embryos are not persons, then they are available for recruitment into the projects of others without serious concern for their interests or well-being.

Viewed through the anthropology of embodiment, none of the arguments for IVF embryo non-personhood are persuasive. All human beings, because of their embodiment, exist on a "scale of disability," with their powers waxing and waning according to age, health, and circumstance. As discussed in the last chapter, living members of the human species need not meet tests for cognitive capacity or possess the abilities of self-reflection and expression necessary to flourish as prescribed by the anthropology of expressive individualism. The vulnerability and dependence of the embryonic human being on others to supply a nurturing environment to support her life and further development (namely, her gestational mother's womb) is no warrant to declare her a non-person available for use or destruction. To the contrary, her vulnerability and dependence—like all human vulnerability and dependence—are a summons for care, concern, and protection. Nor is her small size or fragility a license to treat her as a non-person. The claim that a high rate of embryo demise prior to implantation and birth diminishes the moral worth of embryos is a *non sequitur;* the same logic would lead to the false conclusion that a high infant mortality rate reduces the moral value of babies *in utero.* In any event, the rate of pregnancies initiated per transfer in IVF is quite high—45 percent for nonfrozen embryos and 56 percent for frozen embryos. The overall rate of IVF pregnancies resulting in birth is 81 percent.[105]

Similarly, the claim that IVF embryos are "undifferentiated balls of cells" does not accurately reflect their status as living organisms, biologically or morally. An "organism" is an individual, whole living being composed of parts that function in a coordinated manner to support growth and development of the entity along a species-specific trajectory. Under this definition, the IVF embryo screened and transferred, discarded, or cryogenically stored is manifestly an organism. There is some debate among embryologists about when exactly differentiation and coordination among the component parts of the embryo occur (for example, within moments following sperm-egg fusion or when the maternal and paternal pro-nuclei fuse at syngamy approximately twenty-four hours later). Despite this uncertainty, there is clear evidence of internally directed, coordinated activity from days one to six, relevant to enabling implantation and further development of the embryo.[106] By virtue of its structure, function, and composition, the IVF embryo is a living human organism.

Similarly, the capacity for embryo twinning does not undermine the embryo's status as an individual living human organism. In rare instances (0.4 percent of births in natural reproduction, and two to twelve times higher in IVF), some portion of the cells of an embryo will split off from the whole, and resolve itself into a new, genetically identical "twin."[107] Some point to this unique capacity for regulation and restitution following developmental disruption as evidence that the embryo is not yet "individuated." But this is not persuasive, given that indivisibility is not necessary for individuation in an organism. The individual flatworm has the bodily resilience to survive similar disruptions, with its severed parts sometimes resolving into a new organism. So too with the human embryo at early stages of development. Its resilience is not surprising given the plasticity of its component parts, which give rise to all the tissue types and structures of the mature body. But despite such plasticity, in the absence of disruption, such parts function as a coordinated, integrated whole. In short, as an individual organism.

From the perspective of an anthropology of embodiment, discussing the human organism at this stage as "the embryo" fails to capture its essential identity. This nomenclature trades in the notion of atomization and isolation of expressive individualism. It is not "the embryo," but the particular human offspring of specific genetic parents. *This* embryonic human being emerges from the process of fertilization already embedded in a web of relationships, most notably involving his or her biological progenitors—his or her parents. An anthropology of embodiment is mindful of this connectivity and the obligations and privileges that flow from it that comprise one dimension of the network of giving and receiving necessary to human life and flourishing. The relationship of genetic progenitors to the given embryonic human being conceived is, normatively speaking, that of parent and child. It would take more discussion and reflection to do justice to the richness of this relationship and to unfold the contours of obligation and privilege within this network, but at a minimum, the genetic parents have an obligation to protect and promote the flourishing of their embryonic child. How they might discharge this obligation also requires a great deal more thought and discussion, but the end point of any such pathway of care would have to be the birth of a child who has a place of belonging as a genuine son or daughter in a family that loves him or her unconditionally.

The role of the law is to facilitate this end—to help genetic parents to cultivate their moral imaginations so as to see their child in the embryo in the dish, and to understand their obligations as parents. Should the parents fail in this regard, the law must intervene to do what the parents cannot or will not do—seek a resolution where this embryonic human being ultimately finds a place of unconditional belonging as a son or daughter in a loving family. How the law can accomplish this aspiration, and what kinds of regulatory mechanisms are fitting and appropriate to this end, are a matter for future consideration.

The conclusion as a matter of principle is that embryonic human beings, as embodied living members of the species, must be included in the network of giving and receiving on which all human beings depend for their survival and their flourishing. Their good must be counted as part of the common good, and their vulnerability and dependence are a warrant for protection and support, just as with any other living member of the human family.

How the law might concretely accomplish this end, which of the myriad passive and active tools it should deploy toward these purposes, and what the practice of ART might look like under this new regime are all matters for a future inquiry. One place to start would be to study the rare laws in the United States and abroad that offer protection to all participants in ART through the lens of children and parents. For example, a Louisiana statute declares such embryonic human beings to be "juridical persons," with the attendant privileges and protections owed to such a status.[108] It would be worth knowing whether such a law successfully engenders the understanding that assisted reproduction is a domain of parents and children at all stages of the process. Similar provisions designed to protect parents—genetic, gestational, and rearing—would likewise be worth exploring. These are inquiries for another time, but they must be pursued if the public bioethics of ART is to be responsive to the full range of needs and wants of the embodied beings whose lives are touched by it.

5

Death and Dying

Our discussion so far has focused on the public bioethics concerning the beginning of life. Now, the inquiry shifts to life's other margin, namely, the public bioethics of death and dying. While there are myriad points of entry into this area of the law, including the definition of death, organ donation, and medical futility, the analysis that follows will focus on two fundamental public questions of perennial and crucial import to the law of end-of-life decision-making: refusal or discontinuation of life-sustaining measures, and assisted suicide. As in earlier discussions, there is a need for an anthropological augmentation to the law's foundations in these matters, for more humane, just, and fully human governance.

Before proceeding with the analysis, it is necessary first to define some basic terms for these related but ethically and legally distinct domains. First, "the refusal or termination of life-sustaining measures" refers to a decision to decline or discontinue a medical intervention necessary to preserve one's life. The decision can be made by the patient herself, or by a proxy decisionmaker on her behalf in the event that she is not or has never been competent to do so. The reasons for doing so may vary. Some patients decline or discontinue life-sustaining measures because they regard *the medical interventions at issue* as unduly burdensome or futile. Others may do so specifically in order *to hasten their own death*. These motives are different, even if the result of the decision is the same. In the first case, the patient is choosing against an unwanted treatment with the foreseeable (though perhaps regrettable) consequence of an earlier death. In the second case, the patient is making a choice for the express purpose of hastening dying, perhaps because she judges her current or near-future quality of life as unbearable. As will be discussed at more length below, regardless of one's motives, it is legal in every state in the United States for a patient to decline or discontinue life-sustaining measures.

Second, "physician-assisted suicide," as practiced in the United States, is the intentional taking of one's own life through the self-administration of a lethal drug, prescribed by a physician for these purposes. It is currently legal in ten U.S. jurisdictions (nine states and the District of Columbia).

Euthanasia is the direct and intentional killing of a patient by a third party either based on his request or in the name of his best interests. "Voluntary euthanasia" is the intentional killing of a patient upon his request. "Non-voluntary euthanasia" is the killing of a patient in the absence of any request, on the grounds that it is in the patient's best interests. "Involuntary euthanasia" is the direct killing of a patient over his objections, overriding his preferences in the name of a perceived greater good. All forms of euthanasia are illegal in the United States.

Termination of life-sustaining measures, physician-assisted suicide, and euthanasia are all distinguishable ethically and legally from the aggressive use of palliative techniques, such as the administration of powerful pain medications that carry a serious risk of death for the patient. In such treatment, the purpose of the clinician is to relieve the pain and suffering of a living patient through the use of potentially dangerous pain management techniques and the dosage is adjusted solely to achieve this goal; the aim is not to hasten his death.

THE REFUSAL OR TERMINATION
OF LIFE-SUSTAINING MEASURES

In *Cruzan v. Director, Missouri Department of Health,* the Supreme Court (quoting a prior case) noted that "No right is held more sacred, or is more carefully guarded, by the common law, than the right of every individual to the possession and control of his own person, free from all restraint or interference of others, unless by clear and unquestionable authority of law." In the United States, the law governing the decision to decline or discontinue unwanted medical care (including life-sustaining measures) is generally set forth by the statutes and judicial decisions of the individual states. It is rooted in the common law of battery, which forbids unwanted touching by others. Upon this foundation, the law of informed consent was erected as an additional protection for bodily integrity, specifically in the context of medical care. As the Supreme Court observed in *Cruzan,* "the logical corollary of the doctrine of informed consent is that the patient generally possesses the right not to consent, that is, to refuse treatment."[1] The first case involving the termination of life-sustaining measures was *In re Quinlan*, in 1976.[2] In that case, the Supreme Court of New Jersey declared that there was a right to discontinue such treatment based on the same right to privacy discerned in the United States Constitution by the Supreme Court in *Griswold v. Connecticut* and *Roe v. Wade*.[3]

Since then, numerous state courts have recognized the same right to refuse unwanted treatment, grounding it in the common law of informed consent alone, or in combination with a right to privacy or self-determination.

In *Cruzan*, following a discussion of the common law right to refusal, the Supreme Court observed, in a conspicuous and atypical use of the passive voice, that "[t]he principle that a competent person has a constitutionally protected liberty interest in refusing unwanted medical treatment may be inferred from our prior decisions."[4] Turning to the question of whether this "liberty interest" extends to refusal of artificial nutrition and hydration, the Court again responded with a somewhat qualified reply that "*for purposes of this case*, we *assume* that the United States Constitution would grant a competent person a constitutionally protected right to refuse lifesaving hydration and nutrition."[5]

Whether grounded in a constitutional liberty interest or the common law of informed consent, in every jurisdiction in the United States it is lawful for a competent patient to decline or discontinue unwanted medical care, including life-sustaining measures. The principle normative justification is to protect the autonomy and self-determination of patients of sound mind. This legal framework is not controversial as applied to such individuals.

Difficulties arise, however, when these legal principles are applied to patients who are not capable of making decisions for themselves. This was the context of *In re Quinlan*, involving a young woman in a "persistent vegetative state," a phrase coined in 1972 by Jennett and Plum to describe "a state of wakefulness without detectable awareness."[6] A Multi-Society Task Force convened in 1994 to study the matter reported that "the distinguishing feature of the vegetative state is an irregular but cyclic state of circadian sleeping and waking unaccompanied by any behaviorally detectable expression of self-awareness, specific recognition of external stimuli, or consistent evidence of attention or intention or learned responses."[7] Such patients may move, smile, cry, moan, or scream, but these actions are, according to the diagnosis, not purposeful or evidence of psychological awareness. Patients in a persistent vegetative state are thus unable to make treatment decisions on their own behalf.

In *Quinlan*, the Supreme Court of New Jersey held that the patient's right to privacy (which includes the freedom to decline unwanted life-sustaining measures) should not be extinguished simply because of cognitive disability.[8] The Court allowed the patient's father, acting as guardian, to make a decision on her behalf that, in his best judgment, she would have made for herself if she were able to do so. Accordingly, it authorized her father to direct the withdrawal of her ventilator, subject to confirmation by the physician and hospital ethics committee that Karen Quinlan had no hope of being restored to a "cognitive, sapient state."[9] Ventilation was discontinued, but to the surprise of everyone, Karen Ann Quinlan continued to breathe on her own and survived another ten years.[10]

Since *Quinlan*, in jurisdictions throughout the United States, courts and state legislatures have embraced the notion that the right to decline life-sustaining measures can be exercised on behalf of patients who no longer have the capacity to decide for themselves. While the details of the laws vary somewhat, the common thread is that the patient's actual prior wishes, if discernable, are paramount. If there is decisive written or oral evidence that expresses the patient's preferences for the circumstances at issue, then they are to be implemented. Courts also allow for proxy decisionmakers, under the auspices of a "substituted judgment" standard to make a decision about what the patient would have wanted based on his expressed wishes, values and opinions, and any other evidence indicating what treatment he would choose or decline under the circumstances. Because the goal is to vindicate the patient's autonomy and self-determination, this is meant to be a purely subjective inquiry. As one Florida state court explained:

> One does not exercise another's right of self-determination or fulfill that person's right of privacy by making a decision which the state, the family, or public opinion would prefer. The surrogate decision-maker must be confident that he or she can and is voicing the *patient's* decision.[11]

In the interest of ensuring that the preferences implemented are truly those of the patient, and to avoid possible fraud, mistake, or abuse, many jurisdictions require those seeking to terminate life-sustaining measures for incompetent patients to prove by "clear and convincing evidence" that this is what the patient wanted under the circumstances. This is the highest standard of proof in American civil law and is tantamount to "beyond a reasonable doubt" in the criminal context. The Supreme Court held in *Cruzan* that such a requirement does not violate the incompetent patient's constitutionally protected liberty interest in declining unwanted life-sustaining measures.[12]

If it proves impossible to determine what the patient's actual wishes were prior to losing the capacity to decide for himself, some jurisdictions allow for treatment decisions to be made according to a "best interests" standard. Unlike the "substituted judgment" approach, which is meant to be subjective and entirely tailored to the patient's preferences, the "best interests" standard is meant to be objective, implementing what a reasonable person would choose under the circumstances. If there is any probative evidence of the patient's preferences, it is incorporated into the calculus. If not, the decision is made by weighing benefits and burdens under a reasonableness standard. For example, in the absence of any evidence of the patient's wishes, the New Jersey Supreme Court in *In re Conroy* proposed a "pure-objective standard," under which life-sustaining measures should be terminated when it is demonstrated that "the net burdens of the patient's life with the treatment . . . clearly and markedly outweigh the benefits that the patient derives from life," and the patient is subject to "recurring, unavoidable and severe pain" rendering the continuation of life sustaining treatment "inhumane."[13]

Similarly, the President's Commission for the Study of Ethical Problems in Medicine and Biomedical and Behavioral Research suggested the following framework for discerning "best interests" in this context:

In assessing whether a procedure or course of treatment would be in a patient's best interests, the surrogate must take into account such factors as the relief of suffering, the preservation or restoration of functioning, and the quality as well as the extent of life sustained. An accurate assessment will encompass consideration of the satisfaction of present desires, the opportunities for future satisfaction, and the possibility of developing or regaining the capacity for self-determination.[14]

Under both the "substituted judgment" and "best interests" standards, if the party seeking to discontinue life-sustaining measures fails in its burden of proof, such treatment is continued for the incompetent patient.

In actual clinical practice, nearly all decisions regarding life-sustaining measures are made by families in private deliberation and are never subject to litigation and the publicity that comes with it. It is only in the rare instance where family members or caregivers disagree so strongly that they seek a resolution through the courts and the court of public opinion. Nevertheless, worries about such disputes over life sustaining measures have motivated a widespread public campaign to encourage people to memorialize their treatment preferences in legal instruments to be used to govern their medical care in the event of their future incompetence.

Now every state has laws providing for the creation of some form of "advance directive," meant to guide life-sustaining treatment decisions after the individual loses the capacity to do so, and likewise to excuse health care providers who follow such directives from legal liability. In 1990, Congress passed the Patient Self-Determination Act (PSDA), requiring health care facilities that receive Medicare or Medicaid funds to give patients under their care information about advance directives deemed valid under state law.[15] If such patients have an advance directive, this must be noted in their medical records. These advance directives can take a variety of forms. Instruction directives are written or oral declarations about future treatment preferences, including end-of-life decision-making. A proxy directive (often called a health care power of attorney) designates a person who can make medical decisions in the event the patient becomes incapacitated. Living wills are written instruments that seek to provide instructions for medical care (including termination of life-sustaining measures) when the patient can no longer decide for himself.

According to the President's Council on Bioethics, "[t]he idea of the living will has been enthusiastically endorsed not only by Congress and the courts, but also by state legislatures, the Veteran's Administration, medical and legal associations, doctors, lawyers, ethicists, and patient advocacy organizations."[16]

THE ANTHROPOLOGY OF THE LAW
OF LIFE-SUSTAINING MEASURES

Just as for the law of abortion and assisted reproduction, the anthropology of the law of life-sustaining measures emerges from first considering the goods it means to advance. The primary good that decisively orients the legal framework is autonomy. It single-mindedly seeks to advance the good of being free from unwanted bodily intrusion. Some state courts—referring specifically to abortion jurisprudence—style it as the good of privacy. Others have described it as the "right to possession and control of one's person" or the "right to be left alone."

The form of autonomy conferred on patients by the law of end-of-life decision-making is the freedom to shape their life's narrative, to construct a conclusion that reflects their own self-understanding, and to convey this meaning to others by the choices they make. Legal philosopher Ronald Dworkin wrote that people "want their deaths, if possible, to express and in that way vividly confirm the values they believe most important to their lives."[17]

Thus, the image of the flourishing person that lies beneath the legal mechanisms of this domain is the solitary individual seeking to assert his will in the face of mortality and suffering, to make a final existential choice that will express his deeply held views about the meaning and value of his life and how to live it. This is the protagonist of expressive individualism, authoring the last chapter of his self-constructed story.

As applied to a patient of sound mind, competent to make his or her own treatment decisions, this is a mostly uncontroversial anthropological grounding for the law. To be sure, it fails to account for the diminished agency that comes with suffering, the more complex array of preferences and desires of patients in this context, and the web of other people affected by such decisions. But given the intimate, delicate, and highly personal nature of these choices, there are good prudential reasons to keep the intrusive machinery of the state from interfering with decision-making by competent patients to reject undesired care. Concerns about fraud, abuse, and duress are less grave when a patient can reflect, deliberate, and decline unwanted medical interventions in his or her own voice. Forcing medical care on competent patients against their wishes runs contrary to well settled and widely shared principles of American law and medical ethics.

However, the anthropology of expressive individualism becomes highly problematic when illness or injury has silenced the patient or otherwise rendered her incompetent to make decisions regarding life-sustaining measures. The person as an atomized unencumbered will seeking its own path forward does not match the lived embodied reality of profound vulnerability and dependence of debilitating injury and illness that leaves one unable to reflect and make life and death choices.

And yet, expressive individualism remains the anthropology of the law in these circumstances. The law insists on the fiction that it is possible to exercise autonomy and self-determination once the ability to formulate or express a decision regarding life-sustaining measures is irretrievably lost. It falsely equates the current exercise of autonomy with binding a now-incapacitated patient to previously expressed wishes, either by operation of a living will or by reconstructing his intentions by recalling less solemn forms of communication. To borrow the words of the President's Council on Bioethics, the law's mechanisms of end-of-life decision-making for incompetent patients rest on the anthropological premise that "each individual [can] remain—by this 'remote control'—a self-determining agent, even when he can no longer directly or contemporaneously determine his own fate."[18]

The shortcomings of a legal strategy rooted in autonomy and self-determination for profoundly vulnerable, dependent, and cognitively impaired patients dependent upon life support becomes clear in light of the frustrated aspirations of the nationwide campaign for the living will. Putting aside the fact that only about a quarter of people in the United States have living wills, there is good reason to believe that even for those that do, it is not effective as the sole means to govern end-of-life decision-making once competence is lost.[19] The President's Council on Bioethics, reviewing the social science evidence analyzed by Amy Fagerlin and Carl Schneider, found that many people surveyed preferred to let proxy decisionmakers have leeway to make choices on their behalf.[20] Vulnerable people facing the possibility of life's end do not seek to assert their unencumbered wills. They want help from those who love them or from experts committed to caring for them.

Moreover, "most people find it difficult to accurately predict their preferences 'for an unspecifiable future confronted with unidentifiable maladies with unpredictable treatments.'"[21] A meta-analysis of multiple studies showed that large percentages of people routinely change their preferences regarding life-sustaining measures in a relatively short period of time.[22] This difficulty for strategies of legal "precommitment" becomes especially acute when the young and healthy try to imagine how and whether they would find meaning in a much-diminished state due to disease, injury, or senescence. The President's Council noted that there is "an extensive body of research on how poor we are at predicting our own preferences and desires, especially in regard to choices far off in the future."[23]

Moreover, living wills as drafted are often either underinclusive regarding possible future scenarios or are so overbroad that they do not provide sufficiently concrete guidance.

Schneider and Fagerlin do not blame this problem on poor drafting, but rather the nature of the task itself, namely, trying to predict a highly complex and variable future. Even more problematic is that studies have shown that patients themselves are ambivalent about whether their instructions should be precisely followed.[24]

Some studies have indicated that living wills do not meaningfully improve the accuracy of proxy decisionmakers in predicting the actual preferences of patients. According to the President's Council on Bioethics:

> Strikingly, what the researchers found in this study was that, compared to the control group, *none* of the interventions produced significant improvement in the accuracy of the surrogates' judgment in *any* illness scenario or for *any* medical treatment. When spouses or children of elderly patients made surrogate "decisions" about medical treatment based *only* on their familiarity with the patient, their judgments were *just* as accurate as that of spouses and children who had read or read and discussed a detailed living will drawn up by the patient.[25]

In addition to these concerns, there are problems with holding a now-incompetent patient to past choices to decline life-sustaining measures made when young and in the peak of health. The current patient can no longer revise these choices, even if he derives value from life in his diminished state. The difficulty is illustrated by the hypothetical case of "Margo," derived from Andrew Firlik's account of an Alzheimer's patient suffering from dementia who was quite content with her life of visiting with friends whose names she could never recall, drawing the same picture, and listening to the same songs.[26] Ronald Dworkin suggested that if Margo had previously executed a living will categorically refusing life-sustaining measures in the event of dementia, should she now contract pneumonia, she should be denied life-saving antibiotics. He argued that to provide antibiotics in this scenario would be to engage in an "unacceptable form of moral paternalism," and a violation of the patient's desire to shape the conclusion of her life's narrative in a manner consistent with her self-understanding.[27] Rebecca Dresser, however, pierces the fiction that this is a valid exercise of self-determination for the patient Margo is now: "A policy of absolute adherence to advance directives means that we deny people like Margo the freedom we enjoy as competent people to change our decisions that conflict with our subsequent experiential interests."[28]

While it is not clear what would happen in a real case involving a patient like Margo, the law's preferred approach as a general matter is to bind now-incompetent patients to choices previously expressed either formally through a living will or informally through oral statements and behaviors deemed sufficient to indicate past preferences. But by doing so the law ignores the embodied reality of the profound vulnerability and dependence of the person suffering under the yoke of debilitating cognitive impairment and instead projects onto him a false image of an intact mind and will. At a time when a person is most fragile and dependent on the care of others for basic needs, the law elevates freedom and self-determination as its animating goods. In a moment when the patient cannot speak for himself, the law insists that his voice be heard and heeded. The single-minded focus on autonomy, grounded in the anthropology of expressive individualism thus renders the law unable to respond fully to the unique needs of this stage of life.

What is needed, therefore, is a legal approach rooted in an anthropology of embodiment. Such an approach understands that because persons are bodies, the living patient diminished by injury, illness, or senescence is the *same person* who, when younger and healthier, expressed views about the appropriate use of life-sustaining measures. To honor the person, those views should be honored, but so too should be the needs of the patient he has now become. An anthropology of embodiment would reject here (as it did in the contexts of the beginning of life) the distinction that some draw between living human beings and human "persons" based on cognitive capacity. The patient whose cognition has been irretrievably lost does not likewise lose her personhood. The life cycle of the person even in the very best of circumstances is marked by radical dependence at the beginning of life, development of one's bodily powers as well as cognition and will, followed by a decline into dependence and vulnerability once again.

An anthropology of embodiment recognizes this "scale of disability" as the nature of life humanly lived—the pathway of all persons.

Caring rightly for an incompetent person dependent on life-sustaining measures requires thinking carefully about previously expressed preferences, but it does not end there. It requires a prudential weighing of present needs and circumstances in all their complexity. And this should occur, as in all cases of profound human dependence throughout life's cycle, in networks of uncalculated giving and graceful receiving. This, as elsewhere, requires the practice of the virtues of just generosity, hospitality, and especially accompaniment in suffering (misericordia). The focus of care must be the patient who presents herself, in all her neediness and vulnerability. Care should not be given according to some idealized standard of how we remember her in the past or how we might wish her to be. Nor should care depend on her inability to become again what she once was. Our care is determined by the patient as she is now.

What, then, might a public bioethics of life-sustaining measures look like when augmented by the anthropology of embodiment? Here, as in previous chapters, there are only general principles on offer, with the working out of details deferred to the future.

The first principle is that the law should respond to the unique vulnerability and dependence of this context by strengthening and supporting the networks of giving and receiving necessary to care for such patients. Following the recommendation of the President's Council on Bioethics, the law should encourage the creation of proxy directives, naming those who can make decisions in the event of future circumstances of incompetency. The proxy should carefully consider the preferences expressed by the patient in the past, but also take into account the complexity of present circumstances and the needs of the patient as he currently is. This approach integrates both the good of self-mastery that reflects the freedom and particularity of individuals, as well as the acknowledgement of dependence that is part of every embodied being's story. In the words of the Council:

> The proxy directive does not ignore the significance of our desire to participate (in advance) in shaping treatment decisions made for us at a time in the future when we can no longer participate concurrently. Precisely by naming someone to serve as our proxy, we take that desire seriously. At the same time, however, this approach emphasizes less the importance of self-determination and correspondingly more the importance of solidarity and interdependence. It invites us to move toward our final days and years not in a spirit that isolates our free decisions from the networks of those who love and care for us but, instead, in a spirit that entrusts our dying to those who have supported us in our living. It enlists them to stay by our side, to the very end.[29]

The proxy must resist the temptation to project his own judgment about quality of life, viewed from his perch as an able-bodied and healthy individual. There is a natural temptation to look at those in a diminished state and conclude that theirs is a life not worth living. But if we are demonstrably bad at predicting how we ourselves might derive meaning and joy in a state of disability, we are even worse at judging how others might do so. The temptation to alleviate suffering or disability by eliminating the patient must be resisted. The President's Council offers a useful framework for avoiding this well-meaning and paternalistic but ultimately misguided judgment about a life not worth living. The proxy decisionmaker should focus on the *medical intervention* under consideration. Declining a treatment because it itself is unduly burdensome or futile is different from doing so for the purposes of hastening the end of a life judged by the proxy to be of low quality. Refusing or terminating an unduly burdensome or futile treatment on behalf of an incompetent patient is a choice for a different, perhaps shorter life. It is not a choice for death.

Proxies are less likely to project their own preferences on to the patient in their charge if they remain focused on the intervention at issue, not her underlying condition. Of course, fleshing out the meaning of "burden" and "futility" requires a great deal of fact-bound thought and reflection that is better left to a future inquiry.

For those without family or friends, the law must fill the gap in the network of giving and receiving on which the vulnerable depend. As the Council advises, "[w]e should not too readily acquiesce in a vision that isolates us in the time of our dependency, or a vision that rests on the false notion that individuals can precisely determine and manage every fact of their lives until the very end."[30] The law should here, as elsewhere, work to shore up the networks of giving and receiving throughout society such that the goods of friendship and solidarity will be practiced and well developed, and thus ready to respond to the most pressing crises of care.

ASSISTED SUICIDE

The final "vital conflict" to be examined is the law concerning assisted suicide. While the vast majority of states do not permit assisted suicide and the American Medical Association remains opposed to it, the campaign to legalize the practice appears to have grown in momentum with the passage of laws in seven jurisdictions since 2013. Just as with the other legal frameworks discussed in the preceding pages, this impoverished anthropological foundation renders the law incapable of responding to the full range of neediness of this context, and threatens the especially vulnerable and dependent, who are invisible from expressive individualism's narrow angle of vision. As before, these defects emerge from analyzing the law itself to discern the goods it is meant to serve, and to uncover its underlying premises about human identity and flourishing.

At common law, conventional suicide was a crime punishable by confiscation of the decedent's movable goods (though not real property, as in Roman Law). In America during the prerevolutionary years, it was punished with forfeiture of property and in some cases "ignominious burial," to dishonor the remains of the suicide. Gradually, however, Americans came to see such punishments as unfair to survivors, and unjust to those who commit suicide, as they grew to appreciate that the close relationship between mental illness and suicide diminished the culpability of those who take their own lives.

Accordingly, suicide itself was decriminalized throughout the United States. However, the law continued to regard suicide as a grave harm to be prevented and deterred. The law retained procedures for involuntary civil commitment and other restrictive mechanisms to prevent suicide. Assisting another in suicide remained illegal.

Then in 1994 by referendum the state of Oregon adopted the Death with Dignity Act, legalizing assisted suicide and regulating its practice.[31] After litigation, the law went into effect in late 1997. The state of Washington followed suit in 2008 and legalized assisted suicide by referendum.[32] In 2009, the Montana Supreme Court declared that assistance in suicide is not prohibited by its extant state law.[33] Led by Compassion and Choices, the principal advocacy organization for assisted suicide, there have been a number of initiatives to legalize the practice that have succeeded in seven additional jurisdictions including Vermont (2013), California and Colorado (2016), Washington, D.C. (2017), Hawaii (2018), and New Jersey and Maine (2019).[34] This brings the total number of U.S. jurisdictions where assisted suicide is legal to ten (including the District of Columbia). By contrast, since 1997 eleven states have explicitly banned assisted suicide, and efforts to liberalize existing bans have foundered in others (most notably in Massachusetts in 2012).[35]

In 1997, in the companion cases of *Washington v. Glucksberg* and *Vacco v. Quill*, the U.S. Supreme Court declared that state laws banning assisted suicide do not violate the United States Constitution.[36] The right to assisted suicide is not protected by the Due Process Clause as it is neither "objectively, deeply rooted in the Nation's history and tradition," nor is it "implicit in the concept of ordered liberty" such that "neither liberty nor justice would exist if the right were sacrificed."[37] The Court further held that laws banning assisted suicide do not violate the Equal Protection Clause of the Fourteenth Amendment, distinguishing the freedom of patients to refuse intrusive, unwanted medical care from the right to affirmatively take their own lives with the aid of a physician.[38] The Court concluded that banning assisted suicide is a rational means to advance legitimate state interests, namely, protecting life generally, preventing suicide, safeguarding the integrity of the medical profession and the role of physicians as healers, protecting the vulnerable, poor, elderly, marginalized, and disabled from neglect, abuse, mistakes, bigotry, and pressures to end their own lives, and preventing a move towards direct mercy killing (euthanasia).[39]

More recently, two state courts of last resort in New Mexico (*Morris v. Brandenburg* 2016) and New York (*Myers v. Schneiderman* 2017) reached similar conclusions in analyzing claims under their state constitutions.[40] The Supreme Court of New Mexico rejected the claims by plaintiffs that the state interests cited in *Glucksberg* and *Quill* were based on worries that had proven false in the intervening years.[41] The Court pointed to more recent consideration and renewal of these concerns by the New Mexico legislature as recently as 2015.[42]

Today advocates and opponents of assisted suicide alike perceive that efforts to legalize the practice are advancing. All the laws proposed and adopted are based on the paradigm of Oregon. Thus, it offers an excellent framework for analyzing the anthropological premises of assisted suicide laws in America more broadly. As shown below, the vision of the person and flourishing that underwrites Oregon's law and those modeled upon it is expressive individualism.

The Oregon law authorizes physicians to prescribe a lethal dose of drugs to terminally ill adult Oregon residents, so they may self-administer them for the purpose of ending their lives. The law states that it does not authorize euthanasia.[43] Death by means of assisted suicide is not defined as "suicide" under Oregon law and death certificates list only the underlying terminal illness as the cause of death.[44] Terminal illness is defined as a malady that will produce death in six months or less, but the law does not specify whether this prognosis distinguishes life expectancy with treatment versus without it.[45] Competency under the law is defined as "the ability to make and communicate health care decisions."[46]

To obtain a prescription, eligible patients are required to make two oral requests of a physician (it need not be the same person) separated by at least fifteen days.[47] Recently, the state enacted a waiver provision for cases where the doctor believes that the patient might die during the waiting period. The patient must also issue a written request, signed by two witnesses (though there are no significant restrictions on who these might be).[48] Two physicians—one prescribing and one consulting—must confirm the diagnosis, prognosis, and capability of the patient to make the request. If either physician believes that the patient's judgment is impaired by a psychiatric or psychological disorder, he will refer him for evaluation.[49] There is no mandatory psychiatric or psychological assessment of patients seeking prescriptions.[50] The prescribing physician must advise the patient of alternatives including comfort care, hospice care, and pain control. There is no requirement that the prescribing physician have expertise in any of these fields.[51] The physician may request (though must not require) that the patient advise family or next of kin of the request for prescription.[52] Such physicians are frequently members or affiliates of Compassion and Choices; there is a limited number of doctors in the state willing to prescribe lethal medications.[53] Once the prescription is issued, there is no requirement that any health care professional be present for the administration of the lethal dose. Physicians are immunized from liability if they are found to have made a "good faith" effort to comply with the law—a significantly more permissive standard than the usual framework for malpractice.[54]

Since 1998, 1,459 people have taken their own lives under the Death with Dignity Act.[55] The number of patients ending their lives under the law has steadily increased, doubling from the four-year period of 2008–2012 to 2013–2017.[56] Data is provided to the Oregon Health Authority by prescribing physicians; the state does not have funding or a mechanism to validate or audit such reports. Original reports are destroyed once the state reports its aggregated annual data.[57] One state official famously noted that the Oregon Health Division has no enforcement role and cannot verify the reports they receive from physicians who participate in the regime established by the Death with Dignity Act.[58]

THE ANTHROPOLOGY OF ASSISTED SUICIDE LAWS

As before, the inductive analysis of the law focuses first on the goods it seeks to advance, and then the underlying assumptions of human identity and flourishing on which such goods are premised. The twin goods invoked to support laws such as Oregon's Death with Dignity Act are autonomy and compassion. These aspirations are linked in the very name of the nation's leading assisted suicide advocacy organization: Compassion and Choices.[59]

The law is meant to allow the exercise of self-determination in the face of a terminal illness, to choose the time and manner of one's demise. An array of famous American moral and political philosophers—Ronald Dworkin, John Rawls, Robert Nozick, Thomas Nagel, Thomas Scanlon, and Judith Jarvis Thomson (of the famous violinist analogy discussed in Chapter 3)—filed an amicus brief to aid the Supreme Court in its consideration of *Washington v. Glucksberg* and *Vacco v. Quill*.[60] The "Philosopher's Brief," as it was called, was also published in *The New York Review of Books*. It invoked the precedent of *Planned Parenthood v. Casey* for a broad individual right of self-determination in making the most intimate and important personal choices. The choice of how and when to die, the brief argued, was a pristine example of such a self-defining decision:

> Most of us see death—whatever we think will follow it—
> as the final act of life's drama, and we want that last act to
> reflect our own convictions, those we have tried to live by,
> not the convictions of others forced on us in our most vulnerable moment.[61]

Seventeen years later, the face of the campaign for assisted suicide became Brittany Maynard, a beautiful and dynamic young woman in her twenties who moved to Oregon to take her own life following a diagnosis of terminal brain cancer. She spoke passionately about the freedom to choose the timing and manner of her death, and to avoid the pain and decline of her disease. She situated this choice in the larger context of the freedom to pursue the life of one's dreams: "The reason to consider life and what's of value is to make sure you're not missing out. Seize the day. What's important to you? What do you care about? What matters? Pursue that, forget the rest."[62] The executives of Compassion and Choices were elated to have such an appealing spokeswoman for the right to assisted suicide. They created ad campaigns and websites including such slogans as "My life. My death. My choice. I support Brittany Maynard and all Americans' right to choose #DeathwithDignity."[63] This campaign was influential in the successful push to legalize assisted suicide in California, Maynard's home state.

Alongside the freedom to exercise autonomy in shaping the timing and manner of one's death, advocates cite compassion for the suffering as the second core animating good of assisted suicide legalization. They invoke compelling images of patients suffering from excruciating and refractory pain, which only ends in death. Assisted suicide is thus justified as a compassionate option for those with intolerable suffering to end the pain by ending their lives with the assistance of a physician.

These are compelling arguments, vividly argued. To one who is anticipating a life of decline, pain, and death, the image of the solitary individual imposing the rational mastery of his will on these dire circumstances—at once exercising his fundamental freedom, using it to author the ending to his life's story with the integrity and coherence of his self-understanding, and in so doing, avoiding an undignified and painful decline—might be appealing. It is an image of freedom, choice, and dignity that resonates deeply with rugged American individualism and Romantic expressivism.

But it is a vision that is deeply forgetful of the body, and the profound vulnerability and dependence faced not only by the patients who choose assisted suicide, but also the vulnerable populations who live in jurisdictions that have embraced the law, ethics, and culture of assisted suicide.

CRITIQUING AND REFORMING THE LAW OF ASSISTED SUICIDE

The anthropology of expressive individualism fails to account for the diminished agency at the margins of life for an embodied being in time, overstates the possibility of autonomy in this setting, and underestimates the risks of systemic neglect, fraud, abuse, mistake, and coercion in a legal regime that allows assisted suicide. Accordingly, the law in Oregon (on which other similar state laws are modeled) fails to adopt crucial safeguards to protect the fragile, needy, elderly, poor, stigmatized, and disabled from such threats. Indeed, just as in the previous contexts discussed in the preceding pages, such vulnerable persons are absent from expressive individualism's field of vision. Moreover, the data from Oregon, sparse though it is, undercuts the view that assisted suicide is a panacea for patients with intractable and excruciating pain.

First, the law in Oregon does not take account of the strong correlation between mental illness, especially treatable depression, and suicidal ideation and desires. There is a large body of social science evidence that shows a supermajority of persons with suicidal ideation suffer from mental illness, including a clear majority suffering from treatable depression. A review of the medical literature showed that "[t]he incidence of suicide in someone with a cancer diagnosis is approximately double the incidence of suicide in the general population."[64] For cancer patients, depression was "the major risk factor for suicidality" and such patients "were 4 times more likely to have a desire for hastened death . . . compared with those patients without depression (47 percent versus 12 percent)."[65] The National Cancer Institute also noted a strong correlation between cancer patients suffering from depression and the false sense that they were a burden to their loved ones.[66] Moreover, another study on suicidal ideation in the elderly noted that "[a] universal finding is the strong association with psychiatric illness, particularly depression."[67] It concluded that "the fact that there is a high prevalence of potentially treatable psychiatric illness in those elderly people who have both physical illness and suicidal ideation should be central in any discussion of physician-assisted suicide."[68]

These studies are highly relevant to assessing whether patients in Oregon are capable of the sort of autonomy the law assumes. Seventy-six percent of patients who have died by assisted suicide in the state suffered from cancer, and the median age of all patients was seventy-two.[69] Yet there is no mandatory screening for psychiatric illnesses that might compromise the self-determination of those who request prescriptions to end their lives. Consulting or prescribing physicians are required to order such evaluations only when they feel that a psychiatric condition might impair the judgment of the patient.[70]

The brute numbers confirm without doubt that the physicians administering Oregon's Death with Dignity Act do not regard depression as ever impairing judgment. To wit, in 2018 less than 2 percent of patients were referred for psychiatric or psychological evaluation, despite the fact that the incidence of depression among cancer patients and the elderly expressing suicidal desires is orders of magnitude higher.[71] And there is no information regarding what happened following such consultations—this data is not gathered or reported. It is possible that the small number of physicians in Oregon who participate in the Death with Dignity Act are not able to recognize depression in their encounters with patients. Only 28 percent of Oregon physicians surveyed indicated they feel confident to do so.[72] In any event, all indications are that patients suffering from treatable depression—a major but *reversible* factor in formation of suicidal desires—are regularly being prescribed lethal drugs. This raises serious questions about the reality of the "autonomy" of the patients assumed by the law. Yet later laws modeled on Oregon's have loosened these standards further. For example, in New Jersey and Colorado any psychological evaluation is designed not to discover a depression or other condition that may impair judgment, but only to determine that the patient can absorb information or communicate a decision, regardless of whether his or her judgment is impaired; in New Jersey and Hawaii the evaluation may be done by a clinical social worker instead of a psychologist or psychiatrist.

Most worrisome of all is that there is no requirement to assess voluntariness or competence *at the time the patient ingests the lethal drugs.* The median length of time between first request and death is forty-seven days.[73] Indeed, there is no obligation at all for a physician to attend the self-administration of the drugs.

Unsurprisingly, since 1998 the prescribing physician was confirmed to be present at the time of death in only 15 percent of cases.[74] As a result, Oregon has very little information on complications that arise during self-administration; in 53 percent of cases since 1998 this information is coded as "unknown."[75] Thus, there is simply no rigorous, systematic, and verifiable way to know *anything* about the state of mind of the vast supermajority of Oregon patients when they self-administered lethal drugs to take their own lives.

There is additional evidence that the patients in Oregon are not choosing to die free from internal pressures. In 2018, 54 percent of patients who obtained prescriptions reported that they were seeking to end their lives because they perceived themselves as a burden to family and friends, the highest percentage recorded since 1998.[76] Sixty-eight percent of patients had insurance or received it solely from government sources—Medicare and / or Medicaid.[77] The percentage of patients on government insurance doubled from 2008–2012 to 2013–2017.[78] These programs fully cover "aid in dying," but under Oregon's Medicaid rationing plan have payment caps on other possible life-saving interventions.[79]

The argument that assisted suicide is a necessary and humane response to the intractable suffering of terminally ill patients is somewhat belied by the evidence, scant though it is. For one thing, unlike in Europe, intolerable suffering is not a prerequisite for eligibility for assisted suicide. The threshold condition is a diagnosis of "terminal illness," though this is a famously difficult prediction to make.[80] Only 26 percent of respondents in 2018 reported that "inadequate pain control or concerns about it" motivated them to pursue a lethal prescription. This number has remained relatively stable since 1998.[81] By far the most common rationales cited for seeking assisted suicide were concerns about "losing autonomy" (92 percent) and being "less able to engage in activities making life enjoyable" (91 percent).[82]

For those terminally ill patients who are in intractable pain, there is no requirement that the consulting or prescribing physicians who administer the Death with Dignity Act have expertise or even minimal qualifications to evaluate pain or propose a plan for pain management. As a result, they are severely compromised in their ability to identify and clearly explain to patients the options for pain management or palliative care that could offer an alternative to assisted suicide. In this way, the law does not empower the autonomy of patients, nor does it respond fully to their suffering.

There is evidence that some jurisdictions that have legalized assisted suicide make less use of hospice care as a general matter. Oregon made major strides in developing hospice programs prior to legalizing assisted suicide, but since legalization its hospice utilization has fallen behind the national average rate of use.[83] Washington, Montana, and Vermont—states that have also legalized assisted suicide—likewise fall below the national average in hospice utilization rate.[84]

Concerns about diminished autonomy and lack of meaningful safeguards against neglect, fraud, abuse, duress, and mistake are amplified for vulnerable populations such as the disabled, the elderly, the marginalized, and the poor. In 1994, the New York Task Force on Life and Law, an advisory body to Governor Mario Cuomo, put the problem thus:

We believe that the practices [of assisted suicide and euthanasia] would be profoundly dangerous for large segments of the population, especially in light of the widespread failure of American medicine to treat pain adequately or to diagnose and treat depression in many cases. The risks would extend to all individuals who are ill. They would be most severe for those whose autonomy and well-being are already compromised by poverty, lack of access to good medical care, or membership in a stigmatized social group. The risks of legalizing assisted suicide and euthanasia for these individuals, in a health care system and society that cannot effectively protect against the impact of inadequate resources and ingrained social disadvantage, are likely to be extraordinary.[85]

These worries have been acknowledged by the Supreme Court (in *Glucksberg* and *Quill*) in 1997, and by the courts of last resort in New Mexico and New York in 2016 and 2017, respectively, despite claims that such worries have proven unfounded. There is simply no rigorous, verifiable system of data collection to gather sufficient information to rule out these concerns. Moreover, the absence of any requirements in the law of Oregon (and those modeled upon it) that there be mandatory evaluation for relevant psychiatric or psychological conditions, that voluntariness and competency be assessed at the time the lethal drugs are ingested, that there be consultation with next of kin, or that *anyone be present* at the time of ingestion and death, opens the door to all manner of fraud, abuse, duress, coercion, mistake, or even homicide. In short, the Oregon law's failure to take seriously the dependence, fragility, and diminished agency of embodied beings in the grip of terminal illness poses potentially grave risks for a wide circle of vulnerable people.

The logic of autonomy and compassion that animates the Oregon laws does not contain limiting principles sufficient to restrict the law to a regime of assisted suicide only for the terminally ill. Instead, the full and coherent embrace of these twin normative principles point to the acceptance of direct killing by euthanasia, for any reason, including in the absence of a request. For example, it does not fully respect the autonomy of a patient nor is it compassionate to deny him access to aid in dying because of his reasons for seeking it (for example, because he is not terminally ill). It is not compassionate, nor does it honor his freedom to allow only oral self-administration of lethal drugs as the sole means to end his life. Some patients are not capable of taking drugs orally. Similarly, it is not compassionate to deny aid in dying to those patients, including children and the cognitively disabled, who are not able to make the request on their own behalf. Thus, in countries such as Belgium and the Netherlands, the practice has moved inexorably from assisted suicide to euthanasia and from voluntary to nonvoluntary, allowing, for example, the direct killing of infants under the Groningen Protocol.[86] Moreover, the reasons for euthanasia have expanded rapidly to encompass autism, depression, and even the claim one's life seems "meaningless."

There are already proposals to liberalize the Oregon law further, to relax the definition of "terminal illness" to embrace a very wide array of conditions, to expand the definition of "self-administer" to include other delivery systems besides oral ingestion, and to allow health care providers aside from physicians to make prescriptions.[87]

Vulnerable communities have expressed deep concerns about the risks imposed by legalization of assisted suicide. Organizations that advocate for the rights of the disabled have been especially resistant to legalizing assisted suicide on the grounds that it promotes a social attitude that lives characterized by diminished physical or cognitive functioning are worse than death. Such advocates worry about assisted suicide laws enhancing already entrenched attitudes of bigotry and discriminatory practices towards the disabled. But even more frightening is the prospect of disabled persons being pressured subtly or overtly to end their lives.[88]

Relatedly, many physicians and the American Medical Association itself have opposed legalization of assisted suicide on the grounds that it would transform medicine from a healing art to its opposite and sow doubt and mistrust between doctors and patients. The AMA cautioned against the temptations that it might pose to doctors: "Health care professionals also experience great frustration at not being able to offer the patient a cure. For some, the ability to offer the patient the 'treatment' of assisted suicide may provide a sense of 'mastery over the disease and the accompanying feelings of helplessness.'"[89] Columbia University psychiatrist Paul Applebaum has expressed the worry that assisted suicide will remove incentives to treat difficult cases: "Will psychiatrists conclude from the legalization of assisted death that it is acceptable to give up on treating some patients?"[90] Conversely, he is concerned that the advent of assisted suicide might risk "inducing hopelessness among other individuals with similar conditions and removing pressure for an improvement in psychiatric and social services."[91]

ANTHROPOLOGY OF EMBODIMENT
AND TERMINAL ILLNESS

Drawing implicitly upon the anthropology of expressive individualism, the law of assisted suicide offers the freedom of the atomized individual will in response to the vulnerability, dependence, fragility, and natural limits of embodied life as it nears its end. What it offers concretely is the freedom to choose self-annihilation as a mechanism to control the conclusion of life's narrative. But because the law fails to grasp the diminished agency of a human being whose body is dying, the framework it offers is rife with risks of fraud, abuse, duress, neglect, and coercion, especially for those populations who are already vulnerable because of old age, disability, poverty, or membership in a stigmatized class.

The answer to this failure is not to seek additional processes and procedures that will allow for the autonomy of the solitary individual to annihilate himself, but rather to strengthen and support the networks of uncalculated giving and graceful receiving that cared for him when he was radically dependent as he entered the world, and will do so again as he leaves it. The role of the law is to encourage and reward the practice of just generosity, hospitality, and accompaniment in suffering (misericordia).[92] It should support the opportunities for people to learn and practice gratitude, humility, openness to the unbidden, and the tolerance of imperfection. The law should support the cultivation of the moral imagination to see our neighbor in the suffering other, and for those to see their own intrinsic and equal dignity despite suffering from a diminished and dependent condition.

More concretely, the law must allow for the aggressive palliation of pain. And it must protect vulnerable populations by not creating legal regimes that teach that their lives are not worth living, and in which they might even be pressured or coerced into ending them.

As with the prior chapters, how the law might accomplish these ends is a highly complex question for a future inquiry. Suffice it to say that it does not reflect or advance an anthropology of embodiment to legalize assisted suicide. Rather, private ordering and public action must be mobilized to redouble efforts to care for and accompany the sick and the dying while avoiding the temptation to alleviate suffering by eliminating the patient himself, whether by our hands or his own.

Conclusion

The fundamental purpose of law is to protect and promote the flourishing of persons. Accordingly, the richest understanding of the law is an *anthropological* one, obtained by inquiry into its underwriting premises about human identity and thriving. In order to be fully wise, just, and humane, the means and ends of the law must correspond to the reality of human life, humanly lived.

The defining character of this reality is *embodiment*—the fact that we experience ourselves, one another, and the world around us as living bodies. As living bodies in time, we are vulnerable, dependent, and subject to natural limits, including injury, illness, senescence, and death. Thus, both for our basic survival and to realize our potential, we need to care for one another. We need robust and expansive networks of uncalculated giving and graceful receiving populated by people who make the good of others their own good, without demand for or expectation of recompense. The goods and practices necessary to the creation and maintenance of these networks are the virtues of just generosity, hospitality, and accompaniment in suffering (misericordia), as well as gratitude, humility, openness to the unbidden, tolerance of imperfection, solidarity, respect for intrinsic equal dignity, honesty, and cultivation of moral imagination. Viewed through the lens of the anthropology of embodiment, all living members of the human family are worthy of care and protection, regardless of age, disability, cognitive capacity, dependence, and most of all, regardless of the opinions of others. Everyone can participate in the network of giving and receiving, even if only as the passive recipient of unconditional love and concern. There are no pre- or post-personal human beings in the anthropology of embodiment.

Through the nurture and protection of these networks we survive, and eventually *become* the kind of people who can give to others in proportion to their need, without the hope or expectation of receiving. In this way, we take responsibility for sustaining such networks of care so that they can endure for future generations. But, more deeply, it is through becoming a person capable of unconditional and uncalculated care of others that we become what we are meant to be. By virtue of our existence as embodied beings in time, we are made for love and friendship.

Our modern dominant anthropology in the three perennial conflicts in public bioethics—the legal disputes over abortion, assisted reproduction, and end-of-life decision-making—is insufficient. It is rooted in expressive individualism, a reductive and incomplete vision of human identity and flourishing. While this captures a truth about human particularity and freedom, it misses crucial aspects of embodied reality. Through the lens of expressive individualism, there are no unchosen obligations, relationships are instrumental and transactional, and natural givens offer no guidance for understanding or negotiating the world. Vulnerability and dependence—that of others and even our own—are not intelligible. And those around us whose freedom and agency are diminished or absent because of age, disease, or disability, are invisible and not recognized as other selves to whom we owe duties of care (in the absence of a prior agreement).

The current law of abortion, as was argued, frames the public question as a zero-sum conflict between isolated strangers, one of whom is recognized as person, with the other deemed a sub-personal being whose moral and legal status is contingent upon the private judgment of others. It offers no comprehensive support for the vulnerable persons involved, including especially the unborn child and her mother. The largely unregulated legal landscape of assisted reproductive technology creates a very particular form of "procreative liberty" that does not offer complementary protections for the broad array of uniquely vulnerable persons whose lives are touched by these procedures, including gamete donors (especially women), gestational mothers, genetic mothers and fathers, and the children conceived with the aid of assisted reproductive techniques and practices. At the end of life, the law governing refusal or termination of life sustaining measures for incompetent patients stubbornly clings to a vision of the patient as an atomized autonomous will as its animating premise, when the embodied reality of such patients is precisely the opposite. Its default aspiration is to bind the now-incompetent patient strictly and unreflectively to his prior preferences, rather than promote decision-making by the patient's loved ones, who will consider both his prior wishes as well as the needs of the patient he has now become. The law of assisted suicide similarly rests on the goods of autonomy and compassion premised on a vision of the person reduced to desire and will, neglecting entirely the profound vulnerability, dependence, and concomitant risks both to patients themselves and at-risk populations in those communities that have legalized the practice.

The influence of expressive individualism can be seen in the law's solutions to the problems posed in these domains. In response to the bodily, psychic, and financial burdens of unwanted pregnancy and parenthood, American abortion jurisprudence offers nothing more than a license to terminate the developing human life *in utero*. In response to the pains and desperation of infertility, the essentially unregulated American legal landscape offers nothing more than the freedom to create (and select for) a baby by almost any means possible. In the face of dependence on life-sustaining measures, the law offers incompetent patients the right "to be left alone" and the false promise of directing one's own care by "remote control" after cognitive abilities necessary for competence have been irretrievably lost. In the face of terminal illness, the law of assisted suicide merely offers a right to self-annihilation. These are the rights and privileges suited to atomized individual wills who inhabit a world of strife. They are limited weapons and tools of rational mastery fit for a lonely, disembodied self to defend and pursue its interests. They are not well-designed to address the complex needs and wants of a community of embodied, vulnerable, and interdependent human persons.

For such a community, the anthropology at the core of these vital conflicts of public bioethics must be augmented to correspond to the lived reality of embodiment. Issues and laws must be reframed according to the categories of connectivity of the networks of giving and receiving that embodied beings need to survive and flourish. Reframing abortion as a conflict involving a mother and her child, thus summoning the support and care of the network in which both are embedded, including the father, extended family, community, and polity (including the government itself) opens channels of care, concern, support, and summons the uncalculated giving that *everyone* owes to the mother and her child, before, during, and *after* her birth. Resituated in this way, the law is free to do the difficult work of applying its traditional principles of justification, excuse, and necessity for cases involving the proposed use of lethal force involving a mother and innocent child. Doing so allows for a full examination of the tragic conflict in all its complexity, depending on the concrete facts and circumstances of each case. Needless to say, it is beyond the scope of this inquiry to offer specific rules of application of such principles without such context.

Similarly, the public questions of assisted reproductive technology must be reframed within the anthropology of embodiment and the normative category of *parenthood*—the network of uncalculated giving and receiving *par excellence*—embracing all of the participants including genetic parents, gestational mother, rearing parents, and child to be (at all stages of development from conception to birth). All are entitled to the protection, support, and care of the networks in which they are situated. The fundamental aspiration of the law should be that every child conceived by assisted reproductive technology should find her way to a home with parents who will welcome her as a gift to be loved unconditionally. This ultimate purpose should animate every decision by all involved as people seek medical care in their quest to become parents.

As for the public bioethics of the end of life, the anthropology undergirding the law must be honest in embracing the reality of embodiment in time, with the vulnerability and dependence that follows. Accordingly, the law should adopt measures designed to protect against abuse, abandonment, fraud, and mistake, while facilitating care for the patient in his current state, rather than as he was or as we might wish him to be. The law should encourage and offer care, not open a pathway to suicide by transforming the healing art of medicine into a handmaiden of death.

In all of these vital areas, the role of the law should be to help create, support, and protect the networks of giving and receiving on which we all depend in our vulnerability as embodied beings in time. It should encourage the goods, virtues, and practices that sustain these networks. The law must encourage the cultivation of the moral imagination, allowing persons to see others to whom they owe a duty of care, or from whom they can make a plea for support. And where such networks fail or are altogether absent, the law must intervene to protect the vulnerable from exploitation and harm, and from the temptation to harm others or even themselves in the pursuit of their own desires and interests.

These are, of course, proposals formulated at the level of high principle—purposes and ends—and do not begin speak to the complexities of how one might make them operational in light of the current givens of the American legal (not to mention political) landscape. They do not even specify which of the panoply of mechanisms available to the law might be deployed towards such ends. Such possibilities include a broad spectrum ranging from passive or active encouragement of private ordering within voluntary associations to more intrusive modes of intervention to regulate behavior directly, with many fine-grained alternatives in between.

But before making such changes, we must reorient our thinking toward the meaning and consequences of our individual and shared lives as bodies in time. This book is a proposal, made in friendship and solidarity and intended to be received in this spirit. It is a proposal for a more wise, just, humane, and fully *human* public bioethics that begins by remembering the body.

NOTES

ACKNOWLEDGMENTS

INDEX

NOTES

INTRODUCTION

1. Robert Bellah et al., *Habits of the Heart: Individualism and Commitment in American Life* (Berkeley: University of California Press, 1985), 47; Charles Taylor, *Philosophical Papers,* vol. 2: *Philosophy and the Human Sciences* (Cambridge: Cambridge University Press, 1985), 187–210.

2. Alasdair MacIntyre, *Dependent Rational Animals: Why Human Beings Need the Virtues* (Chicago: Open Court Publishing, 1999), 5.

3. Ibid., 121.

4. Ibid., 119; Michael J. Sandel, *The Case Against Perfection: Ethics in the Age of Genetic Engineering* (Cambridge, MA: Harvard University Press, 2009), 45.

I. A GENEALOGY OF AMERICAN PUBLIC BIOETHICS

1. 45 C.F.R. § 46.102 (2019).

2. Henry K. Beecher, "Ethics and Clinical Research," *New England Journal of Medicine* 274 (1966): 1354–1360.

3. Jean Heller, "Human Guinea Pigs: Syphilis Patients Died Untreated," *Washington Evening Star,* July 25, 1972, A1.

4. Victor Cohn, "Live-Fetus Research Debated," *Washington Post,* April 10, 1973, A1.

5. Vincent J. Kopp, "Henry Knowles Beecher and the Development of Informed Consent in Anesthesia Research," *Anesthesiology* 90 (1999): 1756–1765.

6. Beecher, "Ethics and Clinical Research," 1355.

7. Ibid., 1355.

8. Ibid., 1356.

9. Ibid., 1357.

10. Ibid., 1358.

11. Ibid.

12. Ibid.

13. Ibid., 1354.

14. Ibid.

15. Heller, "Human Guinea Pigs," A1.

16. Ibid.

17. DeNeen L. Brown, "'You've Got Bad Blood': The Horror of the Tuskegee Syphilis Experiment," *Washington Post,* May 16, 2017.

18. Ibid.

19. Ibid.

20. Cohn, "Live-Fetus Research Debated," Al.

21. Ibid.

22. Victor Cohn, "NIH Vows Not to Fund Fetus Work," *Washington Post,* April 13, 1973, A1.

23. Victor Cohn, "Scientists and Fetus Research," *Washington Post,* April 15,1973, A1.

24. Ibid.

25. Geoffrey Chamberlain, "An Artificial Placenta: The Development of an Extracorporeal System for Maintenance of Immature Infants with Respiratory Problems," *American Journal of Obstetrics and Gynecology* 100 (1968): 615–626.

26. Peter A. J. Adam et al., "Cerebral Oxidation of Glucose and Dbeta-Hydroxy Butyrate in the Isolated Perfused Human Head," *Transactions of the American Pediatrics Society* 309 (1973): 81.

27. In May of 2013, Dr. Gosnell would be sentenced to three life terms in prison for murdering three newborns who survived their attempted abortions, and manslaughter for the death of patient Karnamaya Mongar, who died of an overdose of sedatives in his clinic.

28. U.S. Congress, Senate, Committee on Labor and Public Welfare, *Quality of Health Care—Human Experimentation: Hearings before the Subcommittee on Health*, 93rd Cong., 1st sess., 1973.

29. Ibid.

30. National Research Act of 1974, Public Law 93–348, *U.S. Statutes at Large* 88 (1974): 342–354.

31. Ibid., 349.

32. Ibid., 350.

33. Ibid.

34. Ibid., 353.

35. U.S. Congress, Senate, Committee on Labor and Public Welfare, *Fetal Research: Hearing before the Subcommittee on Health*, 93rd Cong., 2nd sess., 1974.

36. Ibid., 98.

37. Ibid., 81.

38. U.S. National Commission for the Protection of Human Subjects of Biomedical and Behavioral Research, *Research on the Fetus* (1975), 74.

39. Ibid., 74.

40. Ibid., 68.

41. The Church Amendments are codified at 42 U.S.C. § 300a–7.

42. Michael J. New, "Hyde @ 40: Analyzing the Impact of the Hyde Amendment," *Charlotte Lozier Institute*, September 2016, 5, https://s27589 .pcdn.co/wp-content/uploads/2016/09/OP_hyde_9.28.3.pdf.

43. *Maher v. Roe*, 423 U.S. 464 (1977).

44. *In re Quinlan*, 355 A.2d 647 (N.J. 1976).

45. Robert D. McFadden, "Karen Ann Quinlan, 31, Dies; Focus of '76 Right to Die Case," *New York Times*, June 12, 1985, A1.

46. Department of Health, Education, and Welfare, Ethics Advisory Board, "Report and Conclusions: HEW Support of Research Involving Human In Vitro Fertilization and Embryo Transfer," *Federal Register* 44, no. 118 (May 4, 1979): 35033–35058.

47. U.S. National Commission for the Protection of Human Subjects of Biomedical and Behavioral Research, *The Belmont Report: Ethical Principles and Guidelines for the Protection of Human Subjects in Research* (1979), https://www.hhs.gov/ohrp/regulations-and-policy/belmont-report/read -the-belmont-report/index.html.

48. President's Commission for the Study of Ethical Problems in Medicine and Biomedical and Behavioral Research, *Defining Death* (1981), 2.

49. *Bowen v. American Hospital Association,* 476 U.S. 610 (1986).

50. Child Abuse Amendments of 1984, Public Law 98–457, *U.S. Statutes at Large* 98 (1984): 1749–1764.

51. National Organ Transplant Act, Public Law 98–507, *U.S. Statutes at Large* 98 (1984): 2339–2348.

52. The Department of Health and Human Services, one of the federal agencies that has adopted the "Common Rule," has codified its regulations in 45 C.F.R. § 46.

53. Health Research Extension Act of 1985, Public Law 99–158, *U.S. Statutes at Large* 99 (1985): 820–886.

54. *Harris v. McRae,* 448 U.S. 297 (1980).

55. *Webster v. Reproductive Health Services,* 492 U.S. 490 (1989).

56. *In re Baby M,* 537 A.2d 1227 (N.J. 1988).

57. Fertility Clinic Success Rate and Certification Act of 1992, Public Law 102–493, *U.S. Statutes at Large* 106 (1992): 3146–3152.

58. *Davis v. Davis,* 842 S.W.2d 588 (Tenn. 1992).

59. *Planned Parenthood v. Casey,* 505 U.S. 833 (1992).

60. National Institutes of Health Revitalization Act of 1993, Public Law 103–43, *U.S. Statutes at Large* 107 (1993): 122–219.

61. Public Law 104–99, *U.S. Statutes at Large* 110 (1996): 34.

62. James A. Thomson et al., "Embryonic Stem Cell Lines Derived from Human Blastocysts," *Science* 282 (1998): 1145–1147.

63. 497 U.S. 261 (1990).

64. William Claiborne, "'Death With Dignity' Measure May Make Oregon National Battleground," *Washington Post,* June 27, 1997, A19.

65. *Washington v. Glucksberg,* 521 U.S. 702 (1997); *Vacco v. Quill,* 521 U.S. 793 (1997).

66. George W. Bush, "President Discusses Stem Cell Research," August 9, 2001, https://georgewbush-whitehouse.archives.gov/news/releases/2001/08/20010809-2.html.

67. Andrew Pollack, "Measure Passed, California Weights Its Future as a Stem Cell Epicenter," *New York Times,* Nov. 4, 2004.

68. The "Weldon" Amendment is now permanently codified. Leahy-Smith American Invents Act, Public Law 112–29, *U.S. Statutes at Large* 125 (2011): 340.

69. Shinya Yamanaka et al., "Induction of Pluripotent Stem Cells from Adult Human Fibroblasts by Defined Factors," *Cell* 131 (2007): 861–872; James A. Thomson et al., "Induced Pluripotent Stem Cell Lines Derived from Human Somatic Cells," *Science* 318 (2007): 1917–1920.

70. "Executive Order 13505 of March 9, 2009, Removing Barriers to Responsible Scientific Research Involving Human Stem Cells," *Code of Federal Regulations*, title 3 (2010): 229–230, https://www.govinfo.gov/content/pkg/CFR-2010-title3-vol1/pdf/CFR-2010-title3-vol1.pdf.

71. *Stenberg v. Carhart*, 530 U.S. 914 (2000).

72. *Gonzales v Carhart*, 550 U.S. 124 (2007).

73. Born Alive Infants Protection Act of 2002, Public Law 107–207, *U.S. Statutes at Large* 116 (2002): 926.

74. Unborn Victims of Violence Act of 2004, Public Law 108–212, *U.S. Statutes at Large* 118 (2004): 568–570.

75. Consolidated Appropriations Act, Public Law 111–117, *U.S. Statutes at Large* 123 (2009): 3034.

76. Fetus Farming Prohibition Act of 2006, Public Law 109–242, *U.S. Statutes at Large* 120 (2006): 570–571.

77. Martin Jinek et al., "A Programmable Dual-RNA-Guided DNA Endonuclease in Adaptive Bacterial Immunity," *Science* 337 (2012): 816–821.

78. Feng Zhang, "Genome Engineering Using the CRISPR-Cas9 System," *Nature Protocols* 8 (2013): 2281–2308.

79. Puping Liang et al., "CRISPR/Cas9-Mediated Gene Editing in Human Triponuclear Zygotes," *Protein & Cell* 6 (2015): 363–372.

80. David A. Prentice, "Modest but Meaningful Protection from Human Embryo Genetic Manipulation," *Townhall*, December 17, 2015, https://townhall.com/columnists/davidaprentice/2015/12/17/modest-but-meaningful-protection-from-human-embryo-genetic-manipulation-n2094746.

81. John Aach et al., "Addressing the Ethical Issues Raised by Synthetic Human Entities with Embryo-Like Features," *eLife* (2017): 1–20.

82. Shoukhrat Mitalipov et al., "Correction of a Pathogenic Gene Mutation in Human Embryos," *Nature* 548 (2017): 413–419.

83. Charlie Osborne, "Meet Lulu and Nana, Claimed to be the World's First Gene-Edited Children," *ZDNet*, November 26, 2018, https://www.zdnet.com/article/meet-lulu-and-nana-the-worlds-first-reported-gene-edited-children/.

84. Debra Goldschmidt, "Jahi McMath, California Teen at Center of Brain-Death Controversy, Has Died," *CNNHealth*, June 29, 2018, https://www.cnn.com/2018/06/29/health/jahi-mcmath-brain-dead-teen-death/index.html.

85. Allan Turner, "Pasadena Man Whose Life-Threatening Illness Spurred Challenge to Texas Law Dies at Hospital," *Houston Chronicle*, December 23, 2015, https://www.chron.com/news/houston-texas/houston/article/Pasadena-man-whose-life-threatening-illness-6717843.php.

86. *Whole Woman's Health v. Hellerstedt*, 136 S.Ct. 2292 (2016).

2. AN ANTHROPOLOGICAL SOLUTION

1. James M. Gustafson, "Genetic Therapy: Ethical and Religious Reflections," *Journal of Contemporary Health, Law, and Policy* 8 (1992): 191.

2. Ernst Cassirer, *An Essay on Man: An Introduction to a Philosophy of Human Culture* (New Haven: Yale University Press, 1992), 1.

3. Whitney J. Oates, ed., *Basic Writings of Saint Augustine*, vol. 1 (Grand Rapids, MI: Baker Publishing Group, 1993), 172.

4. Psalm 8:4 (RSV).

5. Kenneth L. Schmitz, "Reconstructing the Person: A Meditation on the Meaning of Personality," *Crisis Magazine*, April 1, 1999, https://www.crisismagazine.com/1999/reconstructing-the-person-a-meditation-on-the-meaning-of-personality.

6. Boethius, *Theological Tractates and the Consolation of Philosophy*, ed. H. F. Stewart and E. K. Rand (Cambridge, MA: Harvard University Press, 1918); John Locke, *Essay on Human Understanding*, ed. P. H. Nidditch (Oxford: Oxford University Press, 1975); Joseph Fletcher, "Indicators of Humanhood: A Tentative Profile of Man," *The Hastings Center Report* 2 (1972): 1–4; Mary Anne Warren, "On the Moral and Legal Status of Abortion," *The Monist* 57 (1973).

7. Quoted in Edmund D. Pelegrino, "Toward A Richer Bioethics: A Conclusion," in Charles R. Taylor and Robert Dell'Oro, eds., *Health and Human Flourishing: Religion, Medicine, and Moral Anthropology* (Georgetown: Georgetown University Press, 2006), 248.

8. John H. Evans, *What Is a Human? What the Answer Means for Human Life* (Oxford: Oxford University Press, 2016).

9. Robert Bellah et al., *Habits of the Heart: Individualism and Commitment in American Life* (Berkeley: University of California Press, 1985), 27.

10. Roderick T. Long, "The Classical Roots of Radical Individualism," *Social Philosophy and Policy* 24 (2007): 262–297.

11. Tibor R. Machan, *Classical Individualism: The Supreme Importance of Each Human Being* (London: Routledge, 1996).

12. Yehoshua Arieli, *Individualism and Nationalism in American Ideology* (Cambridge, MA: Harvard University Press, 1964).

13. Alexis de Tocqueville, *Democracy in America*, vol. 2, trans. George Lawrence (New York: Harper, 2006), 508.

14. Ibid.

15. Bellah, *Habits of the Heart*, 334.

16. Machan, *Classical Individualism*.

17. Adam Smith, *An Inquiry into the Nature and Causes of the Wealth of Nations* (Oxford: Oxford University Press, 2008).

18. Bellah, *Habits of the Heart*, 47.

19. Charles Taylor, *Philosophical Papers*, vol. 2: *Philosophy and the Human Sciences* (Cambridge: Cambridge University Press, 1985), 189.

20. Ibid., 201.

21. Ibid.

22. Ibid., 202.

23. Long, "The Classical Roots of Radical Individualism," 262–297.

24. Michael J. Sandel, *Public Philosophy: Essays on Morality in Politics* (Cambridge, MA: Harvard University Press, 2005), 160.

25. John Rawls, *A Theory of Justice* (Cambridge, MA: Harvard University Press, 2009), 491.

26. Ibid.

27. Sandel, *Public Philosophy*, 162.

28. Michael J. Sandel, "The Procedural Republic and the Unencumbered Self," *Political Theory* 12 (1984), 87.

29. Sandel, *Public Philosophy*, 164.

30. Bellah, *Habits of the Heart*, 334.

31. Ibid., 33.

32. Ralph Waldo Emerson, *Journals of Ralph Waldo Emerson*, vol. 3 (Boston: Houghton Mifflin, 1912).

33. Bellah, *Habits of the Heart*, 48.

34. Charles Taylor, *Sources of the Self: The Making of Modern Identity* (Cambridge, MA: Harvard University Press, 1989); Charles Taylor, *Malaise of Modernity* (Toronto: House of Anansi, 1991); Charles Taylor, *Multiculturalism: Examining the Politics of Recognition* (Princeton: Princeton University Press, 1993); Charles Taylor, *(1993), A Secular Age* (Cambridge, MA: Harvard University Press, 2007).

35. Taylor, *The Malaise of Modernity*, 16.

36. Ibid., 17.

37. Ibid., 16.

38. Ibid., 17.

39. Taylor, *Sources of the Self*, 375.

40. Plato, *Theatetus*, trans. Robin H. Waterfield (London: Penguin, 1987), 160d9.

41. Charles Taylor, *The Ethics of Authenticity* (Cambridge, MA: Harvard University Press, 1992).

42. Alfred Tennyson, "Ulysses," *Poetry Foundation*, https://www.poetryfoundation.org/poems/45392/ulysses.

43. George Gordon Noel Byron, *Manred: A Dramatic Poem* (London: John Murray, 1817).

44. John Milton, *Paradise Lost*, bk. 5 (London: Penguin, 2000), lines 854–866.

45. Taylor, *Sources of the Self*, 376.

46. Taylor, *The Malaise of Modernity*, 32.

47. Alasdair MacIntyre, *After Virtue: A Study in Moral Theory* (Notre Dame, IN: University of Notre Dame Press, 1981), 11–12.

48. Ibid., 220.

49. Ibid., 75.

50. Sandel, "The Procedural Republic and the Unencumbered Self," 86.

51. Sandel, *Public Philosophy*, 164.

52. Alasdair MacIntyre, *Dependent Rational Animals: Why Human Beings Need the Virtues* (Chicago: Open Court Publishing, 1999), 5.

53. Ibid., 73.

54. Ibid., 108.

55. Ibid., 91.

56. Bertrand de Jouvenel, *The Pure Theory of Politics* (Carmel, IN: Liberty Fund, 2000), 61.

57. Ibid., 60.

58. Milton, *Paradise Lost*, bk. 5, lines 859–861.

59. MacIntyre, *Dependent Rational Animals*, 82.

60. Charles Taylor, *Philosophical Papers*, vol. 2: *Philosophy and the Human Sciences* (Cambridge: Cambridge University Press, 1985), 202.

61. Sandel, *Public Philosophy*, 166.

62. MacIntyre, *After Virtue*, 216.

63. Ibid., 216.

64. Sandel, *Public Philosophy*, 168.

65. Charles Taylor, *Multiculturalism: Examining the Politics of Recognition* (Princeton: Princeton University Press, 1994), 32.

66. MacIntyre, *After Virtue*, 221

67. Michael J. Sandel, *Liberalism and Its Critics* (New York: New York University Press, 1984), 173.

68. Roger Scruton, *On Human Nature* (Princeton: Princeton University Press, 2018), 116.

69. Bertrand de Jouvenel, *Power: The Natural History of its Growth* (London: Batchworth, 1952), 414.

70. Aleksandr Solzhenitsyn, "We Have Ceased to See the Purpose," in Aleksandr Solzhenitsyn, *The Solzhenitsyn Reader: New and Essential Writings, 1947–2005*, eds. Edward E. Ericson and Daniel J. Mahoney (Wilmington, DE: Intercollegiate Studies Institute, 2009).

71. John H. Evans, *What Is a Human? What the Answer Means for Human Life* (Oxford: Oxford University Press, 2016), 13.

72. Ibid., 21.

73. Bellah, *Habits of the Heart*, 38.

74. MacIntyre, *Dependent Rational Animals*, 146.

75. Ibid., 146.

76. Ibid., 119.

77. Ibid., 121.

78. Michael J. Sandel, "The Case Against Perfection," *The Atlantic,* April 2004, https://www.theatlantic.com/magazine/archive/2004/04/the -case-against-perfection/302927/.

79. Michael J. Sandel, *The Case Against Perfection: Ethics in the Age of Genetic Engineering* (Cambridge, MA: Harvard University Press, 2009), 45.

80. MacIntyre, *Dependent Rational Animals,* 91.

81. Blaise Pascal, *Pensées* (London: Penguin, 1995).

82. Michael J. Sandel, "The Case Against Perfection," *The Atlantic,* April 2004, https://www.theatlantic.com/magazine/archive/2004/04/the -case-against-perfection/302927/.

83. Keith Phipps, "Close Encounters of the Third Kind," *Slate,* November 20, 2007, http://www.slate.com/articles/arts/dvdextras/2007/11 /close_encounters_of_the_third_kind.html.

84. Quote available at https://www.officetally.com/the-office-the -whale.

85. Bellah, *Habits of the Heart,* 153.

86. Roscoe Pound, *The Spirit of the Common Law* (London: Routledge, 1999), 13.

87. Mary Ann Glendon, "Looking for 'Persons' in the Law," *First Things,* December 2006, https://www.firstthings.com/article/2006/12 /looking-forpersonsin-the-law.

3. IN CASES OF ABORTION

1. Paul Benjamin Linton, "Enforcement of State Abortion Statutes after Roe: A State-by-State Analysis," *University of Detroit Law Review* 67 (1990): 158–160.

2. *Roe v. Wade,* 314 F. Supp. 1217 (N.D. Tex. 1970).

3. *Griswold v. Connecticut,* 381 U.S. 479, 487–499 (1965) (Goldberg, J., concurring).

4. *Griswold v. Connecticut,* 381 U.S. 479 (1965) (opinion of Douglas, J.).

5. *Griswold v. Connecticut,* 381 U.S. at 487–499 (1965) (Goldberg, J., concurring).

6. *Roe v. Wade,* 314 F. Supp. 1217, 1224 (N.D. Tex. 1970).

7. See United States Courts, "Appellate Courts and Cases—Journalist's Guide," https://www.uscourts.gov/statistics-reports/appellate-courts-and-cases-journalists-guide.

8. *Roe v. Wade*, 314 F. Supp. at 1224.

9. *Roe v. Wade*, 410 U.S. 113 (1973).

10. Ibid., 152–154.

11. U.S. Const. amend. IV.

12. See *Griswold v. Connecticut*, 381 U.S. at 484 (1965) (opinion of Douglas, J.) ("The foregoing cases suggest that specific guarantees in the Bill of Rights have penumbras, formed by emanation from those guarantees that help give them life and substance.").

13. *Roe v. Wade*, 410 U.S. at 152–154.

14. *Lochner v. New York*, 198 U.S. 45 (1905).

15. See *Roe v. Wade*, 410 U.S. at 152 (citing *Palko v. Connecticut*, 302 U.S. 219 [1937]).

16. *Roe v. Wade*, 410 U.S. at 152.

17. Ibid., 152–154.

18. Randolph, A. Raymond, "Before *Roe v. Wade:* Judge Friendly's Draft Abortion Opinion," *Harvard Journal of Law and Public Policy* 29 (2006): 1037–1038.

19. Joseph W. Dellapenna, *Dispelling the Myths of Abortion History* (Durham, N.C.: Carolina Academic Press, 2006), 315.

20. 1867 Ohio Senate J. App., 233–234.

21. *Roe v. Wade*, 410 U.S. at 153.

22. Ibid.

23. Ibid., 163.

24. Ibid., 155.

25. Ibid., 156–159.

26. Ibid., 159.

27. Ibid.

28. Ibid., 162.

29. Ibid., 163.

30. Ibid.

31. Ibid.

32. Ibid., 163–164.

33. *Doe v. Bolton*, 410 U.S. 179 (1973).

34. Ibid., 183.

35. Ibid., 183–184.

36. Ibid., 201.

37. Ibid., 191.

38. Ibid., 191–192.

39. Judith Jarvis Thomson, "A Defense of Abortion," *Philosophy and Public Affairs* 1 (Autumn 1971): 47–66.

40. Ibid., 47.

41. Ibid., 55.

42. Ibid., 58–59.

43. Ibid., 59.

44. Ibid., 64.

45. Ibid., 65.

46. Ibid., 65–66.

47. Ibid., 66.

48. Michael Tooley, "Abortion and Infanticide," *Philosophy and Public Affairs* 2 (Autumn 1972): 37–65.

49. Mary Anne Warren, "On the Moral and Legal Status of Abortion," *The Monist* 57 (January 1973): 43–61.

50. Tooley, "Abortion and Infanticide," 44.

51. Ibid., 45.

52. Ibid., 47.

53. Ibid., 42, 52.

54. Warren, "On the Moral and Legal Status of Abortion," 43.

55. *Roe v. Wade*, 410 U.S. at 156–157.

56. Warren, "On the Moral and Legal Status of Abortion," 50.

57. Ibid., 47.

58. Ibid., 43.

59. Ibid., 52.

60. Ibid., 55.

61. Ibid.

62. Ibid., 56.

63. Ibid., 60–61.

64. Mary Anne Warren, "Postscript on Infanticide, February 26, 1982" in *The Problem of Abortion,* ed. Joel Feinberg (Belmont, CA: Wadsworth Publishing Co., 1984), 117.

65. Ibid.

66. See David Boonin, *A Defense of Abortion* (Cambridge: Cambridge University Press, 2002); Alberto Giublini and Francesca Minerva, "After-Birth Abortion: Why Should the Baby Live?" *Journal of Medical Ethics* 39 (2013): 261–163; Peter Singer, *Practical Ethics* (Cambridge: Cambridge University Press, 2011).

67. *Roe v. Wade,* 410 U.S. at 162.

68. *Thornburgh v. American College of Obstetricians and Gynecologists,* 476 U.S. 747, 794 (1986) (White, J., dissenting).

69. Pennsylvania Abortion Control Act of 1989, 18 Pa. Cons. Stat. § 3201–3220 (1989).

70. *Planned Parenthood v. Casey,* 505 U.S. 833 (1992).

71. *Planned Parenthood v. Casey,* 505 U.S. at 846.

72. Ibid.

73. Ibid. (citing *Daniels v. Williams,* 474 U.S. 327, 331 [1986]).

74. Ibid., 849.

75. Ibid., 850–851.

76. Ibid., 851.

77. Ibid., 852.

78. Ibid.

79. Ibid., 854–864.

80. Ibid., 864–869.

81. Ibid., 856.

82. Ibid., 869.

83. Ibid., 876.

84. Ibid., 878.

85. Ibid., 879.

86. Ibid., 870.

87. Ibid.

88. Ibid., 851.

89. Ibid., 852.

90. Ibid., 856.

91. Martin Haskell, "Dilation and Extraction for Late Second Trimester Abortions," Presented at the National Abortion Federation Risk Management Seminar *Second Trimester Abortion: From Every Angle* (September 13, 1992) 27–34.

92. Ibid., 30.

93. Ibid., 28.

94. Ronald Powers, "Moynihan, in Break with Clinton, Condemns Abortion Procedure," *Associated Press*, May 14, 1996, https://www.apnews.com/6e619434f53783d58df59a7f1331c8b0.

95. David Stout, "An Abortion Rights Advocate Says He Lied About Procedure," *New York Times*, February 26, 1997, A12.

96. Ibid.; Roy Rivenburg, "Partial Truths," *Los Angeles Times*, April 2, 1997, https://www.latimes.com/archives/la-xpm-1997-04-02-ls-44326-story.html.

97. *Stenberg v. Carhart*, 530 U.S. 914 (2000).

98. Ibid., 930.

99. Ibid., 934.

100. See ibid., 964 (Kennedy, J., dissenting) ("The Court awards each physician a veto power over the State's medical judgment that the procedures should not be performed.").

101. Frank Murray, "Daschle Bill May Not Ban Anything; Abortionists Could Use Own Judgment," *The Washington Times*, May 15, 1997, A1.

102. *Stenberg v. Carhart*, 530 U.S. at 935–936.

103. Ibid., 937.

104. Ibid., 937 (O'Connor, J., concurring).

105. Ibid., 972 (Kennedy, J., dissenting).

106. Ibid.

107. Ibid., 1015.

108. Ibid., 966.

109. Ibid., 967.

110. Ibid.

111. Partial Birth Abortion Act of 2003, Public Law 108-105, *U.S. Statutes at Large* 117 (2003): 1201–1208.

112. Ibid., 1207.

113. *Gonzales v. Carhart*, 550 U.S. 124 (2007) [hereinafter *Carhart II*].

114. Ibid., 147.

115. Ibid., 170 (Ginsburg, J., dissenting) (citing *Planned Parenthood v. Casey*, 505 U.S. at 851–85).

116. Ibid., 172 (Ginsburg, J. dissenting).

117. Ibid., 159 (opinion of Kennedy, J.) (citing Brief for Sandra Cano, The Former "Mary Doe" of *Doe v. Bolton*, and 180 Women Injure by Abortion as Amici Curiae in Support of Petitioners, *Gonzales v. Carhart*, 550 U.S. 124 [2007] [No. 05-380]); Avi Selk, "'Jane Roe' Made Abortion Legal. Then a Minister Made Her Rethink," *Washington Post*, February 18, 2017, https://www.washingtonpost.com/news/acts-of-faith/wp/2017/02/18/jane-roe-made-abortion-legal-then-a-minister-made-her-repent/.

118. *Carhart II*, 505 U.S. at 185 (Ginsburg, J., dissenting).

119. Ibid., 183–184 (citing opinion of Kennedy, J., at 159).

120. Ibid., 187.

121. Jon Hurdle and Trip Gabriel, "Philadelphia Abortion Doctor Guilty of Murder in Later-Term Procedures," *New York Times*, May 14, 2013, A12.

122. Sabrina Tavernise, "Squalid Abortion Clinic Escaped State Oversight," *New York Times*, January 23, 2011, A25.

123. *Whole Woman's Health v. Lakey*, 46 F. Supp. 673 (W.D. Tex. 2014), rev'd in part by *Whole Woman's Health v. Cole*, 790 F.3d 563 (5th Cir. 2015).

124. *Whole Woman's Health v. Hellerstedt*, 136 S.Ct. 2292 (2016).

125. Ibid., 2309.

126. Ibid., 2320.

127. Ibid., 2310–2318.

128. Ibid., 2330 (Thomas, J., dissenting) (citing Antonin Scalia, "The Rule of Law as a Law of Rules," University of Chicago Law Review, 56 (1989): 1182).

129. *Whole Woman's Health v. Hellerstedt*, 136 S.Ct. at 2343 (Alito, J., dissenting).

130. S.B. 240, 2019–2020 Gen. Assemb, Reg. Sess. (N.Y. 2019).

131. Ibid.

132. H.B. 2495, 101st Gen. Assemb., Reg. Sess. (Ill. 2019).

133. See *Immigration and Naturalization Service v. St. Cyr*, 533 U.S. 289, 342 (Scalia, J., dissenting).

134. *Hodes & Nauser, MDs, P. A. v. Schmidt*, 440 P.3d 461, 466 (Kan. 2019).

135. Ibid., 520 (Stegall, J., dissenting).

136. Ibid., 480 (per curiam opinion).

137. Ibid., 483.

138. *Planned Parenthood v. Casey,* 505 U.S. at 856.

139. Of course, some commentators will argue that only women are permitted to speak or write about the reality and meaning of procreation, pregnancy, and birth. While this perspective is surely understandable, especially in light of historic unjust and shameful repression of women's voices and exclusion of their essential insights on these and other matters, it is not finally persuasive. Since the first emergence of *homo sapiens,* every human being alive or dead directly experienced and benefitted from a woman's pregnancy, and thus has standing to explore its human meaning, albeit with appropriate trepidation and deference to others who understand it more deeply owing to her personal experience carrying a human life *in utero.*

140. Sidney Callahan, "Abortion and the Sexual Agenda," in *Moral Issues and Christian Responses,* ed. Patricia Beattie Jung and L. Shannon Jung (Minneapolis: Fortress Press, 2013), 365.

141. See Gilbert Meilaender, *Not by Nature but by Grace: Forming Families Through Adoption* (Notre Dame, IN: University of Notre Dame Press, 2016).

142. Carl Schneider, "Bioethics in the Language of the Law," *Hastings Center Report* 24, no. 4 (1994): 21.

143. Alasdair MacIntyre, *Dependent Rational Animals: Why Human Beings Need the Virtues* (London: Duckworth, 1999).

144. Of course, the Court seems to distinguish the moral status of the fetus pre- and post-viability, but even this becomes functionally conflated in light of *Doe v. Bolton's* health exception.

145. This is not to say that other species are not worthy of care, concern, and legal protection.

146. To be clear, this is a proposal very much at odds with the premises held by prominent supporters of abortion rights, including perhaps Justice Ruth Bader Ginsburg. In a recent opinion concurring in part and dissenting in part from the Supreme Court's decision to affirm the constitutionality of an Indiana law requiring the humane disposition of fetal remains following abortion and decline to review the constitutionality of that state's ban on abortions solely for reasons of genetic, racial, or sex discrimination, Justice Ginsburg stated explicitly: "A woman who exercises her constitutionally protected right to terminate a pregnancy is not a

'mother.'" *Box v. Planned Parenthood*, 139 S.Ct. 1780, 1793 n.2 (2019) (Ginsburg, J., concurring in part). She was responding to Justice Thomas's use of the word to refer to a woman who has obtained an abortion, so it is possible that she meant after an abortion is completed, a woman is no longer a mother. But it is also possible she meant to say that it is solely the intention to parent that determines parenthood rather than a biological reality. It is this latter notion that the anthropology of embodiment rejects.

147. Reva Siegal, "Abortion," in *Companion to American Thought*, ed. Richard Wightman Fox and James T. Kloppenberg (Oxford: Blackwell Publishers, 1995), 2.

4. assisted reproduction

John A. Robertson, *Children of Choice* (Princeton, NJ: Princeton University Press, 1994), 4.

Dr. Gerald Schatten, "Session 6: Assisted Reproductive Technologies in the Genomics Era," testimony, President's Council on Bioethics, December 13, 2002.

1. R. G. Edwards, B. D. Bavister, and P. C. Steptoe, "Early Stages of Fertilization *in vitro* of Human Oocytes Matured *in vitro*," *Nature* 221 (1969): 632–635.

2. Suzanna White Junod, "FDA's Approval of the First Oral Contraceptive, Enovid," *FDA*, https://www.fda.gov/media/110456/download.

3. *Roe v. Wade*, 410 U.S. 113 (1973).

4. Victor Cohn, "First U.S. Test-Tube Baby Is Born," *Washington Post*, December 29, 1981, A1.

5. Ibid.

6. Maggie Fox, "A Million Babies Have Been Born in the U.S. With Fertility Help," *NBC News*, April 28, 2017, https://www.nbcnews.com/health/health-news/million-babies-have-been-born-u-s-fertility-help-n752506.

7. Centers for Disease Control and Prevention, American Society for Reproductive Medicine, Society for Assisted Reproductive Technology, "2016 Assisted Reproductive Technology National Summary Report," *US Dept of Health and Human Services*, October 2018, https://www.cdc.gov/art/pdf/2016-report/ART-2016-National-Summary-Report.pdf, 2

[hereinafter "2016 National Summary Report"]; Brady E. Hamilton et al., "Births: Provisional Data for 2016," *CDC*, June 2017, https://www.cdc.gov /nchs/data/vsrr/reporto02.pdf, 1.

8. "2016 National Summary Report," 50.

9. Tamar Lewin, "Industry's Growth Leads to Leftover Embryos, and Painful Choices," *New York Times*, June 18, 2015, A1.

10. See Catherine A. McMahon et al., "Embryo Donation for Medical Research: Attitudes and Concerns of Potential Donors," *Human Reproduction*, 18 (2003): 871–877; Kay Elder, "Human Embryos Donated for Research: A Gift that Goes on Giving," *BioNews*, October 16, 2017, https://www.bionews.org.uk/page_96220.

11. Alan Zarembo, "An Ethics Debate Over Embryos on the Cheap," *Los Angeles Times*, November 29, 2012, https://www.latimes.com/health /la-xpm-2012-nov-19-la-me-embryo-20121120-story.html.

12. David Plotz, "Darwin's Engineer," *Los Angeles Times*, June 5, 2005, https://www.latimes.com/la-tm-spermbank23juno5-story.html.

13. Sarah M. Capelouto et al., "Sex Selection for Non-medical Indications: A Survey of Current Pre-implantation Genetic Screening Practices among U.S. ART Clinics," *Journal of Assisted Reproduction and Genetics* 35 (2018): 412–413.

14. Hannah Devlin, "IVF Couples Could Be Able to Choose the 'Smartest' Embryo," *The Guardian*, May 24, 2019, https://www.theguardian .com/society/2019/may/24/ivf-couples-could-be-able-to-choose-the -smartest-embryo.

15. Ibid.

16. 42 U.S.C. § 263a-7.

17. Annick Delvigne and Serge Rozenberg, "Epidemiology and Prevention of Ovarian Hyperstimulation Syndrome (OHSS): A Review," *Human Reproduction Update* 8 (2002): 559–577.

18. "2016 National Summary Report," 64.

19. Ibid.

20. Ibid., 54.

21. "ART and Intracytoplasmic Sperm Injection (ICSI) in the United States," *CDC*, https://www.cdc.gov/art/key-findings/icsi.html.

22. Ibid.

23. Ibid.

24. Capelouto et al., "Sex Selection for Non-medical Indications," 411.

25. Harvey J. Stern, "Preimplantation Genetic Diagnosis: Prenatal Testing for Embryos Finally Achieving Its Potential," *Journal of Clinical Medicine* 3 (2014): 285.

26. Ibid., 283.

27. Ibid., 284.

28. Capelouto et al., "Sex Selection for Non-medical Indications," 412–413.

29. Ibid.

30. Ibid., 413.

31. Ariana Eunjung Cha, "From Sex-selection to Surrogates, American IVF Clinics Provide Services Outlawed Elsewhere," *Washington Post*, December 30, 2018, https://www.washingtonpost.com/national/health -science/from-sex-selection-to-surrogates-american-ivf-clinics-provide -services-outlawed-elsewhere/2018/12/29/0b596668-03c0-11e9-9122 -82e98f91ee6f_story.html.

32. "2016 National Summary Report," 53.

33. Ibid., 32.

34. Ibid., 56.

35. Ibid., 56–57.

36. Lewin, "Industry's Growth Leads to Leftover Embryos, and Painful Choices."

37. For transfers involving frozen nondonor or donor embryos, the pregnancy rate was 56 percent. "2016 National Summary Report," 16.

38. Ibid., 18. The CDC was unable to determine the number of fetuses for 6.9 percent of pregnancies.

39. See President's Council on Bioethics, *Reproduction and Responsibility: The Regulation of New Biotechnologies*, March 2004, https://bioethic sarchive.georgetown.edu/pcbe/reports/reproductionandresponsibility /fulldoc.html, 43.

40. "2016 National Summary Report," 15. For frozen nondonor embryos, 46 percent of transfers resulted in live birth. For frozen donor embryos, the rate was 45 percent per transfer. Ibid., 44.

41. Ibid., 18.

42. Aniket D. Kulkarni et al., "Fertility Treatments and Multiple Births in the United States," *New England Journal of Medicine* 369 (2013):

2218–2225; Joyce A. Martin et al., "Births: Final Data for 2016," *National Vital Statistics Reports* 67 (2018): 4.

43. Kulkarni et al., "Fertility Treatments and Multiple Births in the United States," 2218.

44. "2016 National Summary Report," 59.

45. Paolo Cavoretto et al., "Risk of Spontaneous Preterm Birth in Singleton Pregnancies Conceived After IVF/ICSI Treatment: Meta-analysis of Cohort Studies," *Ultrasound in Obstetrics and Gynecology* 51 (2018): 43–53.

46. "2016 National Summary Report," 19.

47. Ibid.

48. "ART and Birth Defects," *CDC*, https://www.cdc.gov/art/key-findings/birth-defects.html.

49. Ibid.

50. Michael J. Davies et al., "Reproductive Technologies and the Risk of Birth Defects," *New England Journal of Medicine* 366 (2012): 1803.

51. "Key Findings: The Association between Assisted Reproductive Technology and Autism Spectrum Disorder," *CDC*, https://www.cdc.gov/ncbddd/autism/features/artandasd.html.

52. "ART and Intracytoplasmic Sperm Injection (ICSI) in the United States," *CDC*, https://www.cdc.gov/art/key-findings/icsi.html.

53. Ibid.

54. "2016 National Summary Report," 5.

55. "ART and Gestational Carriers," *CDC*, https://www.cdc.gov/art/key-findings/gestational-carriers.html.

56. Ibid.

57. Ibid.

58. Fertility Clinic Success Rate and Certification Act of 1992, Public Law 102–493, *U.S. Statutes at Large* 106 (1992): 3146–3152.

59. See The President's Council on Bioethics, *Reproduction and Responsibility: The Regulation of New Biotechnologies*, 50.

60. Ibid.

61. Omnibus Consolidated Appropriations Act of 1997, Public Law 104–208, *U.S. Statutes at Large*, 110 (1997): 3009–3270.

62. See "Human Cells, Tissues, and Cellular and Tissue-Based Products; Donor Screening and Testing; and Related Labeling 6/19/2007 Final

Rule Questions and Answers," *FDA,* https://www.fda.gov/vaccines-blood
-biologics/tissue-tissue-products/human-cells-tissues-and-cellular-and
-tissue-based-products-donor-screening-and-testing-and-related.

63. Stuart Nightingale, "Letter About Human Cloning," *FDA,* October 26, 1998, https://www.fda.gov/science-research/clinical-trials-and
-human-subject-protection/letter-about-human-cloning.

64. "Cellular & Gene Therapy Products," *FDA,* https://www.fda.gov
/vaccines-blood-biologics/cellular-gene-therapy-products.

65. See President's Council on Bioethics, *Reproduction and Responsibility: The Regulation of New Biotechnologies,* 62 (citing Kathryn Zoon, Testimony before the Subcommittee on Oversight and Investigations of the Committee on Energy and Commerce [House of Representatives, March 28, 2001]).

66. Consolidated Appropriations Act of 2016, Public Law 114–113, *U.S. Statutes at Large* (2016): 2283.

67. In 2001, fourteen years before the Aderholt Amendment, the FDA intervened to block clinicians at St. Barnabas Hospital in New Jersey from adding third party ooplasm (and thus foreign mitochondrial DNA) to women's eggs before fertilization and transfer. The FDA halted this on the grounds that it was unauthorized gene transfer research, which required agency approval (which would not be forthcoming). See President's Council on Bioethics, *Reproduction and Responsibility: The Regulation of New Biotechnologies,* 62.

68. Ibid., 36–37.

69. See *Kass v. Kass,* 696 N.E.2d 174 (N.Y. 1998); *Litowitz v. Litowitz,* 48 P.3d 261 (Wash. 2002); *In re Marriage of Rooks,* 429 P.3d 579 (Colo. 2018); *Davis v. Davis,* 842 S.W.2d 588 (Tenn. 1992). Finding no enforceable contract, the Tennessee Court ultimately granted custody of the embryos to the ex-husband (who planned to destroy them) so as to vindicate his right to avoid procreation. *Davis v. Davis,* 842 S.W.2d 588 (Tenn. 1992).

70. See *A. Z. v. B. Z.,* 725 N.E.2d 1051 (Mass. 2000).

71. See *J. B. v. M. B.,* 783 A.2d 707 (N.J. 2001); *In re Marriage of Witten,* 672 N.W.2d 768 (Iowa 2003).

72. In the 2018 case of *In re Marriage of Rooks,* the Colorado Supreme Court announced a balancing test for weighing the competing interests, but remanded the case to the lower courts to apply to the facts of the case.

In re Marriage of Rooks, 429 P.3d 579 (Colo. 2018). A small number of intermediate state appellate courts have awarded custody to the party seeking to implant the embryos and give birth to the resulting child, especially where they conclude that this is the only remaining option for procreation available to that party.

73. In 2018, the Arizona legislature passed a law declaring that in the case of a custody dispute over embryos, "the court shall award the *in vitro* embryos to the spouse who intends to allow the *in vitro* embryos to develop to birth." Ariz. Rev. Stat. Ann. § 25–318.03 (2018).

74. See Nicole Pelletiere, "Surrogate Mom Who Kept Baby with Down Syndrome Says Toddler Is Hitting Milestones," *ABC News*, April 19, 2016, https://abcnews.go.com/Lifestyle/surrogate-mom-baby -syndrome-toddler-hitting-milestones/story?id=38486518.

75. See Bradford Richardson, "Surrogate Mother Refused to Abort Baby after Heart Defect Found," *Washington Times*, December 27, 2017, https://www.washingtontimes.com/news/2017/dec/26/surrogate-mother -refused-abort-baby-heart-defect/; Jessica Schladebeck, "Surrogate Calls for Law Change a Year after She Refused to Abort Baby," *NY Daily News*, December 22, 2018, https://www.nydailynews.com/news/national/ny-news -surrogate-law-change-refused-abortion-20181222-story.html.

76. Petition for Writ of Certiorari, *Cook v. Harding*, 139 S.Ct. 72 (2018) (No. 17–1487).

77. "Surrogate Mom Carrying Triplets Fights Biological Parents on Abortion," *CBS News*, December 17, 2015, https://www.cbsnews.com/news /surrogate-mom-with-triplets-fights-biological-parents-on-abortion/.

78. The President's Council on Bioethics, *Reproduction and Responsibility: The Regulation of New Biotechnologies*, xliii.

79. Ibid.

80. Ibid.

81. Ibid., xliv.

82. Ibid.

83. Robertson, *Children of Choice*, 22.

84. Ibid., 4.

85. Ibid.

86. Ibid., 24.

87. Ibid., 35.

88. Ibid., 24.

89. Ibid., 35.

90. Ibid., 30.

91. Ibid., 33.

92. Ibid.

93. Ibid., 102.

94. John Robertson, "Procreative Liberty and Harm to Offspring in Assisted Reproduction," *American Journal of Law and Medicine* 30 (2004): 15.

95. Ibid., 8 (citing Derek Parfit, *Reasons and Persons* [Oxford: Oxford University Press, 1984], chap. 16).

96. Robertson, "Procreative Liberty and Harm to Offspring in Assisted Reproduction," 14.

97. Ibid., 25.

98. Ibid., 39.

99. Dr. Gerald Schatten, "Session 6: Assisted Reproductive Technologies in the Genomics Era" (testimony, President's Council on Bioethics, December 13, 2002).

100. The law need not be frustrated in this aspiration by Robertson's appeal to the "nonidentity" problem. The law is supple and dynamic enough to offer protections to vulnerable persons in the face of highly complex relationships of duty, cause, and effect. There are, in fact, ample resources to draw upon in the law of torts (particularly regarding rules relating to negligence and causation) for guidance. This, however, is beyond the scope of the present inquiry.

101. Gil Meilaender, *Bioethics: A Primer for Christians,* 3rd ed. (Grand Rapids, MI: Williams B. Eerdmans Publishing Company, 2913), 10–25.

102. See Michael Tooley, "Abortion and Infanticide," *Philosophy and Public Affairs* 2 (Autumn 1972): 37–65; Mary Anne Warren, "On the Moral and Legal Status of Abortion," *The Monist* 57 (January 1973): 43–61.

103. Jonathan Alter, "The Pro-Cure Movement," *Newsweek,* June 6, 2005, 27.

104. See, e.g., the statement of Dr. Hynes on Ira Flatow, "Stem Cell Research and Policy," *NPR, Science Friday,* April 29, 2005 (stating that before the primitive streak occurs at 14 days, the embryo is really just an "undistinguished, undifferentiated ball of cells").

105. "2016 National Summary Report," 18, 44.

106. See, e.g., Rita Vassena et al., "Waves of Early Transcriptional Activation and Pluripotency Program Initiation During Human Preimplantation Development," *Development* 138 (2011): 3699–3709 ("Carefully timed genome-wide transcript analyses of single oocytes and embryos uncovered a series of successive waves of embryonic transcriptional initiation that start as early as the 2-cell stage. In addition, we identified the hierarchical activation of genes involved in the regulation of pluripotency."); Anthony T. Dobson et al., "The Unique Transcriptome through day 3 of Human Preimplantation Development," *Human Molecular Genetics* 13 (2004): 1461–1470 ("First, we found that a complex pattern of gene expression exists; most genes that are transcriptionally modulated during the first three days following fertilization are not upregulated, as was previously thought, but are downregulated. . . . Third, we show that embryonic transcriptional programs are clearly established by day 3 following fertilization, even in embryos that arrested prematurely with 2-, 3- or 4-cells.); Michael Antczak and Jonathan Van Blerkom, "Oocyte Influences on Early Development: the Regulatory Proteins Leptin and STAT3 are Polarized in Mouse and Human Oocytes and Differentially Distributed with the Cells of the Preimplantation Stage Embryo," *Molecular Human Reproduction* 3 (1997): 1067–1086 ("The findings demonstrate that both leptin and STAT3 are polarized in the oocyte and, as a consequence of their location and the position of the cleavage planes with respect to these protein domains: (i) differences in allocation of these proteins between blastomeres occur at the first cell division such that by the 8-cell stage; (ii) unique cellular domains consisting of leptin/STAT3 rich and leptin/STAT3 poor populations of cells are generated. By the morula stage, a cell-borne concentration gradient of these proteins extending along the surface of the embryo is observed."); Asangla Ao et al., "Transcription of Paternal Y-linked Genes in the Human Zygote as Early as the Pronucleate State," *Zygote* 2 (1994): 281–287 ("*ZFY* transcripts were detected as early as the pronucleate stage, 20–24 h post-insemination *in vitro* and at intermediate stages up to the blastocyst stage."); P. Braude et al., "Human Gene Expression First Occurs Between the Four- and Eight-Cell Stages of Preimplantation Development," *Nature* 332 (1988): 459–461 ("We describe here changes in the pattern of polypeptides synthesized during the pre-

implantation stages of human development, and demonstrate that some of the major qualitative changes which occur between the four- and eight-cell stages are dependent on transcription."). For data on embryo-directed post-implantation development, see Deglincerti et al., "Self-organization of the *In Vitro* Attached Human Embryo," *Nature* 533 (2016): 251–254; Shahbazi et al., "Self-organization of the Human Embryo in the Absence of Maternal Tissues," *Nature Cell Biology* 18 (2016): 700–708 ("[O]ur results indicate that the critical remodelling events at [days 7–11] of human development are embryo-autonomous, highlighting the remarkable and unanticipated self-organizing properties of human embryos.").

107. Jessica R. Kanter et al., "Trends and Correlates of Monozygotic Twinning After Single Embryo Transfer," *Obstetrics & Gynecology* 125 (2015): 111.

108. La. Stat. Ann. § 9:121–133 (1986).

5. DEATH AND DYING

1. *Cruzan v. Director, Missouri Department of Health*, 497 U.S. at 270.

2. *In re Quinlan*, 355 A.2d 647 (N.J. 1976).

3. Ibid., 663.

4. *Cruzan v. Director, Missouri Department of Health*, 497 U.S. at 278.

5. Ibid., 279 (emphasis added).

6. The Multi-Society Task Force on PVS, "Medical Aspects of the Persistent Vegetative State," *New England Journal of Medicine* 330 (1994): 1499–1508 (citing B. Jennett and F. Plum, "Persistent Vegetative State after Brain Damage: A Syndrome in Search of a Name," *Lancet* 1 (1972): 734–737).

7. Ibid., 1500.

8. *In re Quinlan*, 355 A.2d at 664.

9. Ibid., 671.

10. President's Council on Bioethics, *Taking Care: Ethical Caregiving in Our Aging Society,* September 2005, https://bioethicsarchive.georgetown .edu/pcbe/reports/taking_care/chapter2.html, 60.

11. *In re Guardianship of Browning*, 568 So.2d 4, 13 (Fla. 1990) (citing *In re Guardianship of Browning*, 543 So.2d 258, 269 [Fla. Dist. Ct. App.]).

12. *Cruzan v. Director, Missouri Department of Health*, 497 U.S. at 284.

13. *In re Conroy*, 486 A.2d 1209, 1232 (N.J. 1985).

14. President's Commission for the Study of Ethical Problems in Medicine and Biomedical and Behavioral Research, *Deciding to Forego Life-Sustaining Treatment*, March 1983, https://repository.library.george town.edu/bitstream/handle/10822/559344/deciding_to_forego_tx.pdf ?sequence=1, 135.

15. Patient Self-Determination Act of 1990, Public Law 101–508, *U.S. Statutes at Large* 104 (1990): 1388–115.

16. President's Council on Bioethics, *Taking Care*, 70–71.

17. Ibid., 68.

18. Ibid.

19. "Nearly Two-Thirds of Americans Don't Have Living Wills—Do You?" *PR Newswire*, March 21, 2016, https://www.prnewswire.com/news -releases/nearly-two-thirds-of-americans-dont-have-living-wills—do -you-300238813.html.

20. President's Council on Bioethics, *Taking Care*, 72 (citing N.A. Hawkins et al., "Micromanaging Death: Process Preferences, Values, and Goals in End-of-Life Medical Decision Making," *Gerontologist* 45 (2005): 107–117). The Hawkins study found that "[t]he majority of participants believed that surrogates should have some leeway to override the patients' preferences if they believed it would be best for patients. A substantial proportion of each group believed that surrogates should have 'a lot' or 'complete' leeway, whereas only 9 percent believed the surrogate should have 'no' leeway. Patient–surrogate agreement was somewhat low (40 percent) but better than chance alone (j = .12, p, .001)." Hawkins et al., "Micromanaging Death," 110.

21. President's Council on Bioethics, *Taking Care*, 73 (citing Amy Fagerlin and Carl Schneider, "Enough: The Failure of the Living Will," *Hastings Center Report* 34, no. 2 (2004): 33).

22. President's Council on Bioethics, *Taking Care*, 74 (citing Fagerlin and Schneider, "Enough," 34).

23. Ibid.

24. President's Council on Bioethics, *Taking Care*, 74–75 (citing Fagerlin and Schneider, "Enough," 35).

25. President's Council on Bioethics, *Taking Care*, 77.

26. Andrew Firlik, "Margo's Logo," *Journal of the American Medical Association* 265 (1991): 201.

27. Ronald Dworkin, *Life's Dominion: An Argument About Abortion, Euthanasia, and Individual Freedom* (New York: Knopf, 1993), 221–222.

28. Rebecca Dresser, Dworkin on Dementia: Elegant Theory, Questionable Policy, *Hastings Center Report* 25, no. 6 (1995): 35.

29. President's Council on Bioethics, *Taking Care*, 89.

30. Ibid., 90.

31. Or. Rev. Stat. Ann. § 127.800–897 (1995).

32. Rev. Code Wash. § 70.245 (2009).

33. *Baxter v. State*, 224 P.3d 1211 (Mont. 2009).

34. Vt. Stat. Ann. tit. 18 § 5281–5293 (2013); Cal. Health & Safety Code § 443 (2016); Colo. Rev. Stat. Ann. § 25–48 (2016); D.C. Code § 7–661 (2017); Haw. Rev. Stat. Ann. § 327L (2018); N.J. Stat. Ann. § 26:16 (2019); Me. Stat. tit. 22, §2140 (2019).

35. See "Question 2: Physician-assisted Suicide," *Boston.com*, http://archive.boston.com/news/special/politics/2012/general/mass-ballot-question-2-election-results-2012.html.

36. *Washington v. Glucksberg*, 521 U.S. 702 (1997); *Vacco v. Quill*, 521 U.S. 793 (1997).

37. *Washington v. Glucksberg*, 521 U.S. at 721.

38. *Vacco v. Quill*, 521 U.S. at 807–808.

39. Ibid., 808.

40. *Morris v. Brandenburg*, 376 P.3d 836 (2016); *Myers v. Schneiderman*, 85 N.E.3d 57 (2017).

41. *Morris v. Brandenburg*, 376 P.3d at 848.

42. Ibid., 857.

43. Or. Rev. Stat. Ann. § 127.880.

44. "Frequently Asked Questions: Oregon's Death with Dignity Act (DWDA)," *Oregon Health Authority*, https://www.oregon.gov/oha/ph/providerpartnerresources/evaluationresearch/deathwithdignityact/pages/faqs.aspx#deathcert.

45. Or. Rev. Stat. Ann. § 127–800.

46. Ibid.

47. Or. Rev. Stat. Ann. § 127–840.

48. "Frequently Asked Questions: Oregon's Death with Dignity Act (DWDA)," *Oregon Health Authority*. He or she must also issue a written request, signed by two witnesses (though there are no restrictions on who these might be).

49. Or. Rev. Stat. Ann. § 127-815–820.

50. Or. Rev. Stat. Ann. § 127-825.

51. Or. Rev. Stat. Ann. § 127-815(c)(E).

52. Or. Rev. Stat. Ann. § 127-815(f).

53. See Herbert Hendin and Kathleen Foley, "Physician-Assisted Suicide in Oregon: A Medical Perspective," *Michigan Law Review* 106 (2008): 1628; Oregon Health Authority, Public Health Division, *Oregon Death with Dignity Act: 2018 Data Summary*, April 25, 2019, https://www.oregon.gov/oha/ph/providerpartnerresources/evaluationresearch/deathwithdignityact/documents/year21.pdf, 14.

54. Or. Rev. Stat. Ann. § 127-885.

55. Oregon Health Authority, Public Health Division, *Oregon Death with Dignity Act: 2018 Data Summary*, 5.

56. Ibid., 8.

57. Dr. K. Hedberg of Oregon Department of Human Services, "Assisted Dying for the Terminally Ill Bill, Volume II: Evidence," (testimony, British House of Lords, December 9, 2004), http://www.publications.parliament.uk/pa/ld200405/ldselect/ldasdy/86/86ii.pdf, 62.

58. Center for Disease Prevention & Epidemiology, Oregon Health Division, *A Year of Dignified Death*, March 16, 1999, https://www.oregon.gov/oha/ph/DiseasesConditions/CommunicableDisease/CDSummaryNewsletter/Documents/1999/ohd4806.pdf.

59. The precursor organization to Compassion and Choices was named "The Hemlock Society."

60. Brief for Ronald Dworkin, Thomas Nagel, Robert Nozick, John Rawls, Thomas Scanlon, and Judith Jarvis Thomson as Amici Curiae in Support of Respondents, *Washington v. Glucksberg*, 521 U.S. 702 (1997) and *Vacco v. Quill*, 521 U.S. 793 (1997) (Nos. 95-1858, 96–110).

61. Ibid.

62. John Boone, "11 Emotional Quotes from Brittany Maynard, The Newlywed Choosing to End Her Life at 29," *ET Online*, October 16, 2014, https://www.etonline.com/fashion/152632_11_emotional_quotes

_from_brittany_maynard_the_newlywed_choosing_to_end_her_life _at_29.

63. See "Compassion & Choices Partnership with Brittany Maynard Is Making Historic Success," *Compassion & Choices*, https://compassion andchoices.org/compassion-choices-partnership-brittany-maynard-making -historic-success/.

64. Linda Anguiano et al., "A Literature Review of Suicide in Cancer Patients," *Cancer Nursing* 35, no. 4 (2012): E14.

65. Ibid., E23–E24.

66. National Cancer Institute, "Depression (PDQ®)—Health Professional Version," updated April 18, 2019, https://www.cancer.gov/about -cancer/coping/feelings/depression-hp-pdq (citing Anguiano et al., "A Literature Review of Suicide in Cancer Patients," E23).

67. Henry O'Connell et al., "Recent Developments: Suicide in Older People," *British Medical Journal* 329 (2004): 895–896.

68. Ibid., 897.

69. Oregon Health Authority, Public Health Division, *Oregon Death with Dignity Act: 2018 Data Summary*, 8, 10.

70. Or. Rev. Stat. Ann. § 127.825.

71. Oregon Health Authority, Public Health Division, *Oregon Death with Dignity Act: 2018 Data Summary*, 11. Only 4.5 percent of patients since 1998 have been referred for such evaluation. Ibid.

72. Neil M. Gorsuch, *The Future of Assisted Suicide and Euthanasia* (2006; repr., Princeton, NJ: Princeton University Press, 2009), 118.

73. Oregon Health Authority, Public Health Division, *Oregon Death with Dignity Act: 2018 Data Summary*, 13.

74. Ibid., 12.

75. Ibid.

76. Ibid.

77. Ibid., 10.

78. Ibid.

79. Oregon Health Authority, *Prioritized List of Health Services: January 1, 2020*, "Statement of Intent 1: Palliative Care," SI-1, https://www .oregon.gov/oha/HPA/DSI-HERC/PrioritizedList/1-1-2020%20Priori- tized%20List%20of%20Health%20Services.pdf ("It is NOT the intent of the Commission that coverage for palliative care encompasses those

treatments that seek to prolong life despite substantial burdens of treatment and limited chance of benefit."); see also ibid., "Guideline Note 12, Patient-Centered Care of Advanced Cancer," GN-5 ("Treatment with intent to prolong survival is not a covered service for patients who have progressive metastatic cancer with: A) Severe co-morbidities unrelated to the cancer that result in significant impairment in two or more major organ systems which would affect efficacy and/or toxicity of therapy; OR B) A continued decline in spite of best available therapy with a non-reversible Karnofsky Performance Status or Palliative Performance score of <50 percent with ECOG performance status of 3 or higher which are not due to a pre-existing disability.").

80. For example, among patients who died by assisted suicide in 2018, the longest duration of days between first request for the lethal drugs and the death of the patient was 807 days, far longer than six months. Oregon Health Authority, Public Health Division, *Oregon Death with Dignity Act: 2018 Data Summary*, 13.

81. Oregon Health Authority, Public Health Division, *Oregon Death with Dignity Act: 2018 Data Summary*, 12.

82. Ibid.

83. J. Ballentine et al., "Physician-Assisted Death Does Not Improve End-of-Life Care," *Journal of Palliative Medicine* 19, no. 5 (2016): 479–480.

84. Ibid.

85. Members of the Task Force on Life and the Law, *When Death is Sought—Assisted Suicide and Euthanasia in the Medical Context*, May 1994, https://www.health.ny.gov/regulations/task_force/reports_publications/when_death_is_sought/preface.htm.

86. See Eduard Verhagen et al., "The Groningen Protocol—Euthanasia in Severely Ill Newborns," *New England Journal of Medicine* 352 (2005): 959–962.

87. H.B. 2232, 80th Leg. Assemb., Reg. Sess. (Or. 2019).

88. See National Council on Disability, *The Danger of Assisted Suicide Laws*, October 9, 2019, https://ncd.gov/sites/default/files/NCD_Assisted_Suicide_Report_508.pdf.

89. Brief of the American Medical Association, the American Nurses Association, and the American Psychiatric Association, et al., as Amici Curiae in Support of Petitioners, *Vacco v. Quill*, 521 U.S. 793 (1997)

(No. 95-1858) (citing Herbert Hendin, "Seduced by Death: Doctors, Patients, and the Dutch Cure," *Issues in Law & Medicine* 10, no. 2 (1994): 129).

90. Paul Appelbaum, "Physician-Assisted Death for Patients With Mental Disorders—Reason for Concern," *JAMA Psychiatry* 73, no. 4 (2016): 326.

91. Ibid.

92. A contemporary example of the practice of these goods and virtues can be found in communities such as the Little Sisters of the Poor who dedicate themselves to the genuine and selfless service of and authentic friendship to the elderly poor.

ACKNOWLEDGMENTS

To borrow again the words of Bertrand Jouvenel, alongside my own efforts, this book is the culmination of the "prolonged work of others," to whom I am deeply indebted. I have been the beneficiary of countless mentors, colleagues, students, friends, and family members, without whose support this book would not have been possible.

The ideas for the book were fleshed out and refined at several conferences. I am grateful to the organizers of and participants in the "Editorial Aspirations: Human Integrity at the Frontiers of Biology" conference at Harvard University, especially Ben Hurlbut and Sheila Jasanoff; to Bill Hurlbut and Jennifer Doudna for their roundtable discussion at Berkeley on the ethics of gene editing; to Kevin Donovan and the organizers of the 16th Annual John Harvey Lecture at the Pellegrino Center for Clinical Bioethics at Georgetown University; and to Robert Ingram and the participants in the George Washington Forum at Ohio University.

Heartfelt thanks to all those who generously read and discussed the manuscript in its various developmental phases, including Montse Alvarado, Ann Astell, Frank Beckwith, Father Justin Brophy, Jeff Brown, Paolo Carozza, Monique Chireau, Maureen Condic, Farr Curlin, Barry Cushman, Father Bill Dailey, Patrick Deneen, Richard Doerflinger, Rebecca Dresser, Justin Dyer, Father Kevin Fitzgerald, Father Kevin Flannery, Nicole Garnett, Rick Garnett, Patrizia Giunti, Mary Ann Glendon, Brad Gregory, John Haldane, Jim Hankins, Bruce Huber, Lauris Kaldjian, Peter Kalkavage, Adam Keiper, Bill Kelley, Sean Kelsey, John

Keown, Father John Paul Kimes, Randy Kozel, Jonathan V. Last, Shannon Last, Sean Leadem, Liz Lev, Yuval Levin, Alasdair MacIntyre, Ashley McGuire, Brian McGuire, Gil Meilaender, Anthony Monta, Michael Moreland, Phil Muñoz, John O'Callaghan, Mary O'Callaghan, Gladden Pappin, Dan Philpott, Alex and Stephanie Pitts, April Ponnuru, Ramesh Ponnuru, Vera Profit, John Ritsick, Rev. Eugene and Dr. Jackie Rivers, Andrea Rovagnati, Abe Schoener, Father Michael Sherwin, Andrea Simoncini, David Solomon, Dan Sulmasy, Chris Tollefsen, Luca Vanoni, Lorenza Violini, John Waters, Tom Williams, and Laura Wolk.

Throughout this process I have been blessed by an extraordinary array of research assistants from the University of Notre Dame. Chief among these were Tim Bradley and Aly Cox, whose unparalleled brilliance, grit, and attention to detail were indispensable. Along with Tim and Aly, I received outstanding research support from Brendan Besh, Hadyn Pettersen, Hope Steffensen, Maryssa Gabriel, Gabriela Weigel, Sarah Clore, Audrey Beck, and Micheal Ganley.

I am grateful for the unwavering support of the peerless staff and dedicated advisory board members of the de Nicola Center for Ethics and Culture at Notre Dame, including Laura Gonsiorek, Margaret Cabaniss, Father Terry Ehrman, Pete Hlabse, Petra Farrell, Ken Hallenius, Tracy Westlake, Hannah Brown, and Angie Lehner. Special thanks to Tony and Christie de Nicola, Sean and Kari Tracey, David and Susan Bender, Jen and John Besh, John and Kathy Gschwind, Mark Filip, Tony and Phyllis Lauinger, Kathy Craft, David and Lisa Fischer, Mike and Maureen Ferguson, Terry Seidler, Mary Hallan Fiorito, Joan and Bob Cummins, Steve and Claudia Sefton, Doug and Cher Abell, Patricia Myser, Neil and Anne Ramsey, John and Kristine DeMatteo, Kevin and Fran Fleming, and Steve and Ellen Rasch.

Many thanks to the strong and constant support of my wonderful colleagues at Notre Dame not already mentioned above, including Deans Marcus Cole, Sarah Mustillo, Martijn Cremers, Dean Emeritus John McGreevy, Jerry McKenny, Jess Keating, Dan Kelly, Jeff Pojanowski, Christian Smith, John Finnis, Patrick Griffin, Bill Mattison, and John Cavadini.

I am profoundly grateful for the unflagging and generous support, encouragement, and counsel of my dear friend Steve Wrinn, Director of Notre Dame Press.

I will always be grateful to the members and staff of the President's Council on Bioethics, including especially my treasured mentor and friend, Chairman Leon Kass. In addition to those already mentioned above, I am indebted in particular to the late Ed Pellegrino, Robby George, Frank Fukuyama, Don Landry, James Q. Wilson, Bill May, Michael Sandel, Paul McHugh, Diana Schaub, Eric Cohen, Carl Schneider, Adam Schulman, Dick Roblin, and Dean Clancy.

Special thanks, as always, to my dear longtime mentors and friends, Nick Maistrellis, Judge Paul J. Kelly, Jr., and Peter Edelman.

I owe a particular debt of gratitude for the amazing work and support of my brilliant editor at Harvard University Press, Janice Audet, and her colleagues Emeralde Jensen-Roberts and Diane Cipollone (of Westchester Publishing Services).

Finally, the greatest debt of all is owed to my family, including my mother, Rosemary Snead; my sister and brother-in-law, Kara and Rob Brendle; my in-laws, Dianne and Frank Mrazeck and the late William P. Fitzpatrick; and most of all to my beloved bride Leigh and our beautiful sons, Orlando, Bruno, and Carlo.

INDEX